D1154843

Edgar Allan Poe Revisited

Twayne's United States Authors Series

Nancy A. Walker, Editor
Vanderbilt University

TUSAS 705

EDGAR ALLAN POE
Daguerrotype courtesy of Brown University Library

Edgar Allan Poe Revisited

Scott Peeples

College of Charleston

Twayne Publishers

New York

Twayne's United States Authors Series No. 705

Edgar Allan Poe Revisited
Scott Peeples

Twayne Publishers

1633 Broadway
New York, NY 10019

Library of Congress Cataloging-in-Publication Data

Peeples, Scott.
　　Edgar Allan Poe revisited / Scott Peeples.
　　　　p.　cm.—(Twayne's United States authors series ; TUSAS 705)
　　Includes bibliographical references (p.　) and index.
　　ISBN 0-8057-4572-6 (alk. paper)
　　　　1. Poe, Edgar Allen, 1809–1849—Criticism and interpretation.
　　2. Fantastic literature, American—History and criticism.
　　I. Title.　II. Series.
　　PS2638.P44　1998
　　818'.309—dc21　　　　　　　　　　　　　　98-29014
　　　　　　　　　　　　　　　　　　　　　　　　CIP

This paper meets the requirements of ANSI/NISO Z3948-1992 (Permanence of Paper).

10 9 8 7 6 5 4 3 2

Printed in the United States of America

For Nancy and Alex

Contents

Preface

In the original Twayne's United States Authors Series book on Poe, Vincent Buranelli devoted several pages to Poe's problematic status as a major author, arguing in his subject's defense against such famous detractors as Aldous Huxley and Henry James. Writing over 35 years after Buranelli's first edition (he revised his book in 1978), I am fortunate to be able to regard Poe's significance to both American and world literature as a given, for while his association with cheap horror movies and his popularity with adolescent readers still arouse suspicion among some critics, Poe's position as a major literary figure is by now well established. Dozens of essays and chapters and at least one or two book-length works devoted to Poe appear each year, in addition to the papers presented at numerous academic conferences, including regular sessions at the Modern Language Association and American Literature Association conventions. While Poe's best-known stories—"The Fall of the House of Usher," "The Tell-Tale Heart," "The Black Cat," "The Masque of the Red Death," "The Cask of Amontillado"—continue to draw new interpretations, other works such as *The Narrative of Arthur Gordon Pym,* "The Man of the Crowd," "The Purloined Letter," and *Eureka* have emerged in the last two decades as focal points for new critical approaches.

Like the works of most major authors, the Poe canon has been transformed in recent years by the challenges of those new approaches—not only have previously overlooked texts become more prominent, but the ways of reading Poe have expanded considerably. Recognizing the ways in which Poe toyed with the instability of language and meaning, deconstructionists have found in him a kindred spirit. Feminist responses to Poe have ranged from critiques of his glorification of "the death of a beautiful woman" to trenchant analyses of gender relations in stories such as "Ligeia" and "Usher." New historicists have made intriguing connections between Poe's writings and other nineteenth-century cultural texts, refuting the image of Poe as unconcerned and unconnected with Jacksonian America. But relatively few of the most successful Poe scholars have simply "plugged Poe in" to a single theory or approach; rather, they have used a combination of critical strategies to find new ways to interpret this enduring body of work.

Thus, my strategy here is not to make a case for a single way of reading Poe but to emphasize the great variety of meanings one can derive from his work—and the great variety within the work itself. Poe spoke in many voices: the pedantic critic, the exposer of humbug, the perpetrator of humbug, the aesthetic theorist, the scientist, the tortured romantic artist, the desperate lover, and an array of buffoons, detectives, and obsessed and self-divided criminals. Moreover, he combined narrative modes and stretched generic boundaries, creating texts that leave readers wondering whether they have just read a satire, an allegory, or a Gothic potboiler. A disciplined artist who was also a kind of literary P. T. Barnum—as James Russell Lowell famously put it, "Three fifths of him genius and two fifths sheer fudge"—Poe defies any single perspective on his work.

In this overview of Poe's career and major writings, I have attempted to account for the genius as well as the fudge, to represent both the range of Poe's work and the range of opinion regarding that work. At the same time, I have emphasized certain tendencies as keys to understanding Poe, among them the artist's quest for control—over his audience, his art, and his own career; the "double" or doppelgänger as a model for human consciousness; and speculation on the nature and finality of death. Although these and other themes surface throughout Poe's career, I also try to emphasize thematic and stylistic changes rather than treat his writing as a static body of work. Accordingly, rather than organizing chapters around single genres or themes, I have proceeded chronologically, making a general claim that Poe's writing went through recognizable phases that correspond (roughly) with his stays in different cities—Baltimore, Richmond, Philadelphia, and New York. I introduce four of the chapters with biographical information to suggest this interplay between the course of his career and the evolution of his writing.

Chapter 1 (1809–1831) follows Poe's early career as a poet steeped in romanticism, infatuated with rebellion and the power of art. Chapter 2 (1832–1838) focuses on his provocative early criticism as literary editor of the *Southern Literary Messenger* and on his apprenticeship as a short-story writer, during which he produced the topical satires and "sensational" tales that laid the groundwork for his mature fiction. Chapter 3 is devoted to *The Narrative of Arthur Gordon Pym* (1838), a failed attempt at a popular novel but a fascinating work that defies generic boundaries and other formal conventions. Chapters 4 and 5 (1839–1844) encompass Poe's creative peak, not only the most productive phase of his career but the period during which he wrote his most complex and profound fiction. Self-division and obsession pervade the tales discussed in chapter 4, while in chapter 5 I emphasize texts that concern intellectual competition, particularly confidence schemes and detection. The reviews and tales I analyze in chapter 6 (1845 –1849) reveal a stronger emphasis on vengeance and a darkening vision of human nature and society. But other works from that period, discussed in chapter 7, express faith in the transcendent power of art and beauty, as Poe returned through poetry to the romantic themes of his early work.

While writing this book I have received generous support and encouragement from colleagues, friends, and students. The College of Charleston and the Department of English and Communication provided summer research grants that enabled me to complete the manuscript. The Robert Scott Small Library's interlibrary loan department acquired much-needed books and articles. Todd Hagstette, Randy Beach, Erin Falligant, and Ellen Lamb provided crucial editorial help, and several colleagues gave valuable advice on the manuscript: Tim Caron, Julia Eichelberger, J. Gerald Kennedy, Simon Lewis, Terence Whalen, and series editor Nancy Walker. I owe special thanks to my students at Niagara University and the College of Charleston for sharing their ideas about Poe and for helping me work through mine—and to my family, for their patience and love.

Chronology

1809   Born January 19 in Boston to itinerant actors Elizabeth Arnold Poe and David Poe. Father abandons the family while Edgar is still an infant.

1811   Elizabeth Poe dies December 8. At the urging of his wife, Frances, John Allan, a Richmond importer, takes in Poe but does not formally adopt him.

1815–1820   Travels with the Allans to England and Scotland, where John Allan had hoped to expand his business. Attends boarding school in London, 1818–1820. Family returns to Richmond in 1820.

1824   Writes earliest extant verse. Jane Stanard, a schoolmate's mother to whom Poe was attracted, dies.

1825   Apparently becomes engaged to Elmira Royster, whose parents disapprove of the relationship. Allan inherits considerable wealth and property from his uncle, William Galt.

1826   Attends University of Virginia but does not return after Christmas recess. Allan and Poe quarrel over money, particularly Poe's gambling debts.

1827   Leaves Richmond for Boston, where he enlists in the United States Army. Stationed at Fort Moultrie near Charleston, South Carolina, from November 1827 to December 1828. Publishes first book of poetry, *Tamerlane and Other Poems*.

1829   While stationed at Fortress Monroe, Old Point Comfort, Virginia, Poe hires a substitute and is discharged from the army. Frances Allan dies. Publishes *Al Aaraaf, Tamerlane, and Minor Poems*.

1830   With Allan's help, attains an appointment to West Point and enrolls in May. Allan remarries and severs ties with Poe.

1831   Court-martialed and expelled from West Point for neglecting classes and drills. Publishes *Poems: Second Edi-*

tion with subscriptions from West Point cadets. Moves to Baltimore, where he lives in poverty with his aunt, Maria Clemm, her daughter, Virginia, and his brother, William Henry Leonard Poe, who dies August 1.

1832   The *Saturday Courier,* a Philadelphia magazine, publishes five stories submitted by Poe as entries in a contest.

1833   Plans "Tales of the Folio Club," a story collection. "Ms. Found in a Bottle" wins a contest sponsored by a Baltimore newspaper, the *Saturday Visiter,* which also publishes several of Poe's poems. John Allan writes Poe out of his will.

1834   Publishes "The Visionary" (later called "The Assignation") in the widely circulated *Godey's Lady's Book.* Submits "Tales of the Folio Club" to Carey & Lea, but it is never published. John Allan dies.

1835   Begins writing for T. W. White's fledgling *Southern Literary Messenger,* then moves back to Richmond with his aunt, Maria Clemm, and cousin Virginia Clemm to edit the magazine. Contributes tales, including "Berenice," "Morella," and "The Unparalleled Adventures of One Hans Pfaall," and often scathing book reviews.

1836   Marries 13-year-old Virginia Clemm in May. Edits *Messenger* and reviews dozens of books. Publishes only one new tale, "Four Beasts in One."

1837   Is either fired by White or resigns from editorship of the *Messenger* in February, then moves the family to New York City. Publishes first chapters of *The Narrative of Arthur Gordon Pym* in the *Messenger* and the story "Mystification" in the *American Monthly Magazine.*

1838   Moves to Philadelphia. Publishes "Ligeia" and "The Psyche Zenobia." Harper & Brothers publishes *Pym* in July.

1839   William Burton hires Poe as assistant editor of *Burton's Gentleman's Magazine.* Poe publishes "The Man That Was Used Up" and "The Fall of the House of Usher" in *Burton's,* and "William Wilson" in an annual gift book, *The Gift,* for 1840. In December Lea & Blanchard publishes Poe's first 25 stories as *Tales of the Grotesque and Arabesque.*

sole editor and proprietor, of the *Broadway Journal*. Wiley and Putnam publishes Poe's *Tales* and *The Raven and Other Poems*. New tales include "Some Words with a Mummy," "The Imp of the Perverse," and "The System of Doctor Tarr and Professor Fether."

1846   *Broadway Journal* folds in January. Moves family to a cottage in Fordham, near New York City. Suffers severe illness described by friends as a "brain fever"; Virginia's condition worsens. Writes "Literati of New York City" sketches for *Godey's;* sues Thomas Dunn English for libel when English retaliates with a satirical sketch of Poe. Publishes "The Philosophy of Composition" and "The Cask of Amontillado."

1847   Virginia dies in January. Depressed and ill for most of the year, Poe writes little but does publish "The Domain of Arnheim" and "Ulalume."

1848   Presents lecture on "The Universe," which he expands into the "prose poem" *Eureka,* published by Putnam in June. Desperately courts Sarah Helen Whitman, who breaks their engagement in December, at least partly because of Poe's reputation for drinking and dishonesty. Establishes intimate but apparently platonic relationship with Nancy Richmond, whom he calls "Annie." Probably attempts suicide by overdose of laudanum. Writes "The Bells" and the second "To Helen."

1849   Negotiates with E. H. N. Patterson to establish *The Stylus;* travels south to Philadelphia, then Richmond, where he lectures and solicits subscriptions. In Richmond, courts Elmira Royster Shelton, now a widow. Leaves Richmond on a steamship on September 27; is discovered in a tavern in Baltimore, "in need of immediate assistance," on October 3, and taken to a hospital, where he dies on October 7. Last publications include "Hop-Frog," "Landor's Cottage," "For Annie," "Eldorado," and (posthumously) "Annabel Lee."

Chapter One

"I Have Dreamed of Joy Departed": 1809–1831

While Edgar Allan Poe is best known for his tales, he published three volumes of poetry before he saw his first work of fiction into print. Indeed, in this first phase of his career he saw himself strictly as a poet; in his poems as well as his correspondence he insists that he has a calling not just to write poetry but to *be* a poet. To understand the importance and the nature of this calling for Poe, we must keep in mind that those first three volumes (*Tamerlane; Al Aaraaf, Tamerlane, and Minor Poems;* and *Poems*) are products of youth—and of a particularly troubled youth. Not surprisingly, Poe based most of his early poetry on the belief in the poet's power to create worlds other than the one from which he felt alienated and outcast.

Born in Boston to itinerant actors, Poe was orphaned at age two: his father, David Poe, had abandoned the family before his mother, Elizabeth Arnold Poe, died in 1811 in Richmond. Taken in by Richmond merchant John Allan, apparently at the urging of Allan's wife, Frances, Poe grew up in what would today be considered an upper-middle-class household, although in the 1810s and 1820s middle-class consciousness was just beginning to emerge. In fact, since older, more rigid class distinctions still prevailed, it would have been important to the Allans to be considered members of Richmond society. In this self-consciously Republican era, to be self-made was a badge of honor, yet the "aristocracy of talent" that emerged in the early Republic virtually duplicated the older, "artificial" aristocracy of birthright that it replaced, suggesting that the talents that brought about success were "in the blood" after all. Thus Poe grew up in an aristocratic social world, but with full knowledge that he was not born to it; at the same time, John Allan sought to instill in him the practical values of the business world where he had found success.[1]

Accordingly, as a child Poe may have believed he was destined to be John Allan's heir, a true Virginia gentleman. Allan sent Poe to good schools in Virginia as well as in England and Scotland, where the family

1

lived from 1815 to 1820. During these years Allan seems to have been a proud and affectionate foster father,[2] and yet he never legally adopted Poe; for his part Poe, as an adolescent, began showing signs of rebellion. By 1824 Allan would complain to Poe's brother, Henry, that Edgar "possesses not a Spark of affection for us nor a particle of gratitude for all my care and kindness towards him."[3]

In that same year Poe, as a member of the Richmond Junior Volunteers, participated in ceremonies honoring the Marquis de Lafayette during his highly publicized tour of the United States. While in Richmond, Lafayette visited Poe's grandmother and the grave of his grandfather, who had fought with him in the American Revolution. If Edgar hadn't already begun to identify himself as a Poe in opposition to Allan, Lafayette's visit probably provided the turning point. Poe's earliest surviving verse also dates from 1824; written on a sheet of John Allan's financial calculations, it consists of only two lines ("Last night, with many cares and toils oppress'd, / Weary, I laid me on a couch to rest—") and is signed not "Edgar Allan," as he had been called in England, but "Edgar A. Poe."[4] Both the signature and the placement of the poem suggest a challenge to his foster father and what he must have come to represent to the angst-ridden teenager: conventionality, repression, and obsession with money.

Poe's brooding deepened that same year with the death of Jane Stanard, a schoolmate's mother to whom he felt a strong attachment, perhaps an infatuation. The deaths of his mother, Stanard, Frances Allan in 1829, and his brother, Henry, in 1831 shed light on Poe's recurring association of love and beauty with death. While we should not simply conflate Poe with his literary creations, the personae of the poetry he published before the age of 22 are similarly grief-stricken and rebellious. Indeed, Poe has been a popular subject for biographers largely because his life fits this romantic, "tortured artist" stereotype so well (and in fact helped popularize the stereotype).

If adolescence strained Poe's relationship with John Allan, early adulthood severed it. In 1826 Allan enrolled Poe at the University of Virginia, "to urge [him] to perseverance & industry in receiving the classics, in perfecting [him]self in the mathematics, mastering the French, &c. &c."[5] Poe did in fact excel in his studies of ancient languages and French, but he also indulged in reading fiction, a practice Allan, like many practical-minded men of his generation, frowned upon. Worse, Poe gambled and ran up debts with Charlottesville merchants. Allan and Poe's written exchanges concerning the year at the university show the two men caught in a circular argument, Allan accusing Poe of wasting time and money, Poe charging that Allan never gave him enough to live on.[6] To make matters worse, before leaving for Charlottesville Poe had engaged himself to Elmira Royster of Richmond, but (according to her later accounts) her father had intercepted their correspondence as part of his effort to lead her toward a more prosperous suitor, Alexander Shelton, whom she married in 1828. Poe did not return to the university after Christmas recess, but following a brief stay with the Allans at the beginning of 1827, he left Richmond for the better part of two years.

"My determination is at length taken—," an 18-year-old Poe wrote his foster father in 1827, "to leave your house and indeavor [*sic*] to find some place in this wide world, where I will be treated—not as *you* have treated me" (*Letters,* 1:7). Poe believed he could make his mark in the world either as a soldier, like his illustrious grandfather, or as a poet. As if to affirm his allegiance to his biological rather than his adopted family, he returned to Boston, his hometown, where he published his first volume of poetry and enlisted in the U.S. Army. The army sent him to Fort Moultrie on Sullivan's Island, South Carolina, for a year, and then to Old Point Comfort, Virginia, in December 1828. Poe thrived as a soldier, rising to Sergeant Major, the highest rank for which enlisted men were eligible. Despite that success, he apparently grew impatient with his position, for in 1829 he hired a substitute and began to campaign for an appointment to West Point. From mid-1829 to mid-1830 Poe pursued the appointment, mostly from Richmond and Baltimore, where he reestablished himself with members of his biological family—his brother, Henry, his aunt, Maria Clemm, and her daughter, Virginia, whom he would later marry—and managed to publish *Al Aaraaf, Tamerlane, and Minor Poems.* Eventually, with some help from John Allan, with whom he enjoyed a brief reconciliation following Frances Allan's death, he gained admission to the academy.

At West Point, however, Poe's pattern of proving himself capable and then abandoning his pursuit continued: this time Allan's remarriage and subsequent severing of ties with Poe prompted the rebellion. Poe conceivably could have stayed at West Point without Allan's financial support, but either because his self-image as a gentleman soldier was now shattered (there was no more hope of adoption or inheritance) or because West Point had been a last attempt to prove himself to Allan, Poe gave up on this "respectable" path to success soon afterward.[7] When Allan refused to give written consent to Poe's early withdrawal, Poe simply stopped appearing for drills and classes, bringing about a swift court-martial. Meanwhile, he continued to write poems and collected enough subscriptions from fellow cadets to publish a third volume in New York City after leaving the academy in 1831. Like its predecessors, however, *Poems* found virtually no audience, not even among the cadets who had helped subsidize it; in fact, they were so disappointed that the book did not contain the sort of satirical verse its author had been known for at school that Poe, according to one of his classmates, became "standing material for jests in the corps, and his reputation for genius went down at once to zero" (Thomas and Jackson, 118).[8] Now homeless and penniless, Poe drifted from New York to Baltimore, where he would spend the next few years writing tales for newspapers in poverty and obscurity.

Tamerlane and Other Poems (1827)

Given Poe's age and his experiences through his 18th year, it is not surprising that *Tamerlane and Other Poems* should be preoccupied with dreamworlds, youth, and loss. The title poem's fourteenth-century Middle Eastern setting is itself a kind of dreamworld, far removed from Poe's time and place and re-created without regard for historical accuracy. Similarly, "Dreams," "Evening Star," "Stanzas," and "A Dream" present a speaker looking to imaginary or heavenly realms for inspiration. While the voice of most of Poe's early poetry seems to be that of the poet himself, with Tamerlane he creates a persona other than the poet's personal-voice "I": an ambitious shepherd who leaves his true love to conquer the world and make her his queen succeeds in his worldly quest, and then returns to his home to find her dead. Ironically, or perhaps appropriately, Poe in the first poem of his first book adopts a defeated, world-weary persona, not a young man but an aged warrior on his deathbed *remembering* his youth. With this approach Poe could write about restless, self-destructive youth from an imaginative distance; moreover, youthful dreams and exploits being voiced by a man about to die remind us that the old man is *in* the young man all along and that death is the inevitable outcome of his or anyone's life.

This grim balancing act infuses the poem. Tamerlane inherits shame, "That hated portion, with the fame, / The worldly glory, which has shown / A demon-light around my throne" (ll. 25–27). Beneath Tamerlane's conventional lesson (similar to Shelley's "Ozymandias," 1818) that the proud and ambitious are doomed to fall lies his contention that whatever joy one experiences is only half of an equation, for on the other side lies equivalent sorrow:

> To him, who still would gaze upon
> The glory of the summer sun,
> There comes, when that sun will from him part,
> A sullen hopelessness of heart.
>
> (ll. 366–69)

All happiness is either illusory or fleeting: "The trancient [*sic*], passion-ate day-flow'r, / Withering at the ev'ning hour" (ll. 390–91); "I reach'd my home—my home no more" (l. 392). Even the "bliss" that comes with having a sense of purpose "may be / The worst ill of mortality" (ll. 304–5). Tamerlane's worldview reflects the peripeteia central to the poem's plot: in trying to make a queen of the beloved Ada, he leaves her; having fought and won years of battles for her sake, he returns to find her dead. Appropriately, the poem concludes with an equation, an uneven trade: Tamerlane gets "A kingdom for a broken-heart" (l. 406).

Here and throughout his first volume Poe imitates the style of the English romantics: Tamerlane is a typical Byronic hero, and the poem evokes Coleridge's "Rime of the Ancient Mariner" and "Christabel" in sound as well as in the attempt to create "new" folklore—a tale that only *sounds* as if it were passed down through the ages. Although Poe based Tamerlane on a historical figure, his first endnote begins, almost boastfully, "Of the history of Tamerlane little is known; and with that little, I have taken the full liberty of a poet" (*CW,* 1:26). Late in the poem he teases the reader with a parenthetical reference to what pre-sumably would have been well known to the priest who is listening to Tamerlane's last words:

> (It boots me not, good friar, to tell
> A tale the world but knows too well,
> How by what hidden deeds of might,
> I clamber'd to the tottering height,) . . .
>
> (ll. 349–52)

In his later work Poe would often utilize this technique of referring to "well-known" facts that are never revealed, placing his text in an imagi-nary larger context. Poe's endnotes (deleted from later versions of the poem) emphasize this context and provide the poem with pseudointel-lectual credentials. These strategies give the narrator an upper hand over the reader, who implicitly should—but does not—know the "tale the world but knows too well." As a result, the reader is kept at a distance; it is as if the poet has access not just to the materials of this poem but to a world of experience and knowledge that the reader can only glimpse with the poet's help.

The other poems in *Tamerlane* also contemplate the distance between the dreamlike realms of the imagination and the mundane world that seemed intolerable to young romantics of the early nineteenth century. And yet, in these "Fugitive Pieces" (as they are designated in the 1827 volume) the dreamworld can hardly be called an escape. Rather, it is an intrusion, a "vision" perhaps, that overcomes the Poe-esque speaker/poet, marking him as a poet even as it disturbs or haunts him. "Dreams" presents the commonplace wish for a permanent escape from "dull reality" (l. 5), but it also raises questions about the relationship between those two realms, as well as a more basic interpretive question: Just what kind of dreams are these? In stanza 1, the speaker seems to refer to the dreams that come with sleep, for he says that his "spirit" will not awaken "till the beam / Of an Eternity should bring the morrow" (ll. 2–3). He seems desperate for escape, for even

> tho' [that is, *if*] that long dream were of hopeless sorrow,
> 'Twere better than the dull reality
> Of waking life to him whose heart shall be,
> And hath been ever, on the chilly earth,
> A chaos of deep passion from his birth!
>
> (ll. 4–8)

If chaos and passion characterize waking life, might we assume that, in contrast, dreams are coherent and manageable? That is not how most people would describe night dreams; indeed, Poe's alignment seems reversed—unless, of course, he means daydreams, which the dreamer *can* control. And, in fact, the boyhood "dreams" of the second stanza appear to be fantasies:

> For I have revell'd when the sun was bright
> In the summer sky; in dreamy fields of light,
> And left unheedingly my very heart
> In climes of mine imagining—apart

> From mine own home, with beings that have been
> Of mine own thought—what more could I have seen?
>
> (ll. 13–18)

These products of his "imagining" are, understandably, more attractive than real life; but the tone of the poem shifts again in stanza 3, which, according to Richard Wilbur, answers the question, "What more could I have seen?"

> 'Twas once and *only* once and the wild hour
> From my remembrance shall not pass—some power
> Or spell had bound me—'twas the chilly wind
> Came o'er me in the night and left behind
> Its image on my spirit, or the moon
> Shone on my slumbers in her lofty noon
> Too coldly—or the stars—howe'er it was
> That dream was as that night wind—let it pass.
>
> (ll. 19–26)

Is this his one bad dream? Or is it, as Wilbur suggests, a glimpse of "some spiritual reality" or "some mystical assurance of the transcendental reality of his visions"?[9] In any case, this power or spell is not something the poet/speaker controls, whether it comes from within him or acts upon him in the night. And while he would perhaps like to "let it pass," he cannot, because its image has been left on his spirit. Dreaming is a gift given to the poet, not a simple act of using one's imagination but more like channeling—making contact with—another realm of experience. As Wilbur puts it, Poe saw his poetry "consist[ing] of visionary gropings toward imaginary realms . . . touch[ing] on the mundane only for the sake of negation."[10]

The very lack of clarity in "Dreams," "Tamerlane," and most of the other poems in the first volume reflects Poe's project, which is not merely to escape from "dull reality" but to make contact with some "higher" or more meaningful realm. Getting there involves rejecting our normal way of seeing—spurning logic and clarity in favor of what David Ketterer calls "arabesque reality," which can be seen only with a "half-closing eye" that fuses and distorts ordinary perception.[11] Poe's poetry has often been called "visionary"; it might also be referred to as "abstract" in that he sought not to make things clear but to make them blurry. Thus the description of obsession (for the beloved Ada) in "Tamerlane" could be taken as a prescription for breaking through the normal barriers of perception:

> In spring of life have ye ne'er dwelt
> Some object of delight upon,
> With steadfast eye, till ye have felt
> The earth reel—and the vision gone?
> And I have held to mem'ry's eye
> One object—and but one—until
> Its very form had pass'd me by,
> But left its influence with me still.
>
> (ll. 94–101)

That moment of receiving influence appears in nearly all the remaining poems in the 1827 volume as well, in every case as something that causes dread or fear. In "Visit of the Dead" (later revised as "Spirits of the Dead"), the speaker insists that "thou" will have the sensation of being visited by "spirits." The stars will attend the visitation, though they "shall not look down":

> But their red orbs, without beam,
> To thy withering heart shall seem
> As a burning, and a fever
> Which would cling to thee forever.
>
> (ll. 15–18)

This sensation will pass with the night, the speaker tells us, "But its *thought* thou cans't not banish" (l. 22). Thomas Ollive Mabbott speculates that Poe wrote this poem (which borrows significantly from a portion of Byron's *Manfred* addressed to Lady Charworth) for Elmira Royster, essentially telling her she won't be able to forget him (*CW,* 1:70); the poem may also reflect Poe's loss of his mother—whom he might not have been able to remember *except* as a loss—or of Jane Stanard. Regardless of what the poem might have meant to Poe personally, its description of a seemingly involuntary moment of communion with the dead suggests that the sort of visionary experience with which the poet is privileged may be as much curse as blessing. Similarly, in "Imitation" (again of Byron), "A dark unfathom'd tide / Of interminable pride" overtakes the speaker, but here its poisoning influence is complete:

> And my worldly rest hath gone
> With a sigh as it passed on:
> I care not tho' it perish
> With a thought I then did cherish.
>
> (ll. 17–20)

Poe's description of the "tide" is so vague that it could be anything, from a lover's rejection to a mystical experience as described in "Visit of the Dead." He is slightly more specific in the untitled poem he later called "A Dream":

> In visions of the dark night
> I have dreamed of joy departed—
> But a waking dream of life and light
> Hath left me broken-hearted.[12]
>
> (ll. 5–8)

Here the speaker contrasts his present, "daytime" unhappiness with a joy he can find only in dreams of the past, joy that is inextricable from loss. Ironically, daytime reality is dreamlike, too:

> Ah! what is not a dream by day
> To him whose eyes are cast
> On things around him with a ray
> Turned back upon the past?
>
> (ll. 5–8)

The speaker inverts dreamworld and reality, concluding with the question, "What could there be more purely bright [than this dream] / In Truth's day-star?" (ll. 15–16) He lives in a Catch-22, therefore: his only joy lies in a dream, but because that "dream" is a memory of joy "departed," it, too, evokes melancholy—joy is always experienced as an absence. Similarly, in "The Happiest Day" the speaker insists that his happiest day has passed and the rest of his life is denouement. Even if he could have that "hope of pride and power" back now, he "would not live again":

> For on its wing was dark alloy
> And as it flutter'd—fell
> An essence—powerful to destroy
> A soul that knew it well.
>
> (ll. 21–24)

Hope, Emily Dickinson would later write, "is a thing with feathers." In this poem, hope appears as a bird of prey, for it contains its own opposite—despair—within it. As in the other poems, the speaker remains fixated on "[s]ome object of delight" that, presumably because the object is absent or lost forever, deepens his sadness and threatens a still greater obsession, "powerful to destroy / A soul."

Given these poems' persistent, vague references to memory and loss, a secret grief that haunts the speaker, readers find it hard to resist filling in their blank spaces with Poe biography, then treating the poems as "evidence" of Poe's (presumably tortured) state of mind. While such speculation generally suits biography better than literary analysis, the consistency of theme and voice that leads readers to biographical interpretations remains one of *Tamerlane*'s most interesting features. The same "character"—presumably a descendant of Tamerlane—speaks all the "fugitive poems," and this character defines himself by certain oppositions. He is young yet world-weary, believing that his "happiest day" is passed; he experiences "reality" as if it were a dream and discovers his most vivid, intense moments in reverie; he can experience joy only by dwelling on its absence. Most important, perhaps, his helplessness at the hands of his daemon, that dream of joy departed that sends a "chilly wind" over him in the night, is also his source of power.[13]

Two of *Tamerlane*'s more challenging poems emphasize this poetic power. The speaker of the baffling, untitled poem now known as "Stanzas" begins by describing someone he has known "with whom the Earth / In secret communing held" (ll. 1–2), but by the first line in stanza 2, that someone seems to be himself: "Perhaps it may be that my mind is wrought / To a ferver by the moon beam that hangs o'er" (ll. 9–10). In youth he did not know what had power over his spirit (stanza 1), but now (stanza 2) he considers some possibilities: if it is not lunacy (as "ferver by the moon beam" suggests), then it could be a sign of "sov'reignty" (l. 12), or it could be his own thought's "unembodied essence" (ll. 13–14). In stanza 3 the speaker employs another image of perception to describe his "awakenings":

> . . . as th'expanding eye
> To the loved object—so the tear to the lid
> Will start, which lately slept in apathy?
> And yet it need not be—(that object) hid
> From us in life—but common—which doth lie
> Each hour before us—but *then* only bid
> With a strange sound, as of a harp-string broken
> T'awake us . . .
>
> (ll. 17–24)

It is no wonder that William Carlos Williams, the poet who insisted on looking at commonplace objects and scenes with "new" eyes, would champion Poe in *In the American Grain*.[14] Poe's speaker, like Williams, claims that we fail to see what is "each hour before us" unless we are woken up. But unlike the egalitarian Williams, whose work invites his readers to perceive poetically, Poe insists that this ability, which amounts to seeing into "other worlds" (l. 25), is given "to those alone / Who otherwise would fall from life and Heav'n / Drawn by their heart's passion" (ll. 26–28), that is, to true poets. God both grants poets access to the realm of the ideal and keeps their godlike—thus potentially Satanic—pride and passion in check. The last sentence of "Stanzas" stretches across 13 lines, playing havoc with pronoun reference, but as I interpret the last three lines, it is God's "throne" that "With desp'rate energy't [t = the poet's spirit] hath beaten down; / Wearing its [the spirit's, and thus the poet's] own deep feeling as a crown" (ll. 31–32). For Poe, to be capable of "deep feeling" and to wear it as a crown identify the poet.

The collection's last poem, "The Lake," stands out among Poe's early poetry largely because it has a specific, real setting, the Lake of the Dismal Swamp near Norfolk, Virginia.[15] According to Thomas Moore, who wrote a poem about the same spot in 1803, local legend told of "a young man who lost his mind upon the death of a girl he loved, and who, suddenly disappearing from his friends, was never afterwards heard of. As he had frequently said, in his ravings, that the girl was not dead, but gone to the Dismal Swamp, it is supposed he had wandered into that dreary wilderness, and . . . been lost" (quoted in *CW,* 1:83). Poe, then, may be evoking the legendary lover when he writes,

> Death was in that poison'd wave
> And in its gulf a fitting grave
> For him who thence could solace bring
> To his dark imagining.
>
> (ll. 17–20)

On the other hand, the "terror" he sees in the lake could be the product of the poet's, rather than the lover's, dark imagining. Still other readings present themselves: the speaker could *be* the suicide Moore wrote about, or the poem could spring from the speaker/poet's identification with him. Yet even without the legend, as Wilbur points out, the image of the dark, opaque lake "represents the obscuration of vision; and its depths are the grave of those reflections, those ideal beauties, which were the only diet of the poet's soul before his fall into the everyday."[16] For Wilbur, this explains why the speaker considers the lake "a fitting grave" for himself, and it explains the puzzling last lines, referring to the speaker: "Whose wild'ring thought could even make / An Eden of that dim lake" (ll. 21–22). One might more easily interpret those last lines to suggest the romantic poet's power to see—and thus *create* with his "wild'ring thought"—the Edenic beauty in the sublime terror of the dark lake. Like "Stanzas," and like much of Poe's early poetry, "The Lake" stresses the creative, godlike power of the true poet not merely to escape the "real" world but to transform it.

Al Aaraaf, Tamerlane, and Minor Poems (1829)

With "Al Aaraaf," Poe went further than he had in the previous volume toward creating an alternative world. Partly because its dreamscape makes so little reference to what most people would consider familiar territory and partly because of its numerous vague allusions and long digressions, "Al Aaraaf" is Poe's most challenging, though hardly his most rewarding, poem. No longer entirely under Byron's spell, Poe imitates here the style of Milton's epics as well as Shelley's *Queen Mab.*[17]

Although he would later denounce long poems, Poe speaks in elevated, "epic" language for 422 lines—and yet almost nothing happens. A thumbnail synopsis will suffice here.[18] On the "messenger star" Al Aaraaf, the angel Nesace prays to God to let His wishes be known. God instructs Nesace to visit other worlds and "[d]ivulge the secrets of thy embassy" (1:147)—the importance of ideal beauty, as opposed to intellectual truth—and Nesace calls on the other spirits of Al Aaraaf. Only two lovers, the angel Ianthe and the spirit of the recently deceased Angelo (identified by Poe as Michelangelo), do not answer the call, for they are preoccupied with Angelo's memories of Earth and with "the beating of their hearts" (2:264). As Daniel Hoffman puts it, "If this be an epic, it is an epic without an epic hero; if it be legend, it is the legend of no people" (40).

Indeed, given the penchant for hoaxing that Poe developed later in his career, one might regard "Al Aaraaf" as a kind of joke or mock-epic—Poe would in fact read this obscure poem to "quiz" a Boston Lyceum audience 16 years later. But in all other respects, Poe the 19-year-old soldier presented himself as a deadly earnest poet; if "Al Aaraaf" is a parody, it is out of character with his other early published writings and far more subtle than any of his later parodies, which were nearly all carried out in prose. Instead, we might see the pointlessness of "Al Aaraaf" as the *point* of "Al Aaraaf," for here Poe makes his first claim that beauty should be pursued without concern for truth. In this "world of words" (1:126), Nesace can create by singing, just as the poet wills the planet/poem Al Aaraaf into existence. Within the fiction of "Al Aaraaf," God speaks through the music of the spheres, but He says only what the poet attributes to Him, for He is the poet's God after all. The creative power suggested in the *Tamerlane* poems reaches its logical conclusion here: unsatisfied with waking existence, the poet wills another cosmos and another God into being.[19] And if the world the poet has created is one where beauty exists for its own sake, the poem itself is Al Aaraafian in that it is completely self-referential: what is true of the planet is true of the poem that shares its name. Instructing the angel Ligeia to awaken the other angels with her song, Nesace sings,

> ["]For what can awaken
> An Angel so soon
> Whose sleep hath been taken
> Beneath the cold moon,

As the spell which no slumber
Of witchery may test,
The rhythmical number
Which lull'd him to rest?"
(2:148–55)

The singer/angel Ligeia is being sung into action by Nesace, whose lines are "sung" by Poe. The "spell" induced by the "rhythmical number" is Ligeia's, but as we gallop through these anapestic dimeters, we realize that Nesace/Poe refers to her/his own rhythmical creation of beauty as well. "Al Aaraaf" is the world of poetry, a world whose beauty exists for its own sake and whose only function is to spread that message.[20]

We might regard such a position as either a cowardly retreat from reality into an "ivory tower" of art or as a bold act of defiance. "Al Aaraaf" certainly defied the expectations most readers of poetry are likely to have had in the 1820s and 1830s. The rational, empirical "Common Sense" school of philosophy, which considered literature valuable only insofar as it was useful (as rhetoric), predominated in Poe's America, which glorified utility and commerce.[21] Even the tradition-breaking English romantic poets, while they shifted the emphasis to the individual poet's perception and celebrated themselves as creators, generally arrived at some moral truth in their work and acknowledged some dependence on an everyday world not made by the poet. For Wordsworth, nature provides lessons to the poet; for Coleridge, the imagination "re-creates" an already existing world (see Hoffman, 44–45). But in "Al Aaraaf," Poe annihilates the Earth (although it is unclear whether this annihilation has already come about or is about to) and all earthly things. Even passionate love—a "less holy," earthly pleasure represented by Angelo and Ianthe in the poem's final section—is punished by death, as Poe explains in an endnote and in the poem's last couplet: "They fell: for Heaven to them no hope imparts / Who hear not for the beating of their hearts" (2:263–64). Not all human passions are excluded from Al Aaraaf, however: sorrow exists there, but "it is that sorrow which the living love to cherish for the dead, and which, in some minds, resembles the delirium of opium" (n. 26). Why? Simply because the dead are not *here;* like the beauties of Al Aaraaf, they exist now only in the mind of the mourner/artist. Remembering the dead is an opiate because it takes one out of the here and now and into a realm that, like Al Aaraaf itself, exists only in the mind.

The same note of defiance rings throughout the other poems in the 1829 collection, as Poe lines up the false gods of his age in order to repudiate them. In "To ———" ("The bowers whereat, in dreams, I see") the speaker, whom it is hard not to imagine as Poe in the aftermath of Elmira Royster's marriage, dreams "[o]f the truth that gold can never buy" (l. 11). In "To ———" ("Should my early life seem") he rejects stoicism, perhaps in the face of the same disappointment:

> I laugh to think how poor
> That pleasure "to endure!"
> What! shade of Zeno!—I!
> Endure!—no—no—defy.
>
> (ll. 37–40)

The most famous poem in the collection, an untitled sonnet later named "Sonnet—To Science," rebukes rational knowledge, which has supplanted poetic perception: "Hast thou not dragged Diana from her car? / And driven the Hamadryad from the wood / To seek a shelter in some happier star?" (ll. 9–11) This complaint was common enough among the romantics (see Mabbott, *CW,* 1:90), yet the poem succeeds largely because Poe defends the beautiful against the useful in a form that imposes difficult but useless rules upon language: a sonnet adheres to iambic pentameter and a strict rhyme scheme simply to please listeners. We should also note that in line 2 Poe reverses the roles of art and science as they are usually perceived: it is science that "alterest all things with thy peering eyes," implying that poets see things as they really are, that there is some deeper truth to the myths he alludes to later in the poem, a reality against which science is mere fiction. In "Al Aaraaf," which immediately follows "Sonnet—To Science" in the 1829 volume, he expresses the same sentiment: the planet's inhabitants are "Seraphs in all but 'Knowledge' . . . For what (to them) availeth it to know / That Truth is Falsehood—or that Bliss is Woe?" (ll. 159, 166–67). By turning the tables, Poe introduces a problem that would preoccupy him in much of his fiction: the slipperiness of truth and the inadequacy of the senses, on which science relies, in attaining it.

In "Sonnet—To Science" Poe compares his nemesis to a vulture; in "Romance," also, he describes Time, the parent of Science, as "eternal Condor years" (l. 11). Time suggests change, in opposition to the eternity of art or "romance," but we might also think of "Condor years" as the time that ushers in adulthood, for in the last eight lines of the poem the speaker sounds as if he has found himself suddenly overburdened with practical concerns:

> I have no time for idle cares
> Through gazing on the unquiet sky.
> And when an hour with calmer wings
> Its down upon my spirit flings—
> That little time with lyre and rhyme
> To while away—forbidden things!
> My heart would feel to be a crime
> Unless it trembled with the strings.
>   (ll. 14–21)

The "calmer wings" presumably belong to the bird of Romance the speaker describes in general—but puzzling—terms in the first stanza:

> Romance, who loves to nod and sing
> With drowsy head and folded wing,
> Among the green leaves as they shake
> Far down within some shadowy lake . . .
>   (ll. 1–4)

Either Poe has set the poem in an imaginary underwater world or else Romance can be perceived only as a reflection, and a poor one at that if the lake is "shadowy." In this world of Romance, the senses are not sharpened but dulled, presumably so that other faculties can take over. If those lines were not enough to suggest that the world of imagination is truly unreal, the speaker adds, "To me [Romance] a painted paroquet / Hath been" (ll. 5–6), raising another question: Is the bird "painted" only in that it is colorful, or is it literally a painted, wooden bird?[22] The latter reading heightens one's sense that Poe is rejecting not only Time but, again, reality. Yet this speaker is slave enough to Time that art and dreaming have become "forbidden things"—almost. As the last two lines suggest, when music or poetry can make the heart tremble, the speaker has no choice but to listen. And so the struggle continues: between Time and the Eternal, between the rational and the irrational, between "dull realities" and the world of Al Aaraaf.

It seems unlikely that such a heretical little book would have found an audience even if it had been well distributed. William Wirt, a writer and statesman whose advice Poe sought regarding the title poem, politely replied he was unqualified to judge it, explaining that "old-fashioned readers like myself" would not take to it and wishing Poe success with a more "modern" audience (Thomas and Jackson, 92). A reviewer for the *American Ladies' Magazine* noted that the "author who appears to be very young, is evidently a fine genius, but he wants judgment, experience, tact" (103). Others were less gracious: "Has the poet been struck dumb with palsy?" asked the *Baltimore Minerva and Emerald;* Nathaniel Parker Willis, Poe's future employer and sometime friend, gleefully described burning one of the other poems in the collection, "Fairyland," in the editorial section of his *American Monthly Magazine* (99). Such responses are not surprising, given not only the poems' difficulties but their audacity. While, as the reviewers noted, Poe's poetry remained opaque and often awkward, he had succeeded, as he boasted in a letter to John Allan (May 29, 1829), in rejecting Byron as a model (*Letters,* 1:20)—although in the process he rejected just about everything else as well. While youth had ceased to be one of his primary explicit themes, Poe expressed in *Al Aaraaf, Tamerlane, and Minor Poems* a thoroughly youthful rejection of old values and championed instead poetic energy and irrationalism.

Poems (1831)

Poe's 1831 collection revisits the themes of the two earlier volumes in five revised poems along with the six new ones; his subtitle, "Second Edition," suggests that one of the first two (probably the more poorly circulated *Tamerlane*) did not count and that *Poems* is essentially his only book, edited and improved.[23] And yet, although Poe broke little new ground thematically with the 1831 volume, stylistically he achieved the effects he had been working toward and produced a handful of poems— "To Helen," "Israfel," "The Valley Nis," and "The Doomed City"—more accomplished than anything in *Tamerlane* or *Al Aaraaf.*[24] The 1831 volume revises not only half a dozen poems but also the angry-young-man persona behind them, for Poe remained intensely conscious of the self he was projecting to his largely imaginary audience.

Sometime between *Al Aaraaf* and *Poems,* Poe wrote in a young Baltimore woman's album a 22-line verse that adopts the more mature, reflective voice he would develop in his new poems. "Alone" (as the

poem is known today) bridges the 1829 "Romance" to the 1831 "Introduction" as a brief poetic autobiography, but here we may take more
license in reading the poem's "I" as Poe himself, since he wrote it to an
individual and not for publication.

> From childhood's hour I have not been
> As others were—I have not seen
> As others saw—I could not bring
> My passions from a common spring—
>
>   (ll. 1–4)

> *Then*—in my childhood—in the dawn
> Of a most stormy life—was drawn
> From ev'ry depth of good and ill
> The mystery which binds me still—
>
>   (ll. 9–12)

Poe insists that he was not like other boys, and now he is not like other
men. He modifies the "mystery" with a series of prepositional phrases
that dominate the remainder of the poem (5 of the remaining 10 lines
begin with "From"). The "mystery" binds him, from "torrent," "fountain," "cliff," "mountain," and so on, until finally, in the last line, we discover that it is the mystery "[o]f a demon in my view" (l. 22). As Mabbott points out, in Poe's day the word *demon*, like *daemon*, brought to
mind a powerful, but not necessarily evil, spirit (*CW*, 1:147);[25] still, that
last line, after the suspenseful buildup, achieves its chilling effect. The
theme certainly is not new—it comes directly from "Tamerlane"—but
here the speaker sounds not like a boy pretending to be an old man but
rather like a sincere young man trying to explain his gift/curse, as he
sees it. This new self-assurance shows through the poem's daring technique, similar to Dickinson's in its heavy use of dashes and enjambment.
Stylistically, "Alone" may be Poe's most modern poem; it is certainly one
of the most revealing of his early career.

Poe's revision of "Romance," the "Introduction" to the 1831 volume,
reads like a public version of "Alone." The new second stanza, for instance,
similarly incorporates imagery of storms and clouds to describe the
speaker's adolescence, suggesting, as he had in "The Happiest Day," that
even his "brightest" moments partook of a more fundamental "darkness":

> Succeeding years, too wild for song,
> Then roll'd like tropic storms along,
> Where, tho' the garish lights that fly
> Dying along the troubled sky,
> Lay bare, thro' vistas thunder-riven,
> The blackness of the general Heaven,
> That very blackness yet doth fling
> Light on the lightning's silver wing.
>
> (ll. 11–18)

The next new stanza is even more confessional:

> And so, being young and dipt in folly
> I fell in love with melancholy,
> And used to throw my earthly rest
> And quiet all away in jest—
> I could not love except where Death
> Was mingling his with Beauty's breath—
> Or Hymen, Time, and Destiny
> Were stalking between her and me.
>
> (ll. 27–34)

Here Poe seems less afraid of being understood, and yet the phrases are not clichéd or overly sentimental. Moreover, the lines quoted above present an early example of a classic Poe-esque interpretive crux. The speaker claims that he is cursed, that "Hymen, Time, and Destiny" (the barriers of marriage to another man, age difference, and, finally, death, each of which separated Poe from Jane Stanard) conspire against him; and yet, having fallen in love not with a human being but with melancholy, he somehow *seeks out* only dying beauty, only women who cannot requite his love—that is, he brings this misery on himself.

In the other new stanzas the speaker sounds at first as if he had reached an advanced age, for he complains,

> But *now* my soul hath too much room—
> Gone are the glory and the gloom—

The black hath mellow'd into grey,
And all the fires are fading away.

                              (ll. 46–49)

If we read the poem autobiographically—as Poe seems to expect—these
lines sound inappropriately jaded for a 22-year-old West Point cadet.
Furthermore, he implies that his poetic powers are already waning as the
blackness that charged the lightning (in stanza 2) mellows to grey and
his fires fade. But he responds to this issue in the final stanza:

> Yet should I swear I mean alone,
> By notes so very shrilly blown,
> To break upon Time's monotone,
> While yet my vapid joy and grief
> Are tintless of the yellow leaf—
>   (ll. 58–62)

As someone not yet in the "yellow leaf" or autumn of life, he should
not be talking like this, but apparently he is affected by the same
"imp" (impulse, perhaps suggesting disposition) the "greybeard" has.
He then concludes by confessing his fear that although they share this
world-weary outlook, reinforced by his reference to "grey" in line
48—"even the greybeard will o'erlook / Connivingly my dreaming-
book" (ll. 65–66). Is this just the rhetorical modesty of an introductory
poem, or after publishing two books that almost no one read, is Poe
admitting that he will never achieve the kind of literary renown that
would justify his rejection of John Allan's bourgeois values? Poe, I
believe, answers the question in the first two lines of this last stanza:

> But dreams—of those who dream as I,
> Aspiringly, are damned, and die . . .
>   (ll. 56–57)

The greatness of Poe's ambitions, to defy convention, commerce,
"Hymen, Time, and Destiny," is so great that it is doomed to failure.
    This fear of critical and commercial failure also informs Poe's other
introduction to *Poems*, his "Letter to Mr. —— ——" (possibly his pub-

lisher, Elam Bliss, but identified only as "B"). Poe briefly argues that only poets themselves can judge poetry and that "I would be as much ashamed of the world's good opinion as proud of your own."[26] He explains this by positing, as he would many times in his career, distinct classes of readers. The many, the "fools" as he calls them here, never recognize good poetry because they lack judgment and therefore are either wrong in their opinions or right only when they repeat the opinions of those "gifted individuals, who kneel around the summit, beholding, face to face, the master spirit who stands upon the pinnacle" (*PT,* 11)—in this example Shakespeare, but by implication any great poet. Of course, these sentiments help rationalize Poe's own commercial failure and betray his fear that he would only see more of it. They also reveal Poe's hierarchical habit of mind early in his career. Very soon he would concern himself much more with popular tastes, but in imagining his audience he never abandoned his belief in this fundamental dichotomy between "the few" and "the many."[27]

Despite, or perhaps because of, Poe's apparent debt to Wordsworth in autobiographical poems like "Alone" and "Introduction," he challenges Wordsworth's conception of poetry as a vehicle of instruction while criticizing his verse in the "Letter to Mr. ———— ————." Poe reasons that since happiness (or pleasure) is the goal of human existence (a dubious premise, but a "truism" for Poe), poetry should aim straight for pleasure rather than trying to bring about pleasure through instruction. In opposing Wordsworth, Poe borrows—almost word-for-word—Coleridge's definition of poetry (see Hoffman, 84–85):

A poem is that species of composition, which is opposed to works of science, by proposing for its *immediate* object pleasure, not truth. . . .

(Coleridge)

A poem, in my opinion, is opposed to a work of science by having, for its *immediate* object, pleasure, not truth. . . .

(Poe, *PT,* 17)

Poe had said as much in "Sonnet—To Science" and "Al Aaraaf," where, one might argue, his "saying it" ironically constitutes instruction, violating the rule even as he sets it down. But while Poe, like all poets, "said things" in his poetry, he did not say much, and he particularly avoided moral instruction and narrative, which characterized almost all popular poetry of the era. When Poe allowed something to happen or made a statement through poetry, it usually concerned the writing of poetry itself.

For example, "To Helen," the most famous poem of the 1831 collection, describes a relationship between poet and muse. Poe compares Helen's beauty to a vehicle, "those Nicéan barks of yore," that brought a "wanderer" (implicitly representing the speaker) home. Poe's metaphor literalizes the idea that the speaker is "moved" by Helen's beauty, but we should keep the figurative definition of "move"—to stir the emotions—in mind as well: Helen's Naiad airs bring him "home" not to Richmond or Baltimore but (in the poem's final version) "[t]o the glory that was Greece, / And the grandeur that was Rome" (ll. 9–10).[28] The references to antiquity make it clear that Helen is Helen of Troy. She may at the same time be a real, present Helen, but it hardly matters; what counts is that her beauty, whether seen in the flesh or imagined by the poet, leads him to his poetic home, the "glory" and "grandeur" of those "holy land[s]" of poetry and art. As a statue, or as "Psyche" (soul), Helen embodies the poet's inspiration.

While "To Helen" expresses a longing to emulate the art of antiquity, "Israfel" casts an angelic poet as an analogue to the speaker. "In Heaven a spirit doth dwell / Whose heart-strings are a lute," Poe begins. Israfel's music springs not from his mind but from his heart, the center of emotion. Merely to feel is to play; Israfel's greatness, his "fire," comes from who he is, for he literally "plays his heart," the speaker says, conflating lute and lyre (both string instruments):

> And they say (the starry choir
> And all the listening things)
> That Israfeli's fire
> Is owing to that lyre
> With those unusual strings.
>   (ll. 12–16)

The speaker feels the same *kind* of fire in his own heart but knows that he does not possess it to the same *degree* as the angel.

> If I did dwell where Israfel
> Hath dwelt, and he where I,
> He would not sing one half as well—
> One half as passionately,

> And a stormier note than this would swell
> From my lyre within the sky.
>
> (ll. 39–44)

The poet seems both to worship and to resent Israfel, for he concludes with an obvious claim that would apply to almost any artist: of course an angel would not sing so well if he were mortal, and a mortal poet, if given supernatural powers, would create "stormier notes" than "this" human poetry. And yet Poe bases the poem on the identification the speaker creates with Israfel, suggesting that *he* is the angel's earthly counterpart. His evidence is the poem itself, which, with its short, rhythmic lines and incessant rhyme, approaches the effortless music he associates with Israfel.

In his continuing search for other worlds, Poe had looked to the remote past ("Tamerlane," "To Helen") and to the heavens ("Al Aaraaf," "Israfel"), but in three poems from the 1831 volume he seemed to create fantastic landscapes out of nothing. His revision of "Fairyland" transforms the poem from a detached description into a dramatic monologue spoken by a visitor from earth to his lover on another planet. Though uncharacteristically whimsical, "Fairyland" features Poe's typical inconsistencies. The most musical and amusing lines come early, in the poem's "new" section:

> You know that most enormous flower—
> That rose—that what d'ye call it—that hung
> Up like a dog-star in this bower—
> To-day (the wind blew, and) it swung
> So impudently in my face,
> So like a thing alive you know,
> I tore it from its pride of place . . .
>
> (ll. 11–17)

But later, Poe resorts to shorter lines that depend heavily on parallelism, repetition of words, and common, monosyllabic end-rhymes, creating the monotonous effect that moved Willis to burn the 1829 version:

> Huge moons—see! wax and wane
> Again—again—again— . . .
>
> (ll. 45–46)

> For that wide circumference
> In easy drapery falls
> Drowsily over halls—
> Over ruin'd walls—
> Over waterfalls,
> (Silent waterfalls!)
> O'er the strange woods—o'er the sea—
> Alas! over the sea!
>
> (ll. 57–64)

While "Fairyland" warrants little attention from Poe scholars, two other landscape poems continue to raise interpretive questions. "The Valley Nis," later revised and titled "The Valley of Unrest," contrasts the absolute stillness of the imaginary valley when its inhabitants had "gone unto the wars" with its current state: "*Now* the *unhappy* shall confess / Nothing there is motionless" (ll. 27–28). What has caused the change? Considering that "Nis," as many readers have noticed, is "sin" backwards, perhaps the unrest has resulted from a fall from innocence. Others have suggested that "Nis" names an actual locale ("Innes") in Scotland, where Poe lived briefly as a boy, or that it signifies "is not," reinforcing the fact that the scene is imaginary (see Mabbott, *CW,* 1:190–91, 193–94). Early in the poem, Poe warns that the "Syriac tale" about this place "Time hath said / Shall not be interpreted" (ll. 9–10). And yet in the very next lines he provides hints:

> Something about Satan's dart—
> Something about angel wings—
> Much about a broken heart—
> All about unhappy things . . .
>
> (ll. 11–14)

Furthermore, his description of the unrest in lines 29 through 46 is not otherworldly, suggesting that whether this is a valley in Scotland or the world of sin, it is some representation of the "real," post-Edenic world. And yet Poe hardly seems to be making judgments or even commenting on the effects of sin. Perhaps he uses the word "nis" rather than "sin" to scramble its meaning along with its letters, for this "fall" seems neither fortunate nor unfortunate: the perfectly still valley, devoid of people, where "the sun ray dripp'd all red / Thro' the tulips overhead" (ll. 23–24), was no paradise, and the valley of unrest no wasteland. In the 1836 version of the poem, Poe changed "The *unhappy*" of line 27 to "each visitor," further removing any sense of judgment; in the 1845 version, he removed the word "Nis" and the references to Satan's dart and angel wings. The poem's before-and-after contrast caused, we can assume, by "going to the wars" leads us toward meaning—indeed, the stars over the quiet valley had "a visage full of meaning" (l. 21)—and yet the scene "[s]hall not be interpreted" (l. 10). Once again, Poe deliberately obscures meaning—increasingly with each revision—in order to affirm his poems' independence from referentiality and interpretation.[29]

More bizarre, confusing, and impressive than "The Valley Nis," "The Doomed City" (better known in its revised form as "The City in the Sea") reveals a scene Poe perhaps associated with the Dead Sea but which he describes in otherworldly terms. In the first line Poe tells us the city is Death's domain, but it is neither heaven nor hell, for here "the good, and the bad, and the worst, and the best, / Have gone to their eternal rest" (ll. 4–5).[30] The buildings are "not like any thing of ours" (l. 7), and even the sky is mysteriously starless; instead, "Light from the lurid, deep sea / Streams up the turrets silently" (ll. 22–23). Although Poe alerted readers to the city's physical situation when he changed the title, in "The Doomed City" we do not learn that the structures are (at least) partially submerged until the fourth of five stanzas:

> There open temples—open graves
> Are on a level with the waves—
> But not the riches there that lie
> In each idol's diamond eye,
> Not the gaily-jewell'd dead
> Tempt the waters from their bed:
> For no ripples curl, alas!
> Along that wilderness of glass—
>   (ll. 31–38)

Poe builds mystery and suspense here without narrative, simply by adding detail to the landscape, until the stanza ends with one of his most chilling lines:

So blend the turrets and shadows there
That all seem pendulous in air,
While from the high towers of the town
Death looks gigantically down.

(ll. 41–44)

In the last stanza, something finally happens: the city collapses into the sea, and although "Hell rising from a thousand thrones / Shall do it reverence" (ll. 55–56), the original version closes with the idea that Death will merely seek another throne: "And Death to some more happy clime / Shall give his undivided time" (ll. 57–58). For all the romantic awe the scene inspires, its passing makes little difference. As with "The Valley Nis," Poe will not let us decide whether the place is real or supernatural, whether he is depicting a biblical event (the destruction of Gomorrah? the apocalypse?) or a random earthquake (Mabbott, *CW,* 1:196–98, 203–4), whether the poem has meaning or simply "paints" a fantastic landscape. As Richard Wilbur has demonstrated, Poe's poetry deliberately leaves interpretive blanks that to some extent his tales fill in.[31] Poe's conception of poetry as the product of imagination—as opposed to prose, the product of intellect—helps explain this deliberate vagueness. In the letter that opened the 1831 *Poems,* Poe wrote that indefiniteness was crucial to poetry, distinguishing it from "romance" (that is, fiction): "Music, when combined with a pleasurable idea, is poetry; music without the idea is simply music; the idea without music is prose from its very definiteness" (*PT,* 17). "The Doomed City," like "To Helen" and, to a lesser extent, the other poems of 1831, conveys just enough idea to carry the music.

The first 21 lines of "Irenë" create yet another landscape, a Gothic midnight scene complete with grey towers, fog, a "lone oak that reels with bliss," and "[a]n influence dewy, drowsy, dim" that makes everything from the lake to the "rosemary . . . upon the grave" seem to sleep. Irenë sleeps, too, with the moon humming in her ear, questioning her strange appearance and trying to wake her. The moon's confusion hints at Irenë's true state—" 'Strange are thine eyelids—strange thy dress! / 'And strange thy glorious length of tress!" (ll. 27–28)—before Poe reveals, more than halfway through the poem, "The lady sleeps: the *dead* all sleep— / At least as long as Love doth weep" (ll. 41–42). The suggestion that the dead sleep "[a]t least as long as Love doth weep" resonates throughout the rest of the poem and much of Poe's later work.

As the rest of the stanza makes clear, after mourners' memory fades—"a week or two" (l. 45), according to this poem—Irenë awakes and haunts the places she knew in life. Thus Death can be controlled, but only by the living, through what Poe would later term "mournful and never-ending remembrance." For a young man who had already lost his mother, his stepmother, and his maternal first love, this notion must have provided some comfort even as it perpetuated his brooding over those losses. The poem ends with a kind of prayer that Irenë will be remembered and therefore sleep: the speaker hopes she will rest in a stately family vault "Against whose sounding door she hath thrown, / In childhood, many an idle stone—" (ll. 69–70), for such a resting place, presumably on the family estate, will encourage remembrance. And yet, with one line, Poe allows the physical reality of death and decay to intrude: "The lady sleeps: oh! may her sleep / As it is lasting so be deep— / No icy worms about her creep" (ll. 60–62). It is an appropriately awkward line, for even in trying to transform death into a peaceful sleep, the speaker cannot escape the fact that the person he tries to keep alive through memory is not only lifeless but disintegrating, being reduced to food for worms, to nothing recognizably human.[32]

"Irenë" and the last poem in the 1831 volume, "A Paean," provide us with Poe's earliest use of what he would later claim was "the most poetical topic in the world": the death of a beautiful woman. I will address Poe's depiction of women—nearly always idealized, and more often than not dead, dying, or returning from the dead—in later chapters, but even by 1831 Poe has established a pattern: women in his poetry are rarely present, living human beings. They are almost always either angels or sources of inspiration, like Nesace and Ligeia in "Al Aaraaf" and the "statue-like" Helen, or else they have rejected the speaker ("I Saw Thee on Thy Bridal Day," "To ——") or died. In his fiction as well as his later poetry Poe would explore through male characters extremes of infatuation and grief, but his early poetry resists such passion. Although the speaker of "A Paean" is the husband of the deceased (also named Helen), he seems almost inappropriately resigned to his loss. And while Poe's revision of "Irenë" ("The Sleeper") would expand the speaker's role by attributing to him the moon's lines, in the 1831 version it remains unclear whether the speaker knows anything more about Irenë than her name: if he were her lover, his reaction on finding her dead would presumably be much more emotional. Poe's literary treatment of women would grow stranger and more complex throughout his career, but even from the beginning he seems either unwilling or unable to imagine them as real, living agents; instead, they are distant icons, either projections of the male speaker's inspiration or representations of death or loss.

In his early poetry, Poe drew on the conventions of romanticism in many ways, most significantly by centering his poems on the creative, subjective poet-persona and by insisting on alternatives to rational, empirical ways of knowing. Adopting the romantic self-image of the solitary young poet, Poe rejected the "dull realities" of the world he lived in—the army, John Allan's importing business, Jacksonian politics, the beginnings of industrial capitalism in cities like Richmond and Baltimore, and the pervasive institution of slavery—by denying them a place in his art. Poe had the luxury of this denial up until about 1831; while he had experienced bitter personal losses and frustrations, he had been fairly sheltered, as John Allan's ward and as a student and soldier. Now cut off from Allan, he tried to continue his writing career without steady work, living with poverty-stricken relatives in a tiny Baltimore apartment. The young man who had declared himself "irrecoverably a poet" did not publish another book of poetry until 1845;[33] instead, he turned for inspiration and support to a fast-growing medium that demanded short works of prose: the magazine.

Chapter Two

"Neither in nor out of Blackwood": 1832–1838

Early in 1835 Poe began work on *Politian,* a verse drama that set a well-publicized 1826 Kentucky murder case in sixteenth-century Rome. Although he quickly turned out a nearly complete first draft, he suddenly abandoned the project; his early mentor John Pendleton Kennedy, in introducing Poe to *Southern Literary Messenger* editor T. W. White, explained that he had turned Poe away from his tragedy and toward "drudging upon whatever may make money" (Thomas and Jackson, 149). Poe's attempt to write for the stage midway through the period discussed in this chapter reflects his ambition to reach a wide audience and his willingness to experiment in order to do so. His abandonment of *Politian* in favor of shorter, more salable (or so he hoped) work suggests much the same impulse to adapt to the literary marketplace, which was increasingly oriented toward burgeoning numbers of newspapers and magazines in the 1830s. Indeed, by 1835 Poe had published five tales in the *Saturday Courier* (Philadelphia) and one each in the *Saturday Visiter* (Baltimore) and the more widely circulated *Godey's Lady's Book.* Perhaps Poe at this point still assumed that literary prestige and remuneration (he received little, in some cases nothing, for these early stories) would come, if not from poetry (as he had previously hoped), then from longer, more substantial works—plays or novels. But he was learning that the odds were stacked against realizing such ambitions and that if he were to earn a living by his pen he had better follow the "energetic, busy spirit of the age," as he described it years later, toward "Magazine literature—to the curt, the terse, the well-timed, and the readily diffused, in preference to the old forms of the verbose and ponderous & the inaccessible" (*Letters,* 1:268).

The period between Poe's dismissal from West Point in early 1831 and the beginning of his association with White in mid-1835 constitutes perhaps the most significant blank spot in his biography. Other than the publication of those seven tales and two poems, we know little except that Poe lived mostly in Baltimore, where he became more deeply attached to his aunt, Maria Clemm, his cousin, Virginia, and his brother, William Henry Leonard Poe, and that this new household, in sharp contrast to the Allans's, was very poor. Poe wrote to Allan in November 1831 that he had been "arrested" for debt; in April 1833 he claimed he was "perishing—absolutely perishing for want of aid" and unable to find work.[1] But Allan, who would die the following year, had stopped answering Poe's letters by this point and had written Poe out of his will.

If Poe, with his adopted aristocratic background, was not exactly typical of the urban poor, neither was he an anomaly. Despite the popular perception of the 1830s and 1840s as the Era of the Common Man, a time when democracy and opportunity for economic advancement reached "the masses," throughout these decades wealth and power became increasingly concentrated in the hands of families who had been rich for decades, if not generations. New industries appeared, but for the most part "old money" developed them, hiring former artisans, former farmers, and immigrants to work in shops and factories.[2] Despite the educational advantages Allan had provided, without his financial backing Poe was left to choose between unemployment and "wage slavery." According to some accounts, he worked at a kiln at one point in the early 1830s; he tried but failed to find employment as a teacher and as an editorial assistant (Thomas and Jackson, 127). Meanwhile, he continued to write, casting his eye on the newspaper and magazine market even before he met Kennedy.

The rise of the "penny-press" and the proliferation of magazines in the second quarter of the century turned print communication into one of the country's most rapidly growing industries. Aided by technological breakthroughs such as stereotyping, machine-made paper, and (by the late 1830s) the steam press, printing became cheaper and faster; at the same time, improvements in transportation expanded the geographical market for printed materials. Inexpensive and highly responsive to their audiences, newspapers and magazines had a special appeal for new urbanites, for whom these media provided a sense of communal experience. Between 1833 and 1836 New York's *Sun, Herald,* and *Tribune,* along with their imitators in Philadelphia and Boston, used sensational crime reporting, distribution by roving newsboys, and a one-cent-per-copy price to reach the masses.[3] Meanwhile, the number of U.S. magazines increased from fewer than 100 in 1825 to about 600 in 1850, with an additional 4,000 or so failed attempts in between.[4] Within this barrage of print, weekly newspapers and monthly magazines became the primary outlet for American fiction and poetry. The lack of an international copyright made "pirating" books by proven British authors more profitable and less risky than publishing American novels. Consequently, most fiction writers sold shorter pieces to periodicals, whose editors often needed copy and, as Poe put it, "pay *something*" (*CW,* 2:1207).

Accordingly, while Poe did not quit writing poetry altogether during this period, the two poems he published in the *Saturday Visiter* in 1833, "Serenade" and "To ———" ("Sleep on"), were much more conventional in theme and form—and thus presumably better suited to the expectations of a weekly paper—than most of his earlier verse. Meanwhile, he incorporated his more inventive poems of this period—"To One in Paradise," "The Coliseum," "The Conqueror Worm"—into his tales.

In 1835, having won the *Visiter's* $50 contest prize for "Ms. Found in a Bottle" and with it, the friendship of Kennedy, Poe began writing, from Baltimore, criticism for a new Richmond magazine, the *Southern Literary Messenger.* Within a few months, Poe joined T. W. White in Richmond, soon followed by "Muddy" (as he called his aunt, Maria Clemm) and the 13-year-old Virginia, whom he married the next year (though they may have been secretly married in 1835). White apparently felt a fatherly affection for Poe, but as had been the case with Poe and Allan, Poe and White disappointed each other. Poe's drinking bouts disturbed his sober, moralistic employer; moreover, Poe was much more willing than White to step over the lines of "gentlemanly" good taste in the interest of selling magazines. Defending the ghastly conclusion of "Berenice"—which White published in the *Messenger* before Poe moved to Richmond—Poe wrote to his future employer that "to be appreciated you must be *read,* and these things are invariably sought after with avidity" (*Letters,* 1:58). Following that same principle, Poe wrote a number of infamously acerbic book reviews that earned him a reputation as a "tomahawk man." For his part, White disappointed Poe by not giving him the official title of editor or the control associated with it.

White apparently fired Poe or convinced him to resign; whatever the exact circumstances, Poe left Richmond for New York in February 1837. The *Messenger* job had lifted Poe, his young bride, and his aunt/mother-in-law temporarily out of poverty, but with the move to New York their fortunes plummeted: for the remainder of 1837 and all of 1838 Poe appears to have earned less than $150.[5] Understandably, this second period of extreme poverty, which coincided with the onset of a nationwide economic depression, is another "blank spot" in Poe biography: little is known except that he lived mostly in New York before moving to

Philadelphia (probably in mid-1838), wrote one of his greatest stories, "Ligeia," and published *The Narrative of Arthur Gordon Pym,* which I discuss in chapter 3.

Early Burlesques, Self-Promotion, and Mystification

Most of Poe's early tales are likely to baffle readers who do not have textual notes explaining the objects of his satire and the numerous inside jokes. In fact, scholars have expended a great deal of energy explicating tales that seem incoherent outside their historical context. While Poe sent his tales to the *Saturday Courier* and the *Visiter,* he still hoped to compile them in book form; between 1833 and 1836 he queried publishers about a collection he first called "Tales of the Arabesque" and then "Tales of the Folio Club." By 1836 the proposed book contained not only 17 tales but 17 satirically drawn authors constituting the Folio Club, whose comments on each other's manuscripts would prove a "burlesque upon criticism generally"; Poe assured one publisher that "[t]he critical remarks, *which have never been published,* will make about 1/4 of the whole" (*Letters,* 1:104). Although no publisher ever accepted the proposal, Poe's plan suggests the spirit in which the early tales were intended.[6]

"The Bargain Lost" (later called "Bon-Bon"), for instance, satirizes metaphysical philosophy, particularly its concern with the nature of the soul. Playing off the notion that the devil eats human souls, Poe has Pierre Bon-Bon, renowned chef and metaphysician, drunkenly offer his soul to the devil in order to prove it no shadow, insisting that it would be worthy of a stew or soufflé. But the devil declines, explaining that he is "supplied at present" and unwilling to take advantage of Bon-Bon's "disgusting and ungentlemanly situation" (*CW,* 2:114). Two other Folio Club stories, "A Tale of Jerusalem" and "Four Beasts in One," parody a contemporary vogue for historical fiction with biblical or Middle Eastern settings. In these tales and others, Poe included more pointed satire within the literary parody: "Jerusalem" features a grossly anti-Semitic portrayal of Jewish soldiers, while in "Four Beasts" Poe launches his first fictional attack on mob psychology.

Other Folio Club tales burlesque subjects that seem to have been closer to Poe's heart and literary aspirations. Both "The Duc de l'Omelette" and "Lionizing" lampoon Nathaniel Parker Willis, who had ridiculed Poe's "Fairyland" in his *American Monthly Magazine* in 1829. Willis was an irresistible target: not only had he insulted Poe, but he was on his way to becoming the most successful "magazinist" of his generation. He would make a career of writing amusing sketches of upper-class life, particularly in Europe, and calling attention to himself as an effete, sophisticated dandy. Thus in "The Duc de l'Omelette" Poe takes specific, petty swipes at Willis's refined taste in food, clothes, and furniture, to the point of having the Duc die of shock upon being served an ortolan with no paper covers over its legs (Mabbott, *CW,* 2:38). Like Bon-Bon, the Duc meets the devil but beats him in a game of cards. In "Lionizing" Poe lampoons Willis's seemingly effortless and undeserved rise to literary fame, as Robert Jones, the story's narrator, ascends to the pinnacle of aristocracy in the town of Fum-Fudge by virtue of his enormous nose. Poe thus invokes a contemporary vogue, probably inspired by *Tristram Shandy,* for stories in which the nose is used both to indicate snobbery (turning up one's nose) and as a euphemism for penis.[7] "The first action of my life was the taking hold of my nose with both hands," says Jones (*CW,* 2:178); Poe tosses in puns on "ejaculated" and "coming" before concluding the story by having Jones shoot off the nose of the Elector of Bluddenuff in a duel.[8]

Beyond the absurd, sophomoric humor and the inside jokes directed at Willis, "Lionizing" targets the cult of celebrity that surrounded such writers and the self-obsessed coterie of "lions" Poe himself was trying to break into. The oafish, self-absorbed (as his obsession with his own "nose" suggests) Jones is declared a "Fine writer!" and a "Profound thinker!" by the newspapers of Europe when he publishes his pamphlet on nosology, and his greatest triumphs come when he turns up his nose, first at an artist and then again when he speaks at a gathering of lions: "I spoke of myself;—of myself, of myself, of myself—of Nosology, of my pamphlet, and of myself. I turned up my nose, and I spoke of myself" (*CW,* 2:182). Not surprisingly, the gathering of parodically named scholars Jones describes here recalls Poe's Folio Club. Among such a self-important group, Jones learns that the quickest way to advance one's reputation is through arrogance. But whatever else Poe's absurd ending might suggest, it certainly makes the point that such fame is fleeting; upon shooting off the Elector of Bluddenuff's nose, the narrator learns that his rival has supplanted him in the affections of the aristocracy, for "there is no competing with a lion who has no proboscis at all" (*CW,* 2:183).

In "Lionizing" and in the Folio Club tales as a group, Poe engages in "coterie satire," a form that usually appeals only to those who belong to the exclusive group whose members are the satire's targets. Poe obviously was reading enough contemporary fiction to be able to parody various writers and styles, but as a virtual unknown he could not lay claim to being a true "insider." And yet he claims insider status through such tales as "Lionizing," implying that he already knows how the literature business works. Indeed, Poe not only assumes insider status but, as satirist, positions himself "above" writing such formulaic and/or ridiculous stories—even as he was writing them. Poe, who would be best known as a critic at least until the mid-1840s, approached fiction with the same presumption of authority he would bring to his *Messenger* reviews. At the same time, as Michael Allen and G. R. Thompson have suggested, Poe seems to have intended "the many," the audience of magazine readers beyond the coterie, to enjoy at least some of these early stories without fully appreciating their satire.[9] Scholars today speculate on the extent to which certain Poe tales should be taken seriously or regarded as burlesques, but this interpretive problem might have been Poe's solution, a way to prove his credentials to the literary "few" while appealing to the "many" with, for example, the penis jokes of "Lionizing," the suspense of "Ms. Found in a Bottle," the prophecy and metempsychosis of "Metzengerstein," and the gruesome sensationalism of "Berenice."

Poe invokes similar strategies in the "Autography" series he wrote for the *Messenger* in 1836, in which he evaluated contemporary literary figures by means of a bogus expertise at interpreting handwriting. Poe, assuming the role of editor, obtains a collection of autographs and proceeds to analyze them for the *Messenger*'s readers.[10] In describing the handwriting of each author (their signatures were authentically reproduced in the magazine), Poe slyly offers his opinion of their work, often punning on words like *character* (meaning "letter or symbol," "quality," and fictional personage) and *tail* (referring both to the lower portions of cursive letters and to "tales"). Thus, Robert Montgomery Bird's "characters have the air of not being able to keep pace with the thought" (*CW,* 2:274), while T. S. Fay's tails "are too long" (*CW,* 2:286); Cooper's MS has "no distinctive character about it," and will "probably be different in other letters" (*CW,* 2:268). Meanwhile, John Pendleton Kennedy, Poe's early patron, exhibits the "*beau ideal* of penmanship" (*CW,* 2:273). Here too, then, Poe undertakes a project that assumes some familiarity with these writers (after all, he has their signatures), positioning himself as a literary "player" who can rib the likes of James Fenimore Cooper. "Autography" also contains an element of self-parody, though, for part of the joke hinges on taking seriously the absurd practice of interpreting autographs. By February 1836, when the installment appeared, Poe was gaining a reputation for overly meticulous, pedantic criticism: the minute analysis of handwriting, seals, and paper quality comes across as a burlesque not just of the writers in question but of a critic who takes his work too seriously.

While Poe himself jockeyed for position in the literary marketplace, he wrote stories about using playful writing to gain power over an adversary. In "Mystification" (1837) Baron Ritzer Von Jung, "one of those human anomalies . . . who make the science of *mystification* the study and the business of their lives," deliberately insults Göttingen's foremost authority on the protocols of duelling, then avoids retribution by referring his adversary to a duelling text whose "language was ingeniously framed so as to present to the ear all the outward signs of intelligibility, and even of profundity, while in fact not a shadow of meaning existed" (*CW,* 2:294–95, 303). Hermann, the duelist, unwilling to admit his befuddlement, declares himself satisfied by the explanation offered by the nonsensical passage. Thus, through Von Jung's ability to analyze his opponent and predict his behavior, he gets away with the insult and humiliates Hermann for the private pleasure of himself and his friend the narrator. Von Jung himself is inscrutable, as the narrator's initial description of this consummate intellectual prankster suggests:

> [I]t was impossible to form a guess respecting his age by any data personally afforded. He might have been fifteen or fifty. . . . His forehead was lofty and very fair; his nose a snub; his eyes large, heavy, glassy and meaningless. . . . The lips were gently protruded, and rested the one upon the other after such fashion that it is impossible to conceive any, even the most complex, combination of human features, conveying so entirely, and so singly, the idea of unmitigated gravity, solemnity and repose. (*CW,* 2:294)

Edward Davidson has noted that this description bears a distinct resemblance to Poe,[11] an appropriate touch considering Von Jung's ability to "read" his adversary while remaining unreadable himself, and to manipulate his opponent with the written word. While Von Jung, like "Lionizing" 's Robert Jones, is ultimately a kind of charlatan, Poe portrays him as deserving of his triumph because he knows how to create a desired effect on his audience.

Poe went to greater lengths to contrive the mystification at the center of "The Unparalleled Adventures of One Hans Pfaall," which appeared in the *Messenger* in 1835. Most of the story consists of Pfaall's description of his voyage to the moon—a mixture of mystification and seemingly plausible explanations of how he overcomes such insurmountable obstacles as gravity and lack of oxygen. Poe/Pfaall maintains a serious, even clinical, tone, and footnotes relate his discoveries to other "scientific" texts. Yet Poe "exposes" the hoax by setting it within an obviously fictional frame: the depiction and the names of the Rotterdamians indicate a caricature of the Dutch (similar to his treatment of Germans in the later tale "The Devil in the Belfry"), and Pfaall's narrative is delivered by way of a balloon made of dirty newspapers. This telling detail, along with several other references to papers and printing, underscores the notion that the truth of Hans's unparalleled adventure is strictly textual;[12] that is, the story is true to the extent that a writer can make it function as truth. Like Von Jung's mystification, this "fake" text achieves the effect of what it pretends to be. But unlike Von Jung's baboon story, Pfaall's text mystifies not only its fictional audience (the Rotterdamians) but also the readers of Poe's story. Pfaall's narrative is too long and detailed not to be an attempt to draw readers in, to make them forget the fictional frame. The closing remarks for that reason come as a surprise, and Poe emphasizes the surprise by teasing his readers, placing them in the position of the Rotterdamians who disprove Pfaall's narrative: "Some of the over-wise even made themselves ridiculous by decrying the whole business as nothing better than a hoax. But hoax, with these sort of people, is, I believe, a general term for all matters above their comprehension."[13]

And yet we should take seriously Poe's complaint that certain "over-wise" citizens dismiss as a mere hoax whatever they do not understand, for within Pfaall's narrative there is something to be said for believing what one reads. Pfaall's situation mirrors that of the reader as he gleans the real possibility of a lunar voyage from a pamphlet:

> The limited nature of my education in general, and more especially my ignorance on subjects connected with natural philosophy, so far from rendering me diffident of my own ability to comprehend what I had read, or inducing me to mistrust the many vague notions which had arisen in consequence, merely served as a farther stimulus to imagination; and I was vain enough, or perhaps reasonable enough, to doubt whether those crude ideas which, arising in ill-regulated minds, have all the appearance, may not often in effect possess also the force, the reality, and other inherent properties of instinct or intuition. (IV, 392)

Here Poe posits his own version of what Neil Harris, in his study of P. T. Barnum, calls the " 'operational aesthetic,' an approach to experience that equated beauty with information and technique, accepting guile because it was more complicated than candor." Especially at a time when Americans were becoming increasingly dependent on printed information, to win the reader's belief—or confidence—was to manufacture truth.[14] Poe explicates this principle with a note added to the story in the 1839 *Tales,* in which he compares "Hans Pfaall" to the moon hoaxes of Richard Adams Locke and "one Mr. D'Avisson." Locke's stunt, a newspaper article describing lunar discoveries made with a telescope rather than a journey to the moon, attracted more attention and fooled more people than Poe's not only because its premise was less far-fetched but because Locke sustained the illusion that his was an actual news article. But Poe insists that whereas Locke's article was inconsistent with available scientific knowledge, "[i]n 'Hans Pfaall' the design is original, inasmuch as regards an attempt at *verisimilitude,* in the application of scientific principles (so far as the whimsical nature of the subject would permit), to the actual passage between the earth and the moon" (*IV,* 433). While there is certainly a difference between writing about an actual moon voyage and writing about an imaginary one, Poe implicitly asks whether there is any difference between *reading* about an actual moon voyage and reading about an imaginary one, provided the writer has made the details of the trip plausible and consistent with the known laws of science. In the *Messenger* version, Poe concludes with this bantering assertion: "I wonder, for my part, you do not perceive at once that the letter—the document—is intrinsically—is astronomically true— and that it carries upon its very face the value of its own authenticity."[15] In "Hans Pfaall" Poe not only shows his readers how easily they can be deceived but also questions the distinction between truth and humbug, fiction and nonfiction, when truth and meaning are seemingly guaranteed by the medium of print.[16]

While exploring the possibilities of mystification in these early fictions, Poe, in his role of *Southern Literary Messenger* editor, sought to establish himself as a powerful demystifier and exposer of humbug. In his essay "Maelzel's Chess Player" (1836), Poe analyzed a traveling exhibition of a purported automaton; first displayed by its Hungarian inventor in 1769, by the 1830s the mannequin was attracting American audiences who puzzled either over whether the chess player was in fact a "pure machine" (as Poe phrases it) or, more likely, *how* Maelzel or some other human being controlled the machine's moves. (Maelzel did not explicitly claim his chess player was entirely mechanical, but his exhibition clearly suggested just that.) Although in 1836 machines were not yet displacing American workers in large numbers, new technologies were beginning to alter and in some cases perform what had previously been human tasks, particularly in printing, the trade with which Poe would have been most familiar. As in his later tale "The Man That Was Used Up," here Poe asks where the line between the human and non-human can be drawn in regard to machines built to duplicate human activity, in particular the capacity for reason. To be sure, such concerns predate and antedate Poe's time—they have become central to computer-age consciousness—but at the dawn of the American industrial revolution, the exhibition of a machine that could not merely perform a predictable sequence of actions but could actually "think" must have frightened and fascinated its spectators. Indeed, Poe emphasizes what this invention's significance would be if it were in fact "pure machine," for unlike other automata and calculators, the chess player must reason and adapt to unpredictable, changing circumstances: "There is then no analogy whatever between the operations of the Chess-Player, and those of the calculating machine of Mr. Babbage, and if we choose to call the former a *pure machine* we must be prepared to admit that it is, beyond all comparison, the most wonderful of the inventions of mankind."[17]

Poe makes this point to suggest the high stakes of proving the automaton to be a disguise, and not a replacement, for human intelligence; his claim contributes to the self-promoting pose he assumes throughout the essay. The editor of the *Messenger* presents himself as a public servant who will expose the duplicitous Maelzel, but he does so by revealing the confidence man he could easily be himself, just as his fictional detective C. Auguste Dupin calculates suspiciously like a criminal (see chapter 5). Several of Poe's 17 observations (numbered to emphasize the order and variety of his evidence) are based on this identification with his "opponent" Maelzel—most notably number 6, in which he remarks that the human figure of the chess player is but an "indifferent imitation" of a real person. Judging from Maelzel's other automata, he is capable of creating more lifelike figures and movements to make spectators forget they are machines; therefore, Poe reasons, the "awkward and rectangular manoeuvres," intended to "convey the idea of pure and unaided mechanism," are a sure sign that the chess player is *not* a pure machine (*ER*, 1270). This rather obvious point reveals the importance of intellectual identification in practicing mystification: Maelzel knows how his audience will reason, and Poe in turn knows how Maelzel will reason in regard to his audience. As John Irwin points out in regard to the Maelzel article, thinking several moves ahead in a chess game, which any successful player must do, necessitates being able to read one's opponent, to identify that person's mind with one's own. Thus Poe's analysis describes even as it utilizes the very mental faculty that would make the chess player mankind's "most wonderful invention."[18]

The most ingenious part of Poe's logic is that it looks more ingenious than it is—again, much like the automaton itself. In this respect, Poe not only identifies with the trickster but he *is* a kind of trickster, pretending to do more in this article than he does, for his revelation is rather small, considering that several previous commentators had argued effectively that a human being was concealed inside the "machine." Poe implies that those commentators were far from solving the mystery simply because they did not satisfactorily account for where exactly the human chess player was hiding or where he went when Maelzel opened the playing table for the public's inspection. Poe presents long-established arguments about the chess player as if they were new, making a small piece of detective work seem large and impressive.[19] As Irwin describes it, Poe's "analytical method is often more a rhetorical device to create the appearance of logical rigor than an exercise in rigorous logic."[20] The creator of Von Jung and Hans Pfaall knew that the appearance of profundity could be more valuable than the "substance," particularly as it furthered the power of a writer well versed in mystification.

Yet at the *Messenger* Poe's primary arena for self-promotion through intellectual jousting was the journal's editorial section, devoted largely to book reviews. Before Poe's arrival the *Messenger* had averaged about 4 pages of editorial matter per issue (which would contain about 70 pages total), but the first number Poe edited contained 28 pages of reviews, and the average during Poe's year with White was about 15 pages.[21] As with most magazines of this period, the reviews were often dominated by lengthy excerpts from new books, which was one way of "innocently" pirating published material, particularly from British imprints. But rather than merely piecing together these excerpts with congratulations to the author, Poe brought to White's gentlemanly publication an aggressive reviewing style that established his dubious career-long reputation. Poe was certainly not the only critic given to "using up" authors; in fact, his early reviewing style owed much to *Blackwood's Edinburgh Magazine,* which was more widely distributed in the United States than any domestic periodical. And in defending his reviews from charges of excessive

severity, Poe pointed out that his comments were more often favorable
than unfavorable. And yet his attacks, even when preceded by praise for a
book's merits, certainly defied the proprieties of genteel literary criticism
and the understanding that American writers needed to be "encouraged."
Instead, Poe's criticisms, whether dismissive or painstakingly analytical,
often took the tone of a crusade against overrated writing.

Such is certainly the case with Poe's first controversial review, in the
December 1835 *Messenger,* of Theodore S. Fay's novel *Norman Leslie.*[22]
Poe begins the review by denouncing the hype—the "puffing" reviews
and advance praise—with which Fay's publisher, Harper and Brothers,
and his cohorts at the *New York Mirror* had surrounded the book:

> Well!—here we have it! This is *the* book—*the* book *par excellence*—the
> book bepuffed, beplastered, and be*Mirrored:* the book "attributed to" Mr.
> Blank, and "said to be from the pen" of Mr. Asterisk: the book which has
> been "about to appear"—"in press"—"in progress"—"in preparation"—
> and "forthcoming:" the book "graphic" in anticipation—"talented" *a priori*—and God knows what *in prospectu.* For the sake of every thing puffed,
> puffing, and puffable, let us take a peep at its contents! (*ER,* 540)

Needless to say, Poe castigates Fay's novel, quoting only brief passages to
support sweeping denunciations of its plot ("a monstrous piece of absurdity and incongruity" [*ER,* 546]), characterization ("The characters *have
no character*" [*ER,* 546]), style ("unworthy of a school-boy" [*ER,* 547]),
and grammar ("not a single page . . . in which even a school-boy would
fail to detect at least two or three gross errors" [*ER,* 547]). The fact that
Poe challenges a highly touted novel by a well-connected New York
writer gives the review the tenor of a crusade, launched from the South
against the North, from an upstart magazine against a center of publishing power.[23] Poe's exaggerated, dismissive tone indicates that he does not
take the business of reviewing the likes of *Norman Leslie* seriously (Poe
seems not to have taken the novel as a genre seriously) except as a means
of calling attention to literary humbug and, more important, calling
attention to the *Southern Literary Messenger* and its brazen young editor.

Not surprisingly, Poe treated poetry with more respect, offering
lengthy and minute analyses of contemporaries whose reputations faded
soon after (if not before) their deaths. In a frequently cited review of collections by Joseph Rodman Drake and Fitz-Green Halleck, Poe seems
eager to prove himself as capable of dissecting literary works he considered worth the trouble as he was of butchering the unworthy.[24] Here,

too, Poe begins with a brief sermon, this time against reviewers finding themselves "involved in the gross paradox of liking a stupid book the better, because, sure enough, its stupidity is American" (*ER,* 506). Although as a New Yorker in the 1840s Poe would associate with a group of literary nationalists calling themselves "Young America," as a Virginian in 1836 he argued that promoting American literature at the expense of objective critical standards did more harm than good. Demonstrating his point, Poe provides a balanced, detailed analysis of Drake and Halleck; while he concludes that they do not deserve their popular acclaim, he treats their work respectfully.

But before turning to Drake and Halleck, Poe sets forth his own poetic standards, returning to the aesthetic issues he had addressed in the "Letter to [Mr. B——]." Here, too, he emphasizes originality, opposing imagination or "ideality"—the "Sentiment of Poesy"—to the lesser powers of combination or comparison. But Poe complicates his theory by adding what would seem to be a self-evident point, that the poet must be able to excite the "Faculty of Ideality" *in his readers:* Poe associates that ability with "the powers of Causality—that is to say . . . metaphysical acumen" (*ER,* 511) and claims that someone gifted with those powers, even without great imagination, will produce better poetry than one who possesses great imagination but no "metaphysical acumen." While such logic seems to complicate the issue unnecessarily, it gives Poe room to hedge on his judgments of individual poets: he immediately pays Coleridge an empty compliment, claiming that he "owed his extraordinary and almost magical pre-eminence rather to metaphysical than poetical powers" (*ER,* 512). Poe's analysis of Drake and Halleck suggests that they possess insufficient faculties of ideality *and* causality to inspire the poetic sentiment in their readers, or at least in readers as discriminating as Poe.

Calling attention to that superior discrimination seems to be the goal of both the sarcastic, annihilating *Norman Leslie* review and the judicious, philosophical Drake-Halleck review. As with the Folio Club tales, Poe seeks in these strident reviews to gain the attention of magazine readers, writers, and editors. He seemed to be succeeding: although his claims to have multiplied the *Messenger's* circulation have been debunked, its circulation did increase—by at least 25 percent—during the year Poe served as editor.[25] Its actual readership might have increased even more, along with the name recognition of both the *Messenger* and Edgar Poe. Poe kept the wheels of self-promotion turning through the common practice of reprinting laudatory notices of his magazine from other publications and, perceiving the value of negative publicity, adding to them the admonitions of rival editors. The Drake-Halleck review, for instance, quotes at length the *New York Commercial Advertiser* and the *Philadelphia Gazette*, both criticizing Poe's severity. Poe rebuts their claims, goading their editors to provide more free publicity (which the *Messenger* would return in kind) by continuing the exchange. Southern publications such as the *Newbern {North Carolina} Spectator* and the *Richmond Compiler* also objected to Poe's caustic style and devoted plenty of their own ink to debating Poe and thus promoting his renegade image. Having created a measure of controversy and acclaim with his criticism and with audacious tales such as "Berenice" and "Hans Pfaall" (the *Courier* of Charleston declared Poe "immortalized" by the latter [Thomas and Jackson, 167]), Poe had successfully positioned himself as both an exposer of mystification and hackwork and—let the reader beware—an accomplished trickster and self-promoter, mystifier and hack.

"Sensations Are the Great Things After All"

The parodist and the critic are at once a part of and apart from the "club" of publishing writers, and, as we have seen, Poe used both roles to gain entry into the club. Not surprisingly, then, Poe parodied and criticized the genres he himself worked in and the writing styles that influenced his own—particularly, as Michael Allen has shown, one of his greatest influences, *Blackwood's Edinburgh Magazine*. The Folio Club sketch includes a "Mr. Blackwood Blackwood who had written certain articles for foreign Magazines" (*CW*, 2:205); moreover, Poe refers explicitly to *Blackwood's* in two of his most intriguing satirical tales, "Loss of Breath" and "The Psyche Zenobia." As the former story's subtitle, "A Tale Neither in nor out of Blackwood," indicates, Poe intended "Loss of Breath" (originally titled "A Decided Loss") as Mr. Blackwood's contribution to the Folio Club collection, but the phrase also suggests that the story is neither "in" *Blackwood,* not having appeared in the magazine, nor "out of," that is, beyond the limits of, the *Blackwood* formula.[26] Like Poe's other early burlesques, this tale abounds in inside jokes and topical references: here the principle target is the *Blackwood* "sensation tale," which typically featured the horrific, near-death experiences of a first-person protagonist and a melodramatic narrative style. Since pulp fiction and tabloid journalism have preserved much of what made these stories popular, "Loss of Breath" seems less dated as satire than, say, "A Tale of Jerusalem." But the story works on other levels as well, in that it tries to make us laugh at questions that many of Poe's previous poems and later tales ask us to consider seriously: What would it feel like to be buried alive? What is it like to be dead? Where does one draw the line between life and death?

The death experience is not the only recurring theme this story reduces to the level of burlesque; as Daniel Hoffman demonstrates, "Loss of Breath" can be discussed alongside other tales such as "The Black Cat," "Berenice," and "Ligeia" as a story of a dysfunctional marriage (229–58). Mr. Lackobreath loses his breath while berating his wife on the day after their wedding, a circumstance that, along with Poe's puns and innuendos, hints that his narrator's loss of breath/speech is a metaphor for impotence: "I was preparing to launch forth a new and more decided epithet of opprobrium, which should not fail, if ejaculated, to convince her of her insignificance, when, to my extreme horror and astonishment, I discovered that *I had lost my breath*" (*CW,* 2:62). The panic-stricken narrator responds by kissing his wife on the cheek and then locking himself in the bedroom, before discovering some *"billets-doux"* to his wife from one Mr. Windenough.

The story operates primarily on this level of adolescent humor—and yet the correlation between speech (the lack of which turns out to be the most important manifestation of his condition) and potency suggests, quite seriously, that to be without voice is to be taken for dead. Poe's contemporaries liked to satirize the impersonal nature of modern urban life, a topic Poe would explore more soberly in "The Man of the Crowd." Considering that Poe in 1832 and 1833 was an anonymous slum-dweller trying to be "heard" in print, we might detect a fear shared by many "voiceless" urbanites in his narrator's "calamity calculated, even more than beggary, to estrange the affections of the multitude, and to draw down upon the wretch the well-merited indignation of the virtuous and the happy" (*CW,* 2:65). Lackobreath correctly predicts the reaction of the "multitude," and the comic cruelties he suffers at the hands of coach passengers, tavern-keeper, doctor, cat, and gallows-mob may strike modern readers as a cross between Kafka and Charlie Chaplin. Accordingly, after Lackobreath finds his nemesis Windenough in the sepulchre and reclaims his "breath" from him, the two bring about their rescue by "[t]he united strength of our resuscitated voices." Yet in order to get the public's attention they must first gain the attention of the newspapers: the buried alive are saved by rival editors motivated only by their own controversy concerning "the nature and origin of subterranean noises" (*CW,* 2:74). Thus this sensation tale "neither in nor out of Black-wood" is resolved by editors who, like Blackwood, seek sensations to help sell their publications; their story will become a crowd-pleaser, just as Poe hoped his "Loss of Breath" would, for he revised and republished it throughout the 1830s. Appropriately, in the midst of the story's slapstick we find an image, both comic and disturbing, of a man trying to amuse his public: "My convulsions were said to be extraordinary. My spasms it would have been difficult to beat. The populace *encored.* Several gentlemen swooned; and a multitude of ladies were carried home in hysterics. . . . When I had afforded sufficient amusement, it was thought proper to remove my body from the gallows" (*CW,* 2:69–70).

While Poe probably did not intend this scene to evoke the plight of the modern writer as entertainer, such a connection is consistent with the lessons of his other *Blackwood* spoof, "The Psyche Zenobia." Possibly Poe's best-executed satire, "The Psyche Zenobia" (first published in the *American Museum* in 1838 and republished as "How to Write a Blackwood Article" and "A Predicament") lampoons Blackwood more aggressively and more personally but also refers more obviously than "Loss of Breath" to Poe's own style and reliance on sensational plot devices. The ridiculous central action of Psyche Zenobia's *Blackwood* article, her decapitation by the gigantic minute hand of a clock, reminds modern readers not of *Blackwood* articles, most of which were never republished, but of other Poe stories. Unwittingly or not, then, the disciple/critic of *Blackwood's* includes himself in this satire that decries the debasement of literature in the magazine age, the pandering of authors and editors to the public's appetite for sensation at the expense of good writing.

At the beginning of his lesson, Mr. Blackwood instructs his student that the writer of "intensities" must use very black ink and a very big pen with a very blunt nib. "And, mark me, Miss Psyche Zenobia!" he continues—as Poe puns on the fact that Zenobia is "marking" or writing him into her narrative—

> mark me!—*that pen—must—never—never be mended!* Herein, madam, lies the secret, the soul, of intensity. I assume it upon myself to say, that no individual, of however great genius, ever wrote with a good pen,—understand me,—a good article. You may take it for granted, that when manuscript can be read it is never worth reading. This is a leading principle in our faith, to which if you cannot readily assent, our conference is at an end. (*CW,* 2:339)

Zenobia, of course, assents, considering the proposition obvious; thus Poe the established autographer criticizes the arrogance of professional writers who, unlike himself, exercise poor penmanship and make trouble for editors. But, especially if we keep in mind the fact that Poe used the autography series as a way to comment on writers' literary styles by commenting on their handwriting, this "leading principle" of Mr. Blackwood assumes more importance: in order to succeed, not only the manuscript but the published article ought to be unreadable. In fact, Blackwood provides a formula that Poe would continue to satirize throughout his career: produce magazine copy not by writing in the traditional sense but through a *system* or *method*—if at all possible, one that will produce unreadable text—and you will create sensations and become a successful magazinist. "Sensations," Blackwood reminds Zenobia, "are the great things after all" (*CW,* 2:340), by which he means physical sensations that provide material for *Blackwood* articles—but the word also evokes the sensations such articles create among the public.

First, Zenobia describes how her mentor produces political articles: "Mr. Blackwood has a pair of tailor's-shears, and three apprentices who stand by him for orders. One hands him the 'Times,' another the 'Examiner,' and a third a 'Gulley's New Compendium of Slang-Whang.' Mr. B. merely cuts out and intersperses" (*CW,* 2:338). The slightly more complicated method for composing "intensities" consists primarily of choosing a tone in which to cast one's sensations. But as with creating political articles, composing in any of the tones Mr. Blackwood offers subverts the development of ideas and negates the need for inspiration—not only because the concept is a sort of paint-by-numbers approach but because each offers its own short cuts: the tone laconic avoids writing in paragraphs; the tone elevated is "the best of all possible styles where the writer is in too great a hurry to think" (*CW,* 2:341); with the tone metaphysical, footnotes and foreign sources allow the writer to "look erudite and—and—and frank" (*CW,* 2:342); and the tone transcendental discourages saying what one means. As for the "filling up," as Blackwood calls it, that can be accomplished largely through stock phrases, many of which can be found in a book appropriately titled *Piquant Facts for the Manufacture of Similes* (*CW,* 2:343).

Writing might be unreadable in the same sense that bad music is said to be unlistenable, because the writer is an unskilled hack like Psyche Zenobia; or it might be unreadable because its author, like Von Jung the mystific or his creator Edgar Poe, wants to fool the reader. "The Psyche Zenobia" suggests that the rise of mass-produced literature, of which weekly and monthly periodicals were the vanguard, would multiply the incidence of both kinds of unreadability and perhaps make it more difficult to tell the two apart—from each other, and from the well-crafted tales on which Poe's twentieth-century reputation would rest.

Love and Death

Even the briefest biographies of Poe emphasize the impact that the deaths of loved ones—women especially—had on his work; some scholars, notably J. Gerald Kennedy and Grace Farrell, have gone further to situate Poe within a contemporary cultural preoccupation with death and mourning.[27] The evolution of attitudes toward death in the nineteenth century is complex, but clearly by Poe's time Americans were regarding death differently than previous generations had, and the middle class was increasingly concerned with beautifying death and ritualizing mourning. Even before the nineteenth century the iconography of tombstones had shifted from grim reminders of mortality (such as skulls) to more hopeful images of everlasting life (such as angels). Nineteenth-century mourning rituals also emphasized the hope of keeping alive a person's spirit and in some ways denied the physical fact of death. In the 1830s the rural cemetery movement gave more dignity and individuality to the deceased and encouraged visits from loved ones. As Kennedy points out, such gestures "symbolically extended the relationship severed by death."[28] Indeed, these new conventions sought to make death less final, less frightening, and somehow easier to accept both as a mourner and as a mortal facing the same fate, but they also called more attention to death and the real uncertainties it arouses. Amid the trend toward "domesticating" death, insisting on its benignity while shifting the focus away from the sensations of the dying and the existential uncertainties of the living, Poe constructed allegories that explored the death experience.

"Ms. Found in a Bottle," the story that launched Poe's career, presents the paradox of trying even to imagine postmortem consciousness. Midway through the tale, the narrator, anticipating death while helplessly drifting on a cargo ship caught in a simoom (a tropical wind or storm), is thrust by the ship's lurching onto another, much larger vessel manned by ancient sailors who seem unaware of his presence. Once on board this ghost ship, the narrator describes its drift toward the South Pole: "It is evident that we are hurrying onwards to some exciting knowledge—some never-to-be-imparted secret, whose attainment is destruction" (*CW,* 2:145). Combining two public fascinations—polar exploration and the possibility of transcending death—Poe suggests a parallel between the ship's movement toward the "great secrets" at the South Pole and the narrator's movement toward the great secrets of existence. However, the tale defies any simple allegorical reading, for, as Charles May points out, Poe suddenly shifts "from the realistic to the imaginative plane" during the simoom. Noting that the word *simoom* "derives from an Arabic word meaning 'to poison,' " May explains the shift as resulting from the narrator's ingestion of opium, which must have mixed during the storm with the jageree that the narrator tells us was his only food for five days on the open sea.[29] However the shift in perspective may be explained, most of the story's commentators link it to the narrator's insistence (in the tale's opening paragraphs) that he is skeptical and rational to a fault: "I have often been reproached with the aridity of my genius; a deficiency of imagination has been imputed to me as a crime" (*CW,* 2:135). But once on board the second ship, he undergoes "a sensation which will admit of no analysis. . . . A new sense—a new entity is added to my soul" (*CW,* 2:141). For critics who emphasize Poe's interest in breaking through what Melville's Ahab would call the "pasteboard mask" of visible objects to attain a more profound and meaningful vision of the cosmos, the story depicts the narrator's arousal from a rationalist "waking dream" to a necessarily irrational consciousness, which Poe elsewhere associated with the dreamworld of the poet or artist, and also with death itself.[30]

The narrator regards this new sensation as "a great evil" because of his rational skepticism, and yet in defiance of his conscious efforts he pursues it. He had no practical reason for embarking on the voyage in the first place: "I went as passenger," he tells us, "having no other inducement than a kind of nervous restlessness which haunted me as a fiend" (*CW,* 2:135). The narrator's subconscious desire is literally inscribed in a brief episode on the deck of the phantom ship: "While musing upon the singularity of my fate, I unwittingly daubed with a tarbrush the edges of a neatly-folded studding-sail which lay near me on a barrel. The studding-sail is now bent upon the ship, and the thoughtless touches of the brush are spread out into the word DISCOVERY" (*CW,* 2:142). The literal impossibility of this accidental writing reinforces the impression that the entire manuscript comes from a dream state, opium-induced or not. Moreover, it creates an ironic tableau: a ship at the edge of a precipice with the word "DISCOVERY" written on its sail. Whatever awakening of the senses the narrator experiences leads either to nothingness or to some "never-to-be-imparted secret." Although the narrator's written "DISCOVERY" goes down with the ship, his bottled manuscript survives. As Gerald Kennedy points out, the narrator hopes that the manuscript, springing up from his burial place, will give him a form of life after death. It does not, however, provide readers with a glimpse of "the other side" but instead reveals the paradox of any effort to represent death:[31] compelled, because of death's inevitablilty, to contemplate it, to try to imagine it, to write about it, we "discover" only its inscrutability. As the manuscript's writer says of the ghost ship, "What she *is not,* I can easily perceive; what she *is,* I fear it is impossible to say" (*CW,* 2:142).

Impossible or not, Poe attempted to picture death in other early works. "Shadow" presents another manuscript-in-a-bottle, as its fictional writer presumes that he will be read only after his death. He begins, "Ye who read are still among the living; but I who write shall have long since gone my way into the region of shadows" (*CW,* 2:188). The living voice of the dead narrator reflects the story's life-in-death scenario: seven men reveling in the midst of a plague. Death, not surprisingly, crashes the party, identifying himself by speaking "not [in] the tones of any one being, but of a multitude of beings . . . the well remembered and familiar accents of many thousand departed friends" (*CW,* 2:191). Thus the story "Shadow," ostensibly written by one who has joined those departed friends, duplicates the figure who says "I am SHADOW," for both are "living" reminders of death's presence in life. Another tableau, "Silence" (first published as "Siope—A Fable"), recalls the imagery of "The Valley of Unrest" and "The Doomed City" to equate death with a perfect stillness; the demon-narrator observes that a man can withstand the terrors of desolation, but when the demon invokes "the curse of *silence,*" the man becomes terrified: "And the man shuddered, and turned his face away, and fled afar off, in haste, so that I beheld him no more" (*CW,* 2:198).[32]

Not surprisingly, however, the early tales that have attracted the most readers and anthologists since Poe's time depict some kind of violation of the boundaries between life and death: "Metzengerstein," "The Assignation," "Berenice," "Morella," and "Ligeia." But how seriously should we take these tales? While many read "Berenice" and "Ligeia," for instance, as Gothic classics, the style in which Poe writes them is heavy-handed enough that one might well laugh at them: Egaeus's dental fixation and Rowena/Ligeia's repeated death-and-rejuvenation episodes seem too absurd to frighten anyone, no matter how often they have been packaged as "classic tales of terror." Are they in fact ironic commentaries on Gothicism, as Clark Griffith and G. R. Thompson have suggested, or do they provoke serious consideration of the power of love—or hatred—to overcome death?[33] Given Poe's combined admiration and mockery of the type of story he associated with *Blackwood's,* it should come as no surprise if the answer is "both," as if Poe finds the idea of transcending death absurd, and yet irresistible.

In "Metzengerstein" and "The Assignation," works of art act as conductors of this death-transcending power. In the former (Poe's first published story), a horse represented in a tapestry comes to life as the reincarnated Count Berlifitzing, who was killed in a fire set by his neighbor and ancestral enemy, Baron Metzengerstein. In "The Assignation" the hero unveils a portrait of his lover, the Marchesa Aphrodite, just before poisoning himself, fulfilling his part in their double suicide. David Ketterer pairs these stories, observing that in "Metzengerstein" "the borderline between art and reality becomes radically equivocal" as the tapestry unites Metzengerstein and Berlifitzing with their ancestors; thus the border between the dead and the living is also transgressed by means of the tapestry.[34] The effect of the painting in "The Assignation" is more subtle: the hero seeks escape through art—in this case escaping the fact that his lover is married to another man—arranging a meeting "in that hollow vale" beyond the grave. Taken at face value, then, the stories suggest that art and death are vehicles of transcendence, and, accordingly, "poetic" justice resolves both tales: the dead Berlifitzing returns to life for revenge, and two star-crossed lovers live together in the afterworld.

But another similarity between these stories—their reliance on popular literary references—suggests that here, too, Poe was trying to capitalize on contemporary literary fashions. "Metzengerstein" 's probable sources, as Mabbott points out in his introduction, include two widely read British novels—Walpole's *The Castle of Otranto* (1764), Disraeli's *Vivian Grey* (1826)—and a poem, "The Buccaneer" (1827), by the popular American writer Richard Henry Dana (*CW,* 2:16–17). The similarities are not strong enough to constitute plagiarism, especially given the widespread use of such devices as enchantment and revenge from beyond the grave in early Gothic fiction; moreover, Poe at this stage in his career would not have been so foolhardy as to choose such popular works if he had intended to pass off borrowed plot devices as original. Rather, Poe must have *wanted* readers to recognize the references to other popular works or at least to standard Gothic devices. His inclusion of "Metzengerstein" in the Folio Club collection and the subtitle he appended to it in the *Southern Literary Messenger*—"A Tale in Imitation of the German"—suggests a parody, but at the same time the story's tone is serious enough that it also reads as a magazinist's abridgement of a typical Gothic novel. Similarly, "The Assignation" 's hero is clearly modeled on Byron, while the plot derives from an episode in Goldsmith's *Vicar of Wakefield* (1766) (Mabbott, *CW,* 2:48–49). And yet here, too, "parody" hardly seems the right word.[35] Like the other Folio Club tales, "The Assignation" employs allusions to gain the approval of members of the real Folio Club of authors and editors, but here the effect is not ridiculous, as in "Lionizing" or "The Duc de l'Omelette." "The Assignation" ultimately pays tribute to Byron even as it implicitly mocks slaving imitation or worship of the Byronic hero.

The narrators of "Metzengerstein" and "The Assignation" will their own deaths in quests for unity—with a mortal enemy in one case and an immortal beloved in another. But in Poe's trilogy of tales named for dying women, the reunions take place not in the spirit world but in the world of the still-living male narrators. Like "Ms. Found in a Bottle," "Berenice" centers on its narrator's painful awakening into another way of knowing. Although the visionary Egaeus is a far cry from the rational skeptic of "Ms. Found in a Bottle," he, too, lives mainly through his intellect, born in a library, where he spends seemingly all his time, shunning human contact or emotions. But midway through the story he finds himself suddenly infatuated with his dying cousin:

> During the brightest days of her unparalleled beauty, most surely I had never loved her. In the strange anomaly of my existence, feelings, with me, *had never been* of the heart, and my passions *always were* of the mind. . . . she had flitted by my eyes, and I had seen her—not as the living and breathing Berenice, but as the Berenice of a dream; not as a being of the earth, earthy, but as the abstraction of such a being; not as a thing to admire, but to analyze; not as an object of love, but as the theme of the most abstruse although desultory speculation. And *now*—now I shuddered in her presence, and grew pale at her approach; yet, bitterly lamenting her fallen and desolate condition, I called to mind that she had loved me long, and, in an evil moment, I spoke to her of marriage. (*CW,* 2:213–14)

Egaeus's obsession with Berenice goes beyond his earlier momentary fixations on random inanimate objects. He is entering a world of feeling for which his lifetime of reading and dreaming have not prepared him; appropriately, he uses "simoom"—the same word that the narrator of "Ms. Found in a Bottle" had used to designate the storm that overtook his ship—to describe the onset of the disease that afflicts Berenice and thereby pulls him into this new realm of experience. Egaeus's marriage proposal is an "evil moment" because it leads to his gruesome violation of his wife's grave, but it also suggests the intimacy between love and death, for Egaeus learns to love Berenice only when he knows she is going to die, as if he can know love only through loss. This irony resonates with the string of paradoxes Egaeus lists in the first paragraph: unloveliness in beauty, evil in good, sorrow in joy, agony in ecstasy.

But it is Berenice's live burial that embodies the paradox at the heart of all the stories discussed in this section, that of living through one's own death. Poe foreshadows the transgression of the living/dead boundary in Egaeus's early, seemingly gratuitous reference to his belief in reincarnation and his quotation from *De Carne Christi,* which translates, "The Son of God has died, it is to be believed because it is incredible; and, buried, He is risen, it is sure because it is impossible" (*CW,* 2:213). But Berenice is no Christ figure: she does not defeat death so much as she unwittingly fakes it. Like Mr. Lackobreath, she is taken for dead and, as a result, her "corpse" is violated while she is still alive. Although "Berenice" strikes few readers as a comic story, it burlesques the same idea as the blatantly comic "Loss of Breath"—that one can live beyond the hour of death—as Poe revives Berenice only to have her suffer still more.[36]

Egaeus extracts Berenice's teeth because he believes they are "ideas": he is desperate to have some essential part of her survive her bodily disintegration. Teeth are an oddly appropriate choice because they are unique to the individual and durable enough even to identify otherwise unrecognizable corpses.[37] As if to hint that Egaeus hopes to preserve Berenice's *iden*tity, Poe goes out of his way to provide the French word for teeth, *dents.* If Egaeus's idea that *"tous ses dents sont idées"* is absurd, it is no more absurd than the idea that her identity can live on after her death—and yet Egaeus's obsession with the ideas or identity of Berenice outliving her body leads him to torture and, presumably, kill her.

Read in this way, "Berenice" foreshadows "Morella" and "Ligeia," stories in which the wives' identities do survive their physical deaths by assuming the bodies of their successors—in Morella's case, her own daughter, and in Ligeia's, her husband's next wife. Like Egaeus, the narrators of "Morella" and "Ligeia" are avid readers obsessed with ideas (particularly ideas about the nature of identity), men who live inside their own minds to the point that one suspects that the supernatural events they describe may be projections of their subconscious desires or obsessions. Indeed, in each of these three stories one wonders how much is "real" and how much is the narrator's invention, delusion, or hallucination. But in "Ligeia" Poe compounds this problem, as the unnamed narrator begins by confessing that he cannot remember even Ligeia's family name, much less where, when, or how he met her. "She came and departed as a shadow," he tells us, hinting, as the library-bound Egaeus does, that he has dreamed his fantasy woman to life (CW, 2:311). Moreover, this narrator reminds us repeatedly that after Ligeia's death his perception has been altered by grief and opium. Does the story depict "real" events until Ligeia dies, at which point fantasy takes over? Or does reality break down only in the final scene of Ligeia's rejuvenation? Or does the narrator invent Ligeia and then psychologically torture her opposite, the flesh-and-blood Rowena, for not being or becoming his ideal? Or are both women archetypes, one fair and the other dark, but neither one an actual human being?

To ask such questions is to regard "Ligeia" as a highly symbolic story, even for Poe, and most critics have treated it as such. Kennedy sees Ligeia as Poe's "poetic" ideal of beauty who prevails over the prosaic Rowena, who inspires only "fear and revulsion." Clark Griffith argues that the two women represent competing schools of Gothicism—Ligeia, "dark" German idealism; Rowena, the watered-down Romanticism of "fair England"—and Poe's story satirizes both even as it depicts the triumph of the German school.[38] As Griffith and G. R. Thompson point out, Poe's exaggerated style, along with his career-long ridicule of transcendentalism, the philosophy to which Ligeia indoctrinates the narrator and which her reincarnation symbolizes, certainly allows for an ironic reading. For Thompson, Poe's description of Ligeia's face, with its prominent forehead, huge black eyes, and "teeth glancing back with a brilliancy almost startling," should bring to mind a skull—reversing the impression that Ligeia represents life triumphant over death.[39]

But even while the story operates as a satire on transcendentalism and Gothic conventions, for many modern readers it epitomizes Poe's representation of women as fantasy objects whose seemingly inevitable deaths provide the focal points of his stories only because of the grief they cause the male subject. Like Helen of the 1831 poem, Ligeia is an art object; she, too, has "hyacinthine" hair, as well as a "marble hand" and "skin rivalling the purest ivory" (CW, 2:312, 311). Although the narrator admires her not only for her beauty but also for her intellectual superiority, both qualities in Ligeia serve as self-congratulation for him, as this creature of otherworldly beauty, "immense" learning, and "gigantic" acquisitions expresses "no ordinary passion" for him as she lies dying: "For long hours, detaining my hand, would she pour out before me the overflowing of a heart whose more than passionate devotion amounted to idolatry" (*CW,* 2:317). Joel Porte argues that this dark, Hebraic fantasy woman is a product of the narrator's imagination—he, not she, wills her back into existence: "Through sheer strength of will he *subjectively*—that is, to his own perceiving—converts the blonde Rowena into the raven-haired Ligeia." More specifically, the narrator kills off Rowena for her body, either by frightening her to death with the funereal decorations and phantasmagoric effects of the bridal chamber or by poisoning her wine.[40]

But why choose as a vessel for Ligeia's spirit a woman who appears to be her opposite? Kennedy argues that the narrator psychologically tortures and kills Rowena not because of her origins or appearance but simply because she is a woman: "Little more than a token of gender, she is yet the brunt of a malevolent plot which begins prior to the narrator's remarriage. . . . Displacing the outrage he feels for the dead woman who has left him to languish, he projects on Rowena all his unconscious resentment of Ligeia."[41] Similarly, Leland S. Person reads the story as a cautionary tale against male objectification of women. Ultimately, Ligeia is more powerful than the narrator, he claims: "More than a record of the narrator's hallucination, the tale can be read as a male-female struggle, . . . a battle of wills finally won by a woman."[42] Indeed, although the narrator remains obsessed with Ligeia as his second wife dies (repeatedly), he seems shocked and horrified by the dark lady's reappearance, hardly the reaction of someone who has willed her back to life. It is Ligeia's teaching and her appearance that inspire the narrator's memory of the Glanville passage that serves as the story's epigraph: "And the will therein lieth, which dieth not. . . . Man doth not yield him[self] to the angels, nor unto death utterly, save only through the weakness of his feeble will" (*CW,* 2:314). The narrator merely repeats what she quotes from her deathbed. And it is Ligeia who writes "The Conqueror Worm"—an allegorical poem that, as Porte points out, can be read as Ligeia's vision not of the plight of "man" confronted by death but of the plight of woman confronted by "the conquering male organ."[43] But Ligeia is not conquered. Poe certainly was no feminist, but regardless of his intentions he did create a story that demonstrates the consequences of male objectification or "othering" of women. While it is hard to find any "realistic" characters—male or female—in Poe, Ligeia, more than any other of Poe's women, has presence, has a voice, and ultimately does "take over" the male narrator's story.[44]

Ligeia takes over in another sense as well, for the story achieves an almost uncanny momentum as she returns in the last paragraph:

> One bound, and I had reached her feet! Shrinking from my touch, she let fall from her head the ghastly cerements which had confined it, and there streamed forth, into the rushing atmosphere of the chamber, huge masses of long and dishevelled hair; *it was blacker than the wings of the midnight!* And now slowly opened *the eyes* of the figure which stood before me. "Here then, at least," I shrieked aloud, "can I never—can I never be mistaken—these are the full, and the black, and the wild eyes—of my lost love—of the lady—of the LADY LIGEIA!" (*CW,* 2:330)

We want to laugh off the return of the dark lady, dressed up in Poe's most hyperbolic language, his stacks of prepositional phrases, scattered dashes, italics, and exclamation marks—but if we do, it is with a very nervous sort of laughter. Even as Poe seemingly pasted together borrowed ideas and bits of parody and burlesque to construct these early stories, when he was most successful, as in "Berenice," "Ms. Found in a Bottle," and "Ligeia," we sense something undeniably alive underneath the spare parts. What Gary Lindberg says of Poe's fiction in general is especially true of a story like "Ligeia": "Banal, jerry-built, shabbily imitative, its moving parts open to view, the contrivance somehow works."[45] In the mid-1830s Poe became a "tomahawk man" to attract attention and sell magazines, but while doing so he raised the standards for literary criticism in the United States. Similarly, he approached prose fiction like a hack writer, flaunting his erudition, borrowing plots, appropriating proven formulas, satirizing other writers—but in the process he laid the foundation for the modern short story. He found that within the almost laughable popular conventions of ghost ships, reincarnation, and premature burial lay profound paradoxes surrounding love and death.

Chapter Three

Black and White and Re(a)d All Over: *The Narrative of Arthur Gordon Pym*

Why Did Poe Write *Pym*?

Before leaving the *Southern Literary Messenger* near the end of 1836, Poe had begun his only novel, although that term seems inappropriate for the enigmatic *Narrative of Arthur Gordon Pym of Nantucket*. At once a mock nonfictional exploration narrative, adventure saga, bildungsroman, hoax, largely plagiarized travelogue, and spiritual allegory, *Pym* stands as one of the most elusive major texts of American literature.[1] Apparently Poe and T. W. White had planned to serialize the work in the *Messenger*, but only two installments appeared early in 1837; by that time Poe had moved to New York, where by May he had arranged for Harper and Brothers to publish *Pym* in book form. As Poe's first book of prose and his first book under the imprint of a major publisher, *Pym* represented a golden opportunity for the aspiring 29-year-old author. But the book did not fare well: although better distributed than his volumes of poetry, it met with poor sales and mixed reviews. Poe himself referred to *Pym* as a "silly book" the year after it was published (*Letters,* 1:130), which raises the question of why Poe, acutely aware of the literary market and determined to perfect his craft, would write a book that lacks the coherence he would insist on in his and others' short fiction, a book that either fails to meet or disregards readers' expectations (in his time or ours) in regard to narrative consistency and wholeness of plot.

At the time, writing a book-length narrative must have seemed a necessary career decision to Poe, for it was probably not a labor of love. Although Poe had improved his prospects for a literary career by editing the *Messenger* for a year, he still could not interest publishers in his "Tales of the Folio Club." He had no steady job in New York, and, with the onset of the economic depression of 1837 (which began while Poe was probably still working on *Pym* and which delayed its publication by a year), his future as a professional writer must have seemed dim. While waiting for *Pym* to be published, he was sufficiently discouraged to write to a well-connected author, James Kirke Paulding, asking for help in obtaining a clerkship that would release him from "the miserable life of literary drudgery."[2] Such a gesture suggests that he might have undertaken *Pym* somewhat grudgingly and with a heightened cynicism toward the profession of authorship. In rejecting "Tales of the Folio Club," Harper and Brothers had advised Poe to "lower himself a little to the ordinary comprehension of the generality of readers" and explained that American readers preferred a "single and connected story [that] occupies the whole volume, or number of volumes, as the case may be" (Thomas and Jackson, 193). Although Poe could hardly afford to spend months on a single project (even established authors did not receive advances for books in the 1830s), he might have reasoned that only a popular novel could raise his status and earning power and was therefore worth the gamble.[3]

If Poe's aim was to appeal to a mass audience, a voyage to the South Pole provided ideal subject matter. The abundance of travel writing and sealore in the 1830s—published as pamphlets and books and in weekly and monthly magazines—indicates the popularity of the mode he had chosen for his novel. In the wake of Jeremiah Reynolds's 1829 to 1830 polar expedition and his efforts in 1836 to persuade Congress to sponsor further exploration, Americans had become particularly interested in these uncharted regions. Poe imported facts, plot devices, and sometimes entire passages from Reynolds's published reports (which he reviewed in the same issue of the *Southern Literary Messenger* that included the first installment of *Pym*), as well as Benjamin Morrell's best-selling *Narrative of Four Voyages* (ghost-written by Samuel Woodworth) and dozens of other popular sea narratives.[4]

Poe, then, had legitimate reasons for choosing to write a sea-adventure tale culminating in a polar discovery. But given the novel's timeliness, along with Poe's virtuosity as fiction writer and his awareness of the public demand for "sensations," the question remains why he crafted *Pym* so that it frustrates readers' expectations more often than it fulfills them. One logical but unsatisfying answer is that Poe simply lacked a novelist's "vision" or sensibility, that he would soon champion the "single-effect" theory of the short story because he could not negotiate the multiple interlocking elements of plot or elaborate the depths of character necessary to produce a coherent novel. But regardless of Poe's ability to write a coherent novel, his mixed feelings toward the reading public might have prodded him to concoct a large-scale mystification, a novel that encourages and then subverts its readers' attempts to find meaning. I have already discussed Poe's interest in hoaxes and mystifications up to this point in his career, his desire to appeal to a mass audience while encoding inside jokes and erudite satire for the benefit of a highbrow audience; he might well have responded to the Harpers' practical advice by deliberately writing a novel with all the outward appearances of a best-selling potboiler but with a hole—a vortex, in fact—that would drain away coherence and meaning. If Poe had intended to create a mystification in the spirit of Von Jung, he half succeeded: on the one hand, the Harpers accepted *Pym,* and the book continues to baffle (and perhaps mystify) readers and critics to this day; on the other hand, the book did not gain Poe the literary celebrity or the money that he desperately needed.

Perhaps we should add to the list of reasons for *Pym* turning out as it did Poe's tendency to sabotage his best opportunities to attain professional stability. Biographers almost invariably attribute to Poe a personal "imp of the perverse," as he would later call it; writing against the principles of unity and verisimilitude that Poe and his contemporaries recognized as essential to the novel could be yet another instance of that impulse.[5] Toward the end of the book, in fact, Pym gives in to an overwhelming desire to annihilate himself by plunging off a steep cliff (only to be caught by his companion Dirk Peters): "For one moment my fingers clutched convulsively upon their hold, while, with the movement, the faintest possible idea of ultimate escape wandered, like a shadow, through my mind—in the next my whole soul was pervaded with *a longing to fall;* a desire, a yearning, a passion utterly uncontrollable" (*IV,* 198). Poe's ambiguous use of the word "escape" is worth noting, for while Pym and Peters are trying to escape death, either from starvation or discovery by the Tsalalians, "escape" in this context also suggests the escape *through* death from Pym's predicament, from the nearly constant suffering and terror he has experienced on his journey. Similarly, a frustrated Poe might have seen *Pym* as a means of escape from the life of literary drudgery, either attaining celebrity or committing professional suicide. But like Pym's leap into Peters's arms, Poe's novel-writing plunge provided him no escape.

While I have taken some license in reading Poe's predicament into Pym's plunge into the abyss, other instances of Poe writing himself into his novel are more specific and less speculative. As many critics have pointed out, "Arthur Gordon Pym" sounds somewhat like "Edgar Allan

Poe," with the same number of syllables in each part of both names, the same ending consonants in the first and middle names, and the same initial consonant and number of letters in the last.[6] (As has also been noted, "Pym" is an anagram for "ymp," again suggesting impulse or the imp of the perverse.) Biographers and critics, notably Richard Wilbur and Burton R. Pollin, have called attention to several intriguing biographical echoes, particularly in the earlier chapters; for instance, Wilbur claims that the character of Augustus Barnard is based on Poe's boyhood friend Ebenezer Burling as well as his brother, William Henry Poe (Augustus dies on August 1, the date on which William Henry died in 1832).[7] In the first paragraph of chapter 1 Pym tells us that Augustus's father "has many relations, I am sure, in Edgarton" and also notes that his own grandfather speculated "in the stocks of the Edgarton New-Bank" (*IV*, 57): Poe uses the proximity of Edgartown, Massachusetts, to slip these self-references into Pym's and Augustus's genealogy. He also makes his own birthday, January 19, the date for a turning point late in the novel, the *Jane Guy* crew's fateful meeting with the Tsalalians. A few commentators have seen Poe's preoccupation with food and consumption throughout *Pym* in terms of his own marginal existence, reflecting perhaps the hunger Poe, Virginia, and Muddy experienced as Poe was writing the book, or, as Alexander Hammond claims, invoking a commonplace metaphor of food consumption for the public's purchase and reading of literature, their "consumption" of "the authorial self": "Poe was evidently scripting into the text figures for the threat he felt from the new marketplace in which he labored."[8] Considering the instances in the novel where humans are devoured (by sharks, birds, and even other humans), Poe's fear of his fate as an author in a modern consumer culture must have been unusually morbid as he composed *Pym*. Faint though they may be, the biographical echoes in *Pym* underscore how important this "silly book" must have seemed to its author, who correctly perceived it as a turning point in his career.

Going to Extremes

These instances of self-reference have reinforced many readers' contention that *Pym* should be read strictly on the level of hoax (like many eighteenth- and early-nineteenth-century sensational novels, the book is attributed to its narrator, not to Poe) or satire aimed at the conventions of sea-adventure narratives and popular novels. Against the claims of authenticity suggested by the title page, with its subtitle promising "details of a mutiny and atrocious butchery on board the American brig Grampus," the reference to the town of Edgarton can be read as a tip-off—or reminder—to astute readers that the journey they are about to take has been fabricated by Edgar Poe. More significant are the preface and the concluding note, which at once affirm and question the veracity of Pym's narrative. Like the detailed subtitle, the inclusion of an introduction signed by the fictional author was, by the 1830s, a fairly conventional authenticating device for novelists. But Poe makes the very issue of truth and believability the subject of Pym's preface:

> One consideration which deterred me was, that, having kept no journal during a greater portion of the time in which I was absent, I feared I should not be able to write, from mere memory, a statement so minute and connected as to have the *appearance* of that truth it would really possess. . . . Another reason was, that the incidents to be narrated were of a nature so positively marvellous, that, unsupported as my assertions must necessarily be (except by the evidence of a single individual, and he a half-breed Indian), I could only hope for belief among my family, and those of my friends who have had reason, through life, to put faith in my veracity—the probability being that the public at large would regard what I should put forth as merely an impudent and ingenious fiction. (*IV*, 55)

Racked with anxiety over whether the people who are now reading the preface will believe the narrative, and having given those readers good reasons *not* to believe it, Pym explains that one Mr. Poe assured him that he could "trust to the shrewdness and common sense of the public" (*IV*, 55). Such an assertion, attributed to the master-cryptologist/parodist/hoaxer Poe, is ironic enough, but Poe adds the explanation that the narrative's "very uncouthness, if there were any, would give it all the better chance of being received as truth" (*IV*, 55–56). As concerned as he is that readers will not believe his story, Pym still consents to allow Poe to "draw up, in his own words, a narrative of the earlier portion of my adventures" and to publish it in the *Southern Literary Messenger* "*under the garb of fiction*" (*IV*, 56). Poe—now a character in his own fiction—is apparently confident enough that the "shrewd" public will believe Pym's story that he is willing to publish it *as* fiction—and according to Pym, Poe is right: "I thence concluded that the facts of my narrative would prove of such a nature as to carry with them sufficient evidence of their own authenticity, and that I had consequently little to fear on the score of popular incredulity" (*IV*, 56). Given the series of incredible adventures that make up most of the narrative, readers who return to the preface will recognize the thick sarcasm behind that statement. Poe engineered this series of reversals partly for a practical reason: to explain why the early chapters had appeared under *his* name in the *Southern Literary Messenger*. But in so doing, Poe and Pym proclaim the public's gullibility: if Pym's narrative were true, the best way to get the public to believe it would be to present it as fiction. Poe might well have thought he was letting "the few" in on a joke at the expense of "the many," but it is hard to imagine two distinct groups in this case: Poe insults all his readers and winks at us at the same time. Ostensibly stage setting for a hoax—one that, if reviews are any indication, fooled almost no one—the preface works more effectively as a satire on authenticating devices and readers' willingness to be taken in.

The concluding note, like the preface, pretends to authenticate the narrative while justifying an embarrassing feature of the text, in this case its abrupt, mysterious ending. But here, too, the explanation raises more questions than it answers. Adopting the persona of an editor, Poe opens the note with one of his trademark mystifications, claiming that fictional "facts" need not be given because they are already well known: "The circumstances connected with the late sudden and distressing death of Mr. Pym are already well known to the public through the medium of the daily press" (*IV*, 207). Whatever Pym experienced the moment after he confronted the great white figure, he did not die: the preface, as well as references to his surviving the journey within the narrative, has already established that Pym's manuscript was not found in a (very large) bottle. But are we to imagine that while the circumstances of Pym's death are well known, the circumstances of his earlier survival—whatever headline-making discovery awaited him beyond the white veil—remain *unknown*, 10 years after the fact? Pym's fatal "accident," occurring when the entire book had gone to press except those chapters explaining how he managed to escape an almost certain death, is suspiciously convenient, symptomatic of a writer who had run out of time, or perhaps ingenuity. (Even so, Poe lays the groundwork for a sequel by promising that either the remaining chapters or Dirk Peters will be found.) While covering his tracks, Poe calls the veracity of the entire narrative into question: the editor tells us that Poe will not finish Pym's account because he does not believe "the latter portions of the narration" (the two or three "lost" chapters, or the last published chapters? "the editor" does not say), and he sneeringly points out that the nature and meaning of the hieroglyphic writing, which baffled Pym, also "escaped the attention of Mr. Poe" (*IV,* 207). As J. Gerald Kennedy observes, "This successive discrediting . . . compels us to ask why, in the last analysis, we ought to accept the editor's construction of 'truth' as decisive and definitive";[9] in devising a way to "anchor" the narrative in some kind of truth, Poe has ironically set it even further adrift.

If the suspicious preface and note were not enough, the narrative itself contains enough contradictions and factual errors to arouse suspicion. In his notes to the standard edition of *Pym,* Burton R. Pollin not only points out approximately 200 errors, ranging from nautical calculations to contradictions in *Pym'*s plot, but theorizes as to which errors are intentional on Poe's part and which are not. Regardless of Poe's intentions, however, to read such an error-laden text—assuming one notices the errors—is to be constantly reminded of its fictional nature, no matter how much nautical (and botanical and zoological) detail Poe includes to convince us that the story is "real." In chapter 5, for example, Pym tells us that his breaking a bottle while trapped in the hold of the *Grampus* had saved his life, because Augustus had given up his search and was about to return to the forecastle when he heard the noise. "Many years elapsed, however, before I was aware of this fact. A natural shame and regret for his weakness and indecision prevented Augustus from confiding to me at once what a more intimate and unreserved communion afterward induced him to reveal" (*IV,* 94). However, Augustus dies not many years but only a few weeks later, on the floating wreck of that same ship. Such errors may be attributed to Poe's writing intermittently and more quickly than usual, but in this case he seems to have gone out of his way to make the mistake, for why should Pym mention that Augustus waited years to tell him he had abandoned his search? For that matter, why should Augustus have been ashamed, for as Pym explains, "[H]e had every good reason to believe me dead . . . and a world of danger would be encountered to no purpose by himself" if he did not return to the forecastle (*IV,* 95). The only purpose Augustus's delay of "many years" serves is to be contradicted eight chapters later.

Similarly, Pym points out that Augustus wrote his warning note to Pym in the hold ("*I have scrawled this with blood—your life depends upon lying close*") on "the back of a letter—a duplicate of the forged letter from Mr. Ross," which had bought Pym enough time away from his father to stow away on the *Grampus* (*IV,* 92). This detail serves some purpose, for readers might otherwise wonder how Augustus, a prisoner, would happen to have paper to write on (since he had to use a toothpick and his own blood for pen and ink). Furthermore, there is some irony in the fact that the note that saves Pym from dying in the ship's hold is written on the reverse of (a copy of) the note that got him there in the first place. But the revelation that there was writing on the reverse side of the blood-written note contradicts Pym's earlier assertion that the side of the paper he had first tried to read in the dark using phosphorous matches was "a dreary and unsatisfactory blank" (*IV,* 78). Again, Poe certainly could have forgotten while writing chapter 5 what he had written in chapter 2, but within a novel pervaded by confusion, contradiction, and deception, it is unsafe to assume such things; indeed, as David Ketterer notes in his comments on Pollin's painstaking editorial work, to try to distinguish between "planned absurdities" and "errors" in *Pym* leads one to a subjective interpretation rather than Poe's true intentions: "Pollin, no less than Pym, is ultimately pursuing a chimera, a shadow."[10] Throughout his narrative, Pym constantly seeks truth but finds either that his senses (or his friends, or his enemies) have deceived him or that he was simply unable to read (that is, gain information from) whatever is in front of him. Augustus's three-sided paper symbolizes Pym's *Narrative:* a warning to the reader on one side, a deliberate deception on the other, and on the impossible third side, "a dreary and unsatisfactory blank."[11]

Even readers who overlook such internal contradictions are likely to have a hard time suspending disbelief as Pym comes face to face with death repeatedly throughout his travels. The *Ariel* adventure in chapter 1 establishes the pattern for the rest of the novel. Two unconscious adolescents tossed from a demolished boat would stand a slim chance for survival, even with the *Penguin's* crew searching for them. Incredibly, Augustus is saved because Pym had tied him in an upright position to a portion of the boat that remained afloat; more incredibly, the sailors find Pym fastened to the *Penguin* by a timber-bolt that had pierced his neck. Both in the hold of the *Grampus* and on the wreck of the *Grampus* Pym nearly starves; he survives an attack by a mad dog and a battle with piratical mutineers; he comes within a splinter of being cannibalized; he and Peters survive the massacre on Tsalal only by being buried alive by a landslide and surviving *that;* and although last seen in a canoe heading into a cataract near the South Pole, Pym somehow makes it home to write his story. These nearly continuous hairbreadth escapes seem "too much," even for an adventure novel, but their very implausibility could be satiric, parodying through hyperbole the sensationalistic plots of exploration narratives, both fictional and nonfictional.

Indeed, Pym emphasizes his extreme peril with hyperbolic language, which he uses so often that it seems as if he had taken lessons, along with Psyche Zenobia, from Mr. Blackwood. He tells us, for instance, that his dreams in the hold of the *Grampus* were "of the most terrific description" (*IV,* 72). *Description* in this context means "nature" or "character," but the more common meaning of the word ("representation") also comes to mind: the "events" in *Pym* are not real events at all but mere *descriptions,* so Poe (Pym) assails us with superlatives in a seemingly desperate effort to make those descriptions sufficiently intense. The next sentence, in fact, reads, "*Every* species of calamity and horror befell me" (my emphasis). Pym invokes superlatives so often that these examples could come from almost anywhere in the book: "Never while I live shall I forget the intense agony of terror I experienced at that moment" (*IV,* 60); "My head ached excessively; I fancied that I drew every breath with difficulty; and, in short, I was oppressed with a multitude of gloomy feelings" (*IV,* 71); "Had a thousand lives hung upon the movement of a limb or the utterance of a syllable, I could have neither stirred nor spoken" (*IV,* 72); "My sensations were those of extreme horror and dismay" (*IV,* 75); "I felt, I am sure, more than ten thousand times the agony of death itself" (*IV,* 83); "It was, indeed, hardly possible for us to be in a more pitiable condition" (*IV,* 115); "[E]very particle of that energy which had so long buoyed me up departed like feathers before the wind, leaving me a helpless prey to the most abject and pitiable terror" (*IV,* 134); "I *then* thought human nature could sustain nothing more of agony" (*IV,* 149).

As if to flaunt the fact that his descriptions do not reflect actual events but rather the conceptions of Poe, Pym repeatedly insists that his ordeals are *beyond* conception or too fantastic for words to convey: "[I]t is nearly impossible to conceive" how the rescuers from the *Penguin* escaped destruction (*IV,* 63); in chapter 10 Pym's experiences are "of the most unconceived and unconceiveable character" (*IV,* 122); when Pym, Peters, and Augustus kill Parker for food, he explains, "Such things may be imagined, but words have no power to impress the mind with the exquisite horror of their reality" (*IV,* 135); elsewhere, "It is quite impossible to conceive our sufferings from thirst" (*IV,* 143); "Such weakness can scarcely be conceived" (*IV,* 145); the "agony and despair" Pym and Peters suffer while buried alive "cannot be adequately imagined by those who have never been in a similar situation," as they inspire "a degree of appalling awe and horror not to be tolerated—never to be conceived" (*IV,* 182); finally, "the extreme hazard" of their later escape from the cliff "can scarcely be conceived" (*IV,* 196). Although these oft-repeated assertions lose their force early in the novel, they insist that the author, if he has not *experienced* what other people cannot even imagine, has at least *created* what other people cannot even imagine. For Poe the hoax provides an ideal medium for demonstrating the creative power of the writer—to make the fantastic become "real" for readers. As in his poems and his Folio Club tales, he calls attention to that power, as if afraid the reader will not sufficiently appreciate it otherwise.

The consecutive episodes of extreme peril, then rescue or reprieve (usually followed by an explanation) create a narrative that reads like a series of *Blackwood* articles. Thus, despite the book's shortcomings as a novel, as Bruce Weiner argues, in writing *Pym* Poe perfected the "explained gothic" tale of effect: "Like his Blackwood's counterparts, Pym is rescued and restored to his senses so that he can tell his tale. . . . Establishing natural causes for the most delusive of Pym's sensations, the explanation counteracts the imaginative excesses evoked by the predicament."[12] Much of Poe's later short fiction hinges on explaining the perverse or the mysterious, although explanations are often left up to the reader, as is the case with the last chapter of *Pym.* As Weiner suggests, *Pym* may be best appreciated as a series of rehearsals for the "classic" tales Poe would write between 1838 and 1844.[13] Like many of those tales (to be discussed in chapters 4 and 5), and like Poe's burlesques of *Blackwood, Pym* should probably be read both literally as a sensational adventure narrative and as a parody of sensational adventure fiction. After all, parodies do not always set themselves apart from the genre at which their satire is directed; a parodist can demonstrate an appreciation for the formula or the work he or she is lampooning. Again, the two audiences Poe imagined are really one audience that can see the excesses of a particular style and still appreciate that style.

"We Were Destined to Be Most Happily Deceived"

So far I have described *Pym* as if it should not be taken seriously, except as a particularly intricate example of Poe's propensity for hoax and satire. But I have also tried to suggest that readers need to balance two sets of expectations when reading Poe: on the one hand, the expectations of literary satire, of a bantering relationship between author and reader, of a text whose real subject is other texts, and on the other hand, the expectation that the work has its own subject and its own themes that convey the author's perspective on the "real world" as well as the literary/publishing world. Such is the case with *Pym,* where the writerly deceptions that permeate the narrative reflect a worldview in which to be deceived is simply to be human. Patrick Quinn and Edward Davidson, two of the first critics to devote extended analysis to *Pym,* identify deception as its principal theme, a premise shared by numerous commentators.[14] "Schoolboys," Pym explains, "can accomplish wonders in the way of deception" (*IV,* 64), an assertion he demonstrates repeatedly in the early chapters: he covers up his wounds (incredibly enough) from the *Ariel* incident to fool his parents, forges a letter and impersonates a sailor to get on board the *Grampus,* and plays the role of Hartman Rogers's ghost to frighten the cook's party and help take over the ship. On a larger scale, Pym the writer builds deception into his narrative by chronicling repeated instances in which *he* is deceived, often in matters of life and death. David Ketterer, in *The Rationale of Deception in Poe,* terms the perils from which Pym is rescued "pseudocrises" or "red herrings," as Pym repeatedly explains after the fact why what appeared to be catastrophic proved to be benign if not lucky.[15] As Poe toys with his readers, then, God, fate, or mere chance toys with Pym.

The paradigm for the seemingly countless episodes of deception occurs in the hold of the *Grampus* in chapters 2 and 3. The wooden box in which Pym stows away has been so sumptuously provisioned by Augustus that Pym moves in "with feelings of higher satisfaction . . . than any monarch ever experienced upon entering a new palace" (*IV,* 69), but he also describes it in terms that suggest nothing so much as a coffin: an "iron-bound box, such as is used sometimes for packing fine earthenware [a possible pun hinting that it will hold a corpse]. It was nearly four feet high, and full six long, but very narrow" (*IV,* 69). Indeed, it nearly becomes his coffin, as the mutiny on deck prevents Augustus from freeing him as planned, leaving Pym to wonder why he has been "thus entombed" (*IV,* 75). Even when Pym tries to find his way out, the "labyrinths of the hold" prevent him from getting his bearings. Yet, ironically, his entombment ultimately saves him, for had he found his way to the deck, he probably would have been killed. Pym's disorientation throughout this ordeal initiates him into the world of confusion and deception that he will inhabit for the rest of the novel. His food having spoiled during his first long sleep, Pym's delirium is heightened by hunger and liquor, which becomes his only sustenance. During his second sleep, he awakens from nightmares of suffocation, demons, and serpents to find "[t]he paws of some huge and real monster . . . pressing heavily upon my bosom" (*IV,* 72). As the monster proves to be his faithful dog, Tiger, Pym is happy to have been deceived—until the dog goes mad and does in fact threaten Pym's life. And yet, by bringing Pym the note from Augustus (a note whose writing Pym cannot see, and whose message he can only partially read), Tiger helps save Pym's life as well. Given these reversals and double reversals, to say that nothing is as it seems in these chapters would be an understatement.[16] Drunk, famished, dropping in and out of consciousness, lost in a labyrinth of crates, and constantly in the dark, Pym's senses tell him nothing—at least nothing he can trust.[17]

By the middle of his narrative, several harrowing crises and pseudocrises later, Pym reflects on his changing perspective:

> Notwithstanding the perilous situation in which we were still placed, ignorant of our position, although certainly at a great distance from land, without more food than would last us for a fortnight even with great care, almost entirely without water, and floating about at the mercy of every wind and wave, on the merest wreck in the world, still the infinitely more terrible distresses and dangers from which we had so lately and so providentially been delivered caused us to regard what we now endured as but little more than an ordinary evil—so strictly comparative is either good or ill. (*IV,* 139)

Pym's sanguine outlook smacks of self-delusion, as J. Gerald Kennedy argues: "Pym's interpretation of past events as divinely ordained . . . rationalizes unspeakable happenings. . . . His reckoning betrays an understandable need to construe the horrors that he undergoes as ordered and meaningful rather than random and senseless."[18] Readers, however, are less likely than Pym to see the hand of providence at work on his behalf: true, he keeps escaping, but only to endure the next atrocity. And, as Kennedy notes, by this point Pym has witnessed and participated in more than his share of horrors, among them cannibalizing Parker and encountering the Dutch brig littered with putrescent corpses.[19]

Whereas in the hold of the *Grampus* Pym was relieved upon having his delusions clarified, in both these cases the reality is more horrifying than the misperception. In the case of Parker, the cannibalism proves to have been unnecessary: five days later, Pym remembers where he left an axe that will enable the three survivors to break into the forecastle and obtain food. The meeting with the Dutch brig, which Pym describes in much more gruesome detail, suggests either the absence of providence or a God who mocks his victims. As the brig and the *Grampus* near each other, Pym believes his party is saved. He sees a sailor seemingly "encouraging us to have patience, nodding to us in a cheerful although rather odd way, and smiling constantly so as to display a set of the most brilliantly white teeth" (*IV,* 123). After "pour[ing] out our whole souls in shouts and thanksgiving to God for the complete, unexpected, and glorious deliverance that was so palpably at hand" (*IV,* 124), the castaways discover the true state of things: the sailor's motions, which they had seen as a sign of hope, are caused by a huge seagull on the dead man's back, eating away at his flesh. Perhaps in the wake of this episode, Pym comes to see God's providence in the fact that he and Peters, and at the time Parker and Augustus, are still alive, at least, but the image of the death ship could just as easily be seen as God's ironic answer to their prayers.[20]

If *Pym* is about the human need to "discover" meaning in a world where meaning is either hidden or nonexistent, Poe's abrupt, problematic ending epitomizes that theme (or perhaps we should say "antitheme"). As Paul Rosenzweig points out, Pym's final words in the last published chapter constitute only one of three endings, since the book actually ends with the editor's note, which in turn alludes to another lost ending.[21] Even the ending of the editor's note has a deceptive ring to it: "*I have graven it within the hills, and my vengeance upon the dust within the rock*" only *sounds* biblical, and although it suggests some curse upon the Tsalalians, its meaning is unclear (*IV,* 208).[22] The first ending (chapter 25) also intimates more than it actually delivers, as Pym discovers some incredible phenomenon or vision that he and Peters are pulled toward at a "hideous velocity" through milky waters: "And now we rushed into the embraces of the cataract, where a chasm threw itself open to receive us. But there arose in our pathway a shrouded human figure, very far larger in its proportions than any dweller among men. And the hue of the skin of the figure was of the perfect whiteness of the snow" (*IV,* 206). Read purely on the level of hoax, these sentences do nothing but taunt the reader with the hint of a profound revelation but no substance, and not enough evidence to draw a reasonable inference. Like the "never-to-be-imparted secret" of "Ms. Found in a Bottle," the "truth" about the South Pole—is it, as Poe suggests in both "Ms." and *Pym,* a vortex, a passageway into a hollow earth?—is never revealed.[23] Read as the (anti-) conclusion of a novel about deception, the passage presents one final instance of the protagonist (and, through him, the reader) being mocked either by his unreliable senses or by the natural world: Pym finds at the end of his journey a figure of pure whiteness, a blank, human in form but shrouded. Critics influenced by deconstruction have, in various ways, found the blank, human figure emblematic of the absence of stable meaning, whether textual or spiritual or both. John T. Irwin argues that the white figure is Pym's "unrecognized shadow," suggesting a link between Pym and readers of *Pym:* "[W]hen one finds one, absolutely certain meaning in a situation where the overdeterminedness of the text makes meaning essentially indeterminate, then the reader is likely not to recognize how much that single meaning is a function of self-projection."[24] For other deconstructionist readers (and those who emphasize hoax and satire in *Pym*) the white figure suggests the absence of transcendent meaning or "the body of the narrative" itself, reminding readers how much the novel is about reading and writing, emphasizing Pym's duplicity as a writer and his repeated "misreadings" of messages, appearances, and his own experience.[25]

Critics who find unity, coherence, and meaning in *Pym,* however, tend to regard the white figure as an archetypal symbol, a conclusion to a spiritual journey that has not been aimless after all. Marie Bonaparte, in her groundbreaking psychoanalytic reading of Poe's works, reads the final episode as a "return to the mother" (hence the milky water).[26] Richard Kopley, in a series of articles, has developed an argument for reading *Pym* as a kind of Christian allegory in which the great white figure turns out to be the masthead of the *Penguin* (the ship that rescued Augustus and Pym in the first chapter) and a symbol of Christ resurrected.[27] And Richard Wilbur, in his introduction to a 1973 edition of *Pym,* describes Pym's journey as a spiritual quest that ends with a new self-awareness: "[The figure represents] Anthropos, or the Primal Man, or the snow-white Ancient of Days (Daniel 7:9), or the 'one like unto the Son of man' in Revelation 1:13, whose 'head and . . . hairs were white like wool, as white as snow.' In other words, the figure stands for the coming reunion of the voyager's soul with God or—what is the same thing—with the divinity in himself."[28]

I have dwelt on various interpretations of the ending of *Pym* in order to demonstrate that this book invites, even begs for, analysis, coaxing readers with the promise of another level of meaning behind the hoaxical elements, or just "beyond the veil" of white water in the final scene; and yet, more than most literary texts, *Pym* frustrates any effort to draw firm conclusions and attracts a range of interpretations so wide as to suggest that *Pym's* interpreters have themselves been taken in by a hoax. Of course, *Pym's* commentators have long recognized that they, too,

are part of the audience Poe wished to mystify, that—as the subtitle to
J. Gerald Kennedy's study of the novel suggests—*Pym* is "an abyss of
interpretation." But such self-consciousness of the potential absurdity or
(to use a more Poe-esque word) perversity of trying to explain the unex-
plainable is no more likely to stop Poe's readers than it is to stop Pym
from trying to understand and explain.

A Black-and-White World

Readers of *Pym* who search for the meaning—or exact nature of the non-
meaning—of the white figure must take into account the episode that
precedes it, in which a tribe of dark-skinned "savages" massacres the
Jane Guy's Anglo explorers. In fact, the episode's emphasis on race and
colonial encounter has attracted considerable attention and scholarly
debate. From chapter 17 on, Poe emphasizes a black-and-white color
scheme, with notable touches of red. As the *Jane Guy* cruises south, its
crew discovers a bear with "perfectly white" wool and "blood red" eyes,
and then a smaller mammal, whose hair, although straight, is also "perfectly white," with scarlet claws and teeth. The day after spotting that
animal, Pym notices the sea becoming "extraordinarily dark" as the *Jane
Guy* nears what turns out to be the island of Tsalal. There, virtually
everything—landscape, people, tools—is dark or black. The Tsalalians'
complexions are "jet black," they wear the skins of black animals, and
the shelters of the more important tribesmen are made of black skin
(*IV,* 168, 172–74). Pym observes a "black albatross," "black gannets,"
"blackfish," and "species of bittern, with jet black and grizzly plumage"
(*IV,* 173, 174, 191); he explores pits and chasms of "black granite" (*IV,*
192). The inhabitants of Tsalal recoil or express horror at anything
white: a handkerchief (*IV,* 168); "several very harmless objects" from the
Jane Guy "such as the schooner's sails, an egg, an open book, or a pan of
flour" (*IV,* 170); the white water and white birds that terrify Pym and
Peters's hostage; and, of course, the "white" visitors themselves. In yet
another example of Poe's inconsistency, Peters, previously identified as a
"half-breed Indian," is "white" at the end of chapter 21 (*IV,* 185); in
Pym's color scheme, Peters is now white because he is not black, but in
fact no caucasian, especially after a long voyage, could accurately be
described as "white." Appropriately, Pym's world—or, perhaps, his
worldview—has become polarized as he nears the Antarctic, whiteness
predominating everywhere but on this one dark island where the natives
fear and loathe all things white.

Given the escalating sectional tensions over slavery in the 1830s, it is difficult, if not impossible, to dismiss this black-and-white world as anything less than an allegory of "natural" distinctions between the races. Throughout the decade, Southern states became much more aggressive in their defense of slavery, both practically and philosophically: they passed stricter laws regulating slaves' behavior and censored antislavery writings while defending their system with biblical references and pseudoscientific "evidence" of "black" inferiority. Nat Turner's 1831 rebellion in Southampton, Virginia, along with a growing abolitionist movement in the North, spread the sort of fear that led to this new militancy.

Poe's personal racism and support for slavery have posed a problem for many of his twentieth-century admirers. His "defenders" on race issues point out that he never incorporated *explicit* proslavery arguments into his fiction or poetry, as did many other antebellum Southern authors; relatively little of his fiction is even set in the southern United States; and only a handful of African-American characters appear in his work. But the scarcity of direct references to race and slavery does not justify overlooking the issues when they do appear in Poe's work.[29] Although the larger cultural preoccupation with race provides sufficient reason to read the Tsalal episode in the context of Southern defenses of slavery, we can add to it the near certainty that Poe supported slavery.[30] He had established what literary reputation he had (by 1838) as the editor of a magazine that promoted not only Southern belles lettres but the "peculiar institution," occasionally writing book reviews endorsing proslavery arguments; and whenever Poe did depict an African character in his work, he invoked demeaning racial stereotypes. But Poe does not play the Tsalians for racist laughs as he does Jupiter in "The Gold Bug" and Pompey in "A Predicament"; on the contrary, the Tsalalian "savages" might be Poe's vision of how the "black race" would behave if not for the strict paternalistic control provided by slavery.

Two days before the *Jane Guy* encounters the Tsalalians, the crew spot "a singular ledge of rock . . . projecting into the sea, and bearing a strong resemblance to corded bales of cotton" (*IV*, 165), an image that suggests a correspondence between the black tribe they will soon meet and the Africans who inhabit another "white world," where real bales of cotton are part of the landscape. As Sidney Kaplan notes, Pym describes the Tsalalians in terms that closely resemble a popular caricature of Africans: "[A]bout the ordinary stature of Europeans, but of a more muscular and brawny frame," with "thick and long woolly hair," "thick and clumsy" lips, and childish mannerisms (*IV*, 168, 174).[31] The polar relatives of African slaves differ only by being more purely "black": they have "jet black" skin and black teeth (*IV,* 205). Poe's fictitious editor deciphers the characters suggested by the chasms as the Ethiopian verbal root, "to be shady" (*IV,* 207), and the inscription on the chasm wall as an Arabic-Egyptian cognate meaning "to be white—the region of the South" (*IV,* 208). Furthermore, Kaplan translates from Hebrew the name of the chief Too-wit, "to be dirty"; Klock-Klock, the name of the town, "to be black"; Tsalemon, the king of the archipelago, "to be shady"; and Tsalal itself, "to be dark."[32] Tsalal, then, is the home not just of a tribe of dark-skinned people but the home of blackness itself.

In Christian typology black is associated with Satan; moreover, Genesis establishes the snake as an animal form the devil is likely to take, and the Tsalalians "do not fear the 'formidable' serpents that cross their path [and] they pronounce the names of their land and king with a 'prolonged hissing sound.' "[33] Kaplan concludes that Tsalal is Hell;[34] at the least, it is a cursed land inhabited by what appear to be Hebrew-speaking descendants of Canaan, Noah's grandson who was punished when Ham, Canaan's father, saw the nakedness of his own father, Noah: "Cursed be Canaan! The lowest of slaves shall he be to his brothers" (Genesis 9:25). When Poe makes Hebrew the Tsalalian language, inscribes into the landscape hieroglyphic messages that put Pym in mind of "descriptions . . . of those dreary regions marking the site of degraded Babylon" (*IV,* 198), and concludes *Pym* with a pseudobiblical curse ("I have graven it within the hills, and my vengeance upon the dust within the rock"), he invokes an audacious but well-circulated Southern justification for slavery. Surrounded by the whiteness that torments them, perhaps even under the watchful gaze of the Great White Father, the Tsalalians seem "the most barbarous, subtle, and bloodthirsty wretches that ever contaminated the face of the globe," elsewhere described as "the most wicked, hypocritical, vindictive, bloodthirsty, and altogether fiendish race of men" (*IV,* 180, 201).[35]

Of course, that assessment of the Tsalalians, like everything else in the narrative, comes from the decidedly unreliable A. Gordon Pym. This observation does not "clear" Poe from responsibility for creating a racist fantasy, but it does point toward yet another interpretive wrinkle. Pym has misread appearances throughout his journey, and Poe provides considerable evidence to contradict him in this episode as well. Dana Nelson regards the encounter on Tsalal as an illustration of how colonizers misperceive indigenous peoples by assuming that "white is right."[36] In the tradition of European (and American) imperialism, the crew of the *Jane*

Guy clearly intends to exploit the Tsalalians: "We established a regular market on shore, just under the guns of the schooner, where our barterings were carried on with every appearance of good faith, and a degree of order which their conduct at the village of *Klock-klock* had not led us to expect from the savages" (*IV*, 177). Pym's reference to the "appearance of good faith" foreshadows the later massacre by the Tsalalians, but in the same statement he reveals that the *Jane Guy*'s crew conducts business not on good faith but "under the guns of our schooner." Furthermore, the high "degree of order" with which the Tsalalians trade should tip Pym off to their intelligence and organizational ability, but ethnocentrism and greed blind him to such a possibility.[37]

In chapters 19 and 20, Pym proudly expounds on the value of bêche-de-mer and the ease with which they can be obtained and processed by natives who apparently do not know their value on the world market. As Nelson points out, when the natives prove shrewd enough to coax the crew into a false sense of security and to engineer the landslide that buries their enemies, Pym "shift[s] his cognitive framework from 'ignorant' to 'treacherous' to explain the event."[38] But the ambush may be best seen not as Pym sees it but as a necessary preemptive strike: especially if these were not the first "white" men the Tsalalians had encountered, the natives knew that their way of life was being threatened and that they would be slaughtered in an open battle with men who were, as Pym puts it, "armed to the teeth" (*IV*, 180). When the crew first ventures onshore, Too-wit, the Tsalalian chief, tells them "there was no need of arms where all were brothers" (*IV*, 180). The explorers "took this in good part," assuming that Too-wit is announcing the Tsalalians' peaceful intentions (*IV*, 180); in hindsight, Pym regards it as simple deception. But while Too-wit probably intends the remark to be misunderstood, his literal, truthful meaning is that the *Jane Guy*'s crew have already shown, by brandishing weapons, that they do not come in peace.[39] Pym and his crewmates do not realize it, but at that point the battle has already begun.

Through Pym, Poe casts the Tsalal episode in ethnocentric terms, feeding his readers' racism, but at the same time he undermines that worldview, showing the fatal consequences of misreading the ethnic "other." Indeed, while no single concept can be said to unify *Pym*, Pym's misreading pervades a novel that is itself "unreadable"—that is, impossible to interpret without encountering contradictions and gaps of meaning. Why does Tsalal appear black and white to Pym? Few who have read his narrative would be comfortable with the answer "because that's how it really is," for nothing up to the Tsalal chapters has been as it seems to Pym. Perhaps Pym sees predominately in black and white in the last chapters because those colors are the easiest for reading. And yet, metaphorically, to "see everything as black or white" is to oversimplify and therefore to misunderstand, to settle for easy answers to complex questions. Here and throughout *Pym* Poe explores, in terms of reading and misreading, the difficulty of interpreting the world; in this case readers of *Pym* are literally looking at the black-and-white world of the printed page as they vicariously experience the black-and-white world of Tsalal and the region to the south. The traces of red on Tsalal may suggest the bloodthirstiness of the natives, but they also suggest a pun on which a famous children's riddle is based: What's black and white and re(a)d all over? "A newspaper" is the typical answer. But Tsalal, as seen by Pym, is also black and white and read all over, for the writer of the editorial note and generations of critics have "read" the hieroglyphic messages—"to be shady" (or dark) and "to be white"—that baffled Pym and "escaped the attention of Mr. Poe" (*IV,* 207). Finally, like newspapers, books (such as *The Narrative of Arthur Gordon Pym*) also fit the black-and-white-and-read description, again suggesting a correspondence between Pym's failed attempts to read the physical world and his readers' futile attempts to interpret his narrative.

In *An Anthropologist on Mars,* neurologist Oliver Sacks describes "the case of the color-blind artist," who, after a car accident, suddenly saw only in black and white, losing all awareness and memory of color. For several days, he also suffered from alexia, a sudden loss of the ability to read.[40] The two phenomena are medically and, as applied to *Pym,* thematically linked. Although Pym does not literally suffer from these neurological symptoms, his limited perception "creates" a monochromatic world that *seems* easy to read but is actually easy to *mis*read. While Poe does not lead us to any clear conclusion or theme with *Pym,* he does, perhaps inadvertently, expose a paradox of the human predicament. Whether classifying people by race, trusting our senses—or other texts—for information, or seeking the one true meaning behind Poe's only novel, our desire to understand and explain blinds us, because explanations are always incomplete. As we interpret our experience ever more aggressively, we risk narrowing our vision and reducing our own stories, our own world, to black and white.

Chapter Four

Double Vision and Single Effect: 1839–1844

After *Pym,* Poe spent most of the next six years, beginning in 1838, in Philadelphia before moving back to New York in 1844. He was incredibly prolific during this period, writing dozens of book reviews and miscellaneous articles, editing *Burton's Gentleman's Magazine* (1839–1840) and then *Graham's Magazine* (1841–1842), delivering lectures on American poetry, and, most significantly, publishing 36 tales, including most of those for which he is best known: "William Wilson," "The Fall of the House of Usher," "The Tell-Tale Heart," "The Black Cat," "The Pit and the Pendulum," "The Masque of the Red Death," "The Gold Bug," "The Murders in the Rue Morgue," and "The Purloined Letter." In many respects Poe seems to have found success in the early 1840s. Philadelphia and New York formed the country's "publishing axis,"[1] so Poe drew considerably more attention as an arbiter of literary taste than he had in his days with the *Southern Literary Messenger.* In 1840 he finally managed to publish a collection of his stories, the two-volume *Tales of the Grotesque and Arabesque;* he even met privately with the most famous English writer of his time, Charles Dickens, when Dickens toured the United States in 1842.

Poe used that occasion to ask Dickens to help him find an English publisher, a maneuver typical of his nearly relentless self-promotion. He wrote anonymously in *Alexander's Weekly Messenger* praising his own work in *Burton's* and inserted four pages of favorable reviews into the front of *Tales of the Grotesque and Arabesque.* In the spirit of his earlier detective work on Maelzel's chess player, he presented himself as an invincible decoder of "cryptograms" in *Alexander's Weekly Messenger* in 1839 and early 1840. Poe began the series by proclaiming that he could solve any and all coded messages readers sent to him, although obviously he could choose which ones to solve and publish.[2] Similarly, in the "Marginalia" series that he began in the *Democratic Review* in 1844, he presented himself as a gentlemanly man of letters whose books (presumably constituting an impressive library) were filled with pithy observations. In a more blatant and potentially embarrassing act of self-promotion from this era, Poe ghostwrote his own biographical essay for the *Saturday Museum* in 1843, in which he shamelessly exaggerated his publishing success and fabricated a patrician background and romantic wandering (to Russia, where he had to be "extricated" by the American consul). Poe used more conventional means to advertise himself as well, writing more reviews that would add to his reputation as a "tomahawk man" and presenting several public lectures on American poetry.

Despite these efforts, and despite the fact that he had reached his creative and productive peak, Poe remained frustrated with his career, for good reason. In 1841, his best earning year, he probably made about $1,100, just above poverty-level wages by the standard of the time.[3] Moreover, he seems to have been nearly obsessed with the prospect of controlling his own magazine—first called the *Penn,* then the *Stylus*—but although he enlisted some subscribers and contributors, publication remained just beyond his reach. Poe blamed, among other things, working for *Graham's:* "I was continually laboring against myself. Every exertion made by myself for the benefit of "Graham," by rendering that Mag: a greater source of profit, rendered its owner, at the same time, less willing to keep his word with me. At the time of our bargain (a verbal one) he had 6000 subscribers—when I left him he had 40,000. It is no wonder that he has been tempted to leave me in the lurch" (*Letters,* 1:205). Specifically, Poe is referring to his employer's (George Rex Graham) backing out of plans to finance the *Penn,* but throughout the early 1840s Poe *was* laboring against himself. Working on behalf of the sort of magazine he wanted to compete against—he later referred to the "namby-pamby" contents of *Graham's*—he found that as an editor for hire, he could not put together enough time or money to get his own publication started. Poe faced the sort of double bind that often traps would-be entrepreneurs, believing that he would never realize his dream while working for someone else, "coin[ing] one's brain into silver, at the nod of a master" as he called it, but also knowing that he would have no reliable income if he quit (*Letters,* 1:172). He quit anyway, giving up an influential post with one of the most successful magazines of the era, arguably the best job he ever had.

Poe found other ways to subvert his own interests during this period. With the encouragement of his friend Frederick W. Thomas, who had landed a sinecure under the Tyler administration in 1841, Poe actively sought a similar appointment, "so that I have something independent of letters for a subsistence."[4] Denied a position with the Philadelphia Custom House, he traveled to Washington in March 1843, planning to present his case, with Thomas's help, to the president's son, Robert Tyler (and perhaps to the president himself), and also to solicit subscriptions and contributions to the *Stylus*. But when Poe arrived, Thomas was too ill to serve as his guide in Washington, and Poe drank himself into a stupor over the course of his visit, reportedly insulting the people who might have done him the most good.

Poe would later claim that his sporadic but heavy drinking during these years resulted from grief over his wife's tuberculosis, which became apparent in January 1842 in what must have been a terrifying episode. While singing one evening, Virginia began hemorrhaging from the lungs, blood running from her mouth.[5] A neighbor later described her illness:

> She could not bear the slightest exposure, and needed the utmost care; and all those conveniences as to apartment and surroundings which are so important in the care of an invalid were almost [a] matter of life and death to her. And yet the room where she lay for weeks, hardly able to breathe except as she was fanned, was a little place with the ceiling so low over the narrow bed that her head almost touched it. But no one dared to speak—Mr. Poe was so sensitive and irritable; "quick as steel and flint," said one who knew him in those days. And he would not allow a word about the danger of her dying—the mention of it drove him wild.[6]

Weak as she was, Virginia lingered for five years before dying. Her husband described her illness in terms that echo "Ligeia" and other tales of dying women in its repetition of death and revivification and its expression of the male lover's desperation and loss of sanity:

> Each time [she came close to death] I felt all the agonies of her death— and at each accession of the disorder I loved her more dearly & clung to her life with more desperate pertinacity. But I am constitutionally sensitive—nervous in a very unusual degree. I became insane, with long intervals of horrible sanity. During these fits of absolute unconsciousness I drank, God only knows how often or how much. (*Letters,* 2:356)

According to most accounts, Poe could stay sober for fairly long periods but drank desperately once he started. "[I]f he took but one glass of beer or cider," wrote Thomas, "the Rubicon of the cup was passed with him, and it almost always ended in excess and sickness" (*Letters,* 1:230).

Not only did Poe's drinking endanger his health and apparently cause him to lose out on a government job, but it made him an easy target for his literary enemies throughout the 1840s. For example, in 1843 Poe's onetime friend Thomas Dunn English included a minor character obviously based on Poe in his temperance novel *The Doom of the Drinker.* English alluded to Poe's weakness for wine while depicting him as brilliant but dishonest, someone who "made no ceremony . . . in appropriating the ideas of others when it suited his turn, and as a man, was the very incarnation of treachery and falsehood" (quoted in Thomas and Jackson, 443). English and Poe would continue to spar in print—and in court—throughout the 1840s. Meanwhile, Poe also entered into a strange and ultimately devastating professional rivalry with his successor at *Graham's,* Rufus Griswold.

Poe's personal struggles and conflicts connect him to mainstream antebellum culture: he was a magazinist at a time when periodicals were the vanguard of print culture; he tried to attain a sinecure when the "spoils system" was a major source of political controversy; an alcoholic, he became a caricature in a temperance novel, one of the most popular literary genres of his day and a weapon in one of the major reform movements of the century; even his wife's tuberculosis made Poe's experience somewhat typical, putting him in intimate contact with the most notorious disease of nineteenth-century America. His fiction from the early 1840s reflects this immersion in his own place and time. To be sure, Poe's artistic techniques and insight into human psychology have given many of his stories the seemingly ahistorical status of "classic" literature, but we should also bear in mind that he wrote his tales primarily for a mid-nineteenth-century American audience, whose frames of reference were in many respects different from those of late-twentieth-century readers.

In the 1980s and 1990s literary scholars have been more inclined to read "classic" texts in light of their historical moment, in part to reconstruct those largely forgotten frames of reference. David S. Reynolds, in his landmark study *Beneath the American Renaissance,* situates "The Tell-Tale Heart" and "The Black Cat" within subgenres of popular literature, pointing out the popularity of the "cool criminal" figure and "dark temperance" fiction. While Poe's stories transcend these forms, Reynolds argues, they were written to appeal to popular tastes, and some elements that seem bizarre or grotesque to modern readers were in fact conventional. If anything, Poe tended to tone down the sensational elements his stories share with then-popular writers such as George Lippard and George Thompson. Like Reynolds, T. J. Matheson reads "The Black Cat" in terms of contemporary temperance literature to argue that Poe sought to challenge the way writers who were associated with the temperance movement sentimentalized and simplified the problem of alcoholism and the road to recovery. Examining another contemporary frame of reference, John Cleman considers both stories as commentaries on the controversy over the insanity defense during Poe's time.[7] Such readings, which emphasize the historical contexts for Poe's writing, are not really opposed to those that focus on "eternal" questions of identity, love, and fear of death. The way people think about those questions, and the context in which those issues become real for people, change over time. Greater awareness of, for instance, the nineteenth-century insanity-defense controversy helps us to understand what forces shaped Poe's writing about identity, because that very argument over what makes a person legally rational or insane helped to shape Poe's vision—and his society's vision—of human identity. Similarly, the issue of alcoholism (and the attitudes Poe's contemporaries held toward it) in "The Black Cat" feeds into the broader issues of self-control, perversity, and the lengths to which a character like the black cat's owner will go to avoid intimacy. Perhaps one can best appreciate Poe's fiction by exploring the interplay between the concerns of his historical moment and the eternal questions that his best work unflinchingly confronts.

"William Wilson" and "The Fall of the House of Usher"

Two stories published in 1839 signaled a new level of maturity in Poe's fiction as well as a new direction. Inspired, perhaps, by an awareness of his own tendency to labor against himself or—through despair and alcohol abuse—to "become someone else," Poe began to use doubling patterns extensively in his stories' imagery and, on occasion, to create doubles as characters. With "William Wilson" Poe contributed what has become a key text in the tradition of doppelgänger literature, a tradition that Poe probably knew mainly through the work of E. T. A. Hoffmann and Germanic folklore. A more immediate inspiration for the story seems to have been a sketch by Washington Irving involving "the personification of conscience," the outline of a story in which a masked "mysterious stranger" stalks the main character, who then kills his nemesis only to discover his own image beneath the mask: "the spectre of himself—he dies with horror!" (Mabbott, CW, 2:423). But Poe has done more than flesh out Irving's parable of conscience. "William Wilson" makes its readers reconsider the very meaning of conscience and examine the construction of individual indentity. To appreciate the way Poe takes this story beyond conventional notions of conscience, consider it alongside a more straightforward doppelgänger narrative, Mark Twain's "The Facts Concerning the Recent Carnival of Crime in Connecticut" (1876). The identity of Twain's conscience—"a far-fetched, dim suggestion of a burlesque upon me, a caricature of me in miniature"—is no mystery to Twain or to the reader; Twain has his double explain that conscience will badger a person no matter what he does, as he ridicules his victim: "Ass! I don't care *what* act you may turn your hand to, I can straightaway whisper a word in your ear and make you think you have committed a dreadful meanness. It is my *business*—and my joy—to make you repent of *every*thing you do."[8] When Twain at last succeeds in killing his conscience, he does not kill himself or die with horror, but rather he becomes a free and happy criminal. If not based exclusively on "William Wilson," Twain's story certainly parallels Poe's by having the double whisper in the ear of the protagonist and by having the protagonist kill the conscience en route to a carnival of crime. Twain subverts the conventional morality of "William Wilson" not only by making conscience a kind of monster who delights in torturing and dominating his victim but by allowing his triumphant persona to live happily without one. Even so, to fulfill his satirical purposes, Twain holds to a rather simple notion of what conscience is and never suggests that his grotesque doppelgänger might be more than that. Poe's message in "William Wilson" is less clear, but perhaps no less subversive.

Poe encourages us to read the second William Wilson as a personification of conscience in the story's epigraph, but—unlike Twain's double—the second Wilson represents more to the first Wilson than moral reprimands or the guilt that prevents him from doing wrong. Most of the details in the first half of the story describe the second Wilson as inherent to the first—they share a birthday as well as a name, they enter Dr. Bransby's school on the same day, and although Wilson I is more conscious of a physical resemblance than his schoolmates are, some of the other boys believe they are brothers.[9] But such a relationship, however close, does not necessarily make Wilson II merely the conscience of Wilson I, particularly if we equate conscience with a strictly moral, guilt-producing faculty. While Wilson II does give Wilson I moral advice, "not openly given, but hinted or insinuated" (*CW,* 2:435), he also competes with Wilson I, imitates him, and, if we can believe the narrator, "chuckle[s] in secret over the sting he had inflicted" (*CW,* 2:435). The two Wilsons appear to be rival components within a single personality, which it is up to the narrator—the "conscious" Wilson—to reconcile. His downfall results from his failure to reconcile himself with seemingly foreign parts of his personality. In Valentine C. Hubbs's formulation, Wilson II is the Jungian "shadow" of Wilson I, "consist[ing] of undifferentiated functions and repressed characteristics which are not compatible with the lifestyle of the conscious ego."[10] The nature of the advice that Wilson II gives Wilson I at Dr. Bransby's (described by Wilson in very general terms), along with his later interventions, suggests that a social awareness, a consideration for other people's dignity and well-being, is the most important repressed characteristic that Wilson II represents, a notion consistent with reading Wilson II as a conscience. But regarding Wilson II as a "shadow" also allows one to read the story as a broader commentary on attempting to repress any such incompatible elements. The results of such repression are tragic, as Hubbs suggests: the murder of Wilson II, the "final act of repression, which destroys any hope of Wilson One to attain psychic harmony, turns him into the guilt-ridden neurotic who has narrated the story."[11]

Poe suggests this broader reading by having Wilson infuse his description of Bransby's school and its grounds with images of repression and self-division. He subtly animates the wall and gate by describing them as "ponderous," while the shape of the enclosure, like the human mind, has "many capacious recesses" (*CW,* 2:429). The schoolhouse itself is unknowable even to the boy who lives there; accordingly, Wilson describes its mysteriousness in terms that suggest the paradox of the inability of the mind to comprehend itself:

> There was really no end to its windings—to its incomprehensible subdivisions. It was difficult, at any given time, to say with certainty upon which of its two stories one happened to be. . . . [T]he lateral branches were innumerable—inconceivable—and so returning in upon themselves, that our most exact ideas in regard to the whole mansion were not very far different from those with which we pondered upon infinity. During the five years of my residence here, I was never able to ascertain with precision, in what remote locality lay the little sleeping apartment assigned to myself and some eighteen or twenty other scholars. (*CW,* 2:429)

It is appropriate that the schoolhouse should symbolize his mind. Not only has his mind presumably developed more "subdivisions" and "lateral branches" as a result of formal education, but Bransby's school has forced Wilson to encounter other boys, who inevitably influence him and complicate his sense of self.

Similarly, Wilson sees in his teacher, Dr. Bransby, an image of his own predicament as an individual with contradictory "sides" to his personality, noting that he is both school principal and church pastor: "This reverend man, with countenance so demurely benign, with robes so glossy and so clerically flowing, with wig so minutely powdered, so rigid and so vast,—could this be he who, of late, with sour visage, and in snuffy habiliments, administered, ferule in hand, the Draconian Laws of the academy? Oh, gigantic paradox, too utterly monstrous for solution!" (*CW,* 2:428–29). The description reveals more about Wilson than it does about Bransby, of course: one man being both minister and principal seems natural enough, yet Wilson regards the combination as a gigantic, monstrous paradox. He insists on a greater consistency of identity than one has any reason to expect and so must regard himself, the body that houses both Wilsons, as an even greater monster than Bransby. Maddened by this failure to know himself, Wilson (at two points in the story) projects onto his double the essential questions of his own existence: "But who and what was this Wilson?—and whence came he?—and what were his purposes?" (*CW,* 2:439).

Poe, then, is using the double to raise fundamental issues of human identity, issues that carried the weight of a national mythology in the United States of the 1830s and 1840s. At the time Poe wrote "William Wilson" Ralph Waldo Emerson had already published his influential essay *Nature,* delivered his "American Scholar" and "Divinity School" addresses, and would soon publish the essay collection that would include "Self-Reliance." For Emerson, individual identity is something discovered by studying oneself and nature, not something shaped by social custom and circumstances or developed through negotiation with other people—indeed, those forces impede self-discovery and self-reliance. "[I]f the single man plant himself indomitably on his instincts, and there abide, the huge world will come round to him," writes Emerson in "The American Scholar."[12] While much of the substance of Emerson's philosophy was probably lost on the audiences who attended his lyceum lectures, his talks and essays contributed to a national self-image of "rugged individualism" and personal freedom.[13] Perhaps because there was considerable pressure toward social conformity during this period, Emerson's professions of nonconformity struck a chord with the American public. Wilson could be regarded as a tragic Emersonian.

Although he is not so much nonconformist as he is outlaw, he shares with Emerson a disdain for the conformist mob and a belief in the primacy of his own will—hence the pseudonym *William Wilson*.[14] Emerson's American scholar must "feel all confidence in himself, and . . . defer never to the popular cry";[15] Wilson has distorted this part of Emerson's thought into a childish egoism, explaining that as a boy he "grew self-willed," that he was left "to the guidance of my own will, and became, in all but name, the master of my own actions" (*CW,* 2:427). Emerson would exhort his readers to "[t]rust thyself: every heart vibrates to that iron string";[16] Wilson refers to his school days, which were "replete with . . . intense excitement," as "*le bon temps, que ce siecle de fer!*" (what a good time it was, that age of iron!; *CW,* 2:430–31).

Because Wilson wants to continue to assert himself as an autonomous, self-willed individual, he bristles at suggestions of his own commonness. Having revealed early on that William Wilson is a pseudonym (on the pretense that his real name "has been already too much an object for the scorn—for the horror—for the detestation of my race" [*CW,* 2:426]), at two later points he expresses shame for having such an "uncourtly patronymic" (*CW,* 2:434): "[N]otwithstanding a noble descent, mine was one of those everyday appellations which seem, by prescriptive right, to have been, time out of mind, the common property of the mob" (*CW,* 2:431). When describing the second Wilson's mocking whisper of his own name, he again calls it "very common, if not plebeian," and calls the "words" of his name "venom in my ears" (*CW,* 2:434). Despite his "noble descent," Wilson is a "commoner" at Oxford, although wealth and personal magnetism have made him, paradoxically, the school's "noblest and most liberal commoner" (*CW,* 2:440). To be common in any sense of the word galls Wilson: he even points out that when Wilson II disrupts his profane toast at Eton, he is dressed in a "novel fashion," which Wilson II imitates. Wilson II's mission is not simply to reprimand the narrator for his profanity but to remind him, as he always has, that he is not "his own man," not the unique Emersonian individual, for his name, his voice, and even his novel fashion sense are also someone else's. Even at Bransby's school, although other students rarely noticed the Wilsons' similarities, "nothing could more seriously disturb" him than having them pointed out (*CW,* 2:434).

Is the second Wilson, then, the conscience of the first, a repressed part of the first Wilson's psyche, or a symbol of Wilson's commonness, his connectedness to other people? The answer is all three. The story suggests that self-reliance, as Wilson understands it, is immoral, that the self-reliant man, by deliberately forgetting his dependence on others, has repressed a vital part of himself. Theron Britt links Poe's critique of individualism to Alexis de Tocqueville, who, a year after "William Wilson," challenged Americans' faith in democratic self-reliance: "[N]ot only does democracy make men forget their ancestors, but also clouds their view of their descendants and isolates them from their contemporaries. Each man is forever thrown back on himself alone, and there is danger that he may be shut up in the solitude of his own heart."[17]

The English setting of "William Wilson," like the pseudonym, is a kind of mask, for the story addresses one of the most enduring issues in American culture.[18] Does the cult of individualism and personal freedom, which reached new heights of expression in Poe's America, promote a harmonious community of self-reliant, self-actualizing individuals, or does it alienate those individuals from each other, and ultimately from themselves? For that matter, is the individual at odds with society, as Emerson and Thoreau claimed, or is he inseparable from society, in the sense that to set oneself against society is to repress a part of oneself, the part that is not autonomous but that is formed by the culture in which one lives? Another bit of description from Dr. Bransby's school offers an analogy for the development of personality: "Interspersed about the [class]room, crossing and recrossing in endless irregularity, were innumerable benches and desks, black, ancient, and time-worn, piled desperately with much-bethumbed books, and so beseamed with initial letters, names at full length, grotesque figures, and other multiplied efforts of the knife, as to have entirely lost what little of original form might have been their portion in days long departed" (*CW,* 2:430). The "original" Wilson was a willful child who changed as he was "written upon," as all individuals are, by the people he lived with—specifically, the same schoolchildren who altered the benches and desks. Tragically, he regards these influences as a violation of his originality rather than normal human development.[19] The "vulgar airs of patronage and protection" (*CW,* 2:432) that he sees in his double are precisely what he resents: having to live within a community based on mutual dependency when he imagines himself independent, uncontaminated by the ties of obligation and indebtedness. Readers often note that at the story's end it is difficult to tell which Wilson is which, for the narrator himself is confused: "It was Wilson; but he spoke no longer in a whisper, and I could have fancied that I myself was speaking" (*CW,* 2:448). At that moment, he sees Wilson II's image as his own, just as, throughout the story, he has recognized his own voice in the voice of the "mob" to whom his name belongs, and vice versa. In erasing the communal writing from his personality, he finds nothing underneath but a blank slate.

The attempt to shut oneself off from outside influences lies at the heart of "The Fall of the House of Usher" as well. Here, as in "William Wilson," Poe uses doubling to suggest the tragic nature of his central character. The instance of doubling that frames the story and infuses the title is, of course, the correspondence between house and family, particularly Roderick. The narrator dwells on the "perfect keeping of the character of the premises with the accredited character of the people," revealing that "House of Usher" had come "to include, in the minds of the peasantry who used it, both the family and the family mansion" (*CW*, 2:399). Although still standing at the beginning of the tale, the house, like the "race" of Ushers, is on the brink of collapse and will collapse upon Roderick and Madeline's fatal embrace. The house is also doubled by its reflection in the tarn, which only intensifies its "capacity for sorrowful impression" and strengthens the connection with the Ushers by mirroring what now appear to be "vacant and eye-like windows" (*CW*, 2:398). Moreover, Roderick believes the house is sentient and that its decay has had an "importunate and terrible influence" on his family and "made *him* what I [the narrator] now saw him" (*CW*, 2:408).

Since there is usually some logic to the reasoning of madmen in Poe's stories, Roderick's support for his theory is worth noting: "Its evidence—the evidence of the sentience—was to be seen, he said, (and here I started as he spoke,) in the gradual yet certain condensation of an atmosphere of their own about the waters and the walls" (*CW*, 2:408). Indeed, the property seems to have an atmosphere all its own, shutting it off from its surroundings. Inside the house, too, the narrator "breathe[s] an atmosphere of sorrow" (*CW*, 2:401). The narrator chooses not to comment on Roderick's belief in the sentience of the mansion, but he shares Roderick's sense of the character of this *atmosphere:*

> I had so worked up my imagination as really to believe that about the whole mansion and domain there hung an atmosphere peculiar to themselves and their immediate vicinity—an atmosphere which had no affinity with the air of heaven, but which had reeked up from the decayed trees, and the gray wall and the silent tarn—a pestilent and mystic vapor, dull, sluggish, faintly discernible, and leaden-hued. (*CW*, 2:399–400).

The fact that the atmosphere seemingly "reeks up" from the terrain not only suggests its hellish nature but contributes to the impression that the atmosphere has hermetically sealed the mansion and grounds, a notion the narrator reinforces when he observes that "there was much [in the house's physical condition] that reminded me of the specious totality of old wood-work which has rotted for long years in some neglected vault, with no disturbance from the breath of external air" (*CW,* 2:400). No wonder the peasantry equate house with family: the house is atmospherically isolated just as the family has isolated itself.

Surprisingly, most critics manage to discuss "Usher" without mentioning the fact that Roderick and Madeline are children of incest and quite possibly practice it themselves. Mabbott rejects the idea because "conscious use of such a theme is contrary to Poe's general practice" (*CW,* 2:395). Still, in this case the "theme" of incest is hard to deny: "I had learned, too, the very remarkable fact, that the stem of the Usher race, all time-honored as it was, had put forth, at no period, any enduring branch; in other words, that the entire family lay in the direct line of descent, and had always, with very trifling and very temporary variation, so lain" (*CW,* 2:399). In the next sentence the narrator refers to this circumstance as a "deficiency," and Roderick later explains that his sickness is "a constitutional and a family evil" (*CW,* 2:402). Roderick's sickness could well be a blood disease brought on by inbreeding. But incest is not the great "hidden meaning" that readers are supposed to discover; it can hardly be said to be *hidden* at all. Rather, the incestuousness of the Ushers is itself a symptom of a malady similar to William Wilson's: they want to live in their own world on their own terms. Although Poe does not specify the story's setting, the Ushers, in their resistance to change and foreign intrusion, prefigure the families of modern Southern Gothic literature from G. W. Cable to Tennessee Williams. Poe would address the consequences of trying to lock out some perceived evil in "The Masque of the Red Death" as well, with a similar conclusion: whether it be a plague or the impurity of non-Ushers or the material world in general, the "enemy" either finds a way inside or is already there. Thinking their "race" could be brought down only by outsiders, the Ushers become victims of their isolation, their hermetically sealed environment.

As twins who look alike despite their gender difference, the Ushers are doubles of each other, which increases our sense of the family's isolation and narcissism: even when Roderick looks at the only significant other in his life, he may as well be looking in a mirror. Thus, as Roderick watches his sister die, he feels as if he is witnessing his own death. As J. Gerald Kennedy argues, Madeline comes to represent death itself for Usher, and her revivification is the surfacing of Roderick's repressed fear and acknowledgment of death.[20] The image of Madeline, "lofty and enshrouded," with "blood upon her white robes," coming for Roderick certainly suggests death personified (*CW,* 2:416). Death comes to Roderick in the form of an embrace with a loved one uncannily like himself. Representative of his "house," Usher suffers and dies as punishment—not strictly for violating the incest taboo but for overindulging the self-love and isolation that incest represents in this story.[21]

While Usher is terrified by Madeline's imminent death and then by her imminent resurrection, her demise also unlocks his creative powers, as Daniel Hoffman observes:

> For instance, while Madeline is sick, but not yet thought to be dead, Roderick is already busy composing *dirges.* The beloved sister is still on her sickbed while Roderick finds solace in one of his favorite books, a Latin office for the *dead.* His visionary painting is of a vault exactly like the vault in which he will inter her, a vault illuminated by that eerie light cast by the energy of the dead which we have seen to shine upwards from the ruins of the City in the Sea. No wonder, then, that Usher's aborted poem foretold the dissolution of his "lofty intellect." He could not become an artist *until he had wished his sister dead.* (Hoffman, 309)

The painting "doubles" not only Madeline's vault but also the vaultlike atmosphere of the whole place. Usher's song "The Haunted Palace," meanwhile, is a *mise en abyme,* a miniature double of the tale itself. Moreso than the tale, in fact, the song creates a precise parallel between house and man of the house: golden banners represent hair, "two luminous windows" are eyes, and the "pearl and ruby" of the "palace door" are the teeth and lips. The "ruler of the realm"—the mind—maintains perfect order until (in the fifth stanza) "evil things, in robes of sorrow, / Assailed the monarch's high estate." The last stanza describes the changes this sorrow brings, madness in thoughts and words, and a "door" turned pale:

> And travellers now within that valley,
>   Through the red-litten windows, see
> Vast forms that move fantastically
>   To a discordant melody;
> While, like a rapid ghastly river,
>   Through the pale door,

A hideous throng rush out forever,
And laugh—but smile no more.
(*CW,* 2:406–7)

The poem does not help to explain the story, but it does show us that Roderick is obsessed with his own deterioration and that he has made it the subject of his art. Hoffman sees Madeline as Roderick's muse, reasoning that "Poe makes the artist a cannibal or vampire whose subject *must die* so that there may be art" (Hoffman, 310–11); Usher's subject, however, is himself as much as it is Madeline.

At the story's climax, a work of art not created by Usher "doubles" his experience: as the narrator reads from "The Mad Trist" of Sir Launcelot Canning (a work almost certainly invented by Poe [Mabbott, *CW,* 2:395]), he and Usher hear the book's sounds in the storm and in Madeline's approach. Since at that point we are about to learn that Madeline has revived from her cataleptic stupor and clawed her way out of a screwed-down coffin lid and a copper-plated burial vault, it seems gratuitous to point out that the correspondence between "The Mad Trist" and Madeline's return is rather far-fetched. And yet, even amid those other implausibilities, the correspondence seems not just far-fetched but unnecessarily so.[22] Why, then, does Poe include it? Does "The Mad Trist" conjure Madeline from her vault? Or, given Usher's and the narrator's states of mind, does the cheap Gothic climax of Sir Launcelot's novel—the "well-known portion of the story" (*CW,* 2:413)—lead them to *imagine* Madeline's reappearance? Whether one chooses to go that far, the interpolated Gothic story puts Usher and the narrator in the same position as readers of Poe's Gothic story—and ideal readers that they are, they give in completely to the fiction, despite its "uncouth and unimaginative prolixity" (*CW,* 2:413).

Keeping in mind that Usher and the narrator are *readers* in that final scene, we may better understand the role of the narrator throughout the story. Many readers see Roderick, his sister, and his house as projections of the narrator's psyche,[23] but since all we know of the narrator is what we learn of him at the house of Usher, it seems logical to regard him in terms of Usher rather than the other way around—specifically, to see the narrator as a "reader" or audience for the Gothic-romantic artist Roderick Usher. He "surrenders" to Usher's art, his house, and his character in the same way he *and* Usher surrender to Sir Launcelot. As the audience member or reader who identifies himself with the artist, the narrator becomes yet another double. In the story's first sentence the narrator seems to have been wandering: "I had been passing alone," he says, and simply "found myself, as the shades of evening drew on, within view of the melancholy House of Usher" (*CW*, 2:397). Only after describing the house does he reveal that Usher has summoned him there, so that what appeared to be happenstance or the result of the narrator's will is actually directed by Usher. After staring at the house and its reflection in the tarn, he moves gradually into Usher's world: "I rode over a short causeway. . . . I entered the Gothic archway. . . . On one of the staircases, I met the physician. . . . The valet now threw open a door and [note the pun] ushered me into the presence of his master" (*CW*, 2:400–401). Eventually, Usher becomes the narrator's master, too, in a sense: "It was no wonder that his condition terrified—that it infected me. I felt creeping upon me, by slow yet certain degrees, the wild influences of his own fantastic yet impressive superstitions" (*CW*, 2:411). On the night of Madeline's return, Usher "roamed from chamber to chamber with hurried, unequal, and objectless step" (*CW*, 2:410), while the narrator, as if in sympathy, "endeavored to arouse myself from the pitiable condition into which I had fallen, by pacing rapidly to and fro through the apartment" (*CW*, 2:412). The narrator has become the ideal audience, controlled by and in sympathy with the artist: Roderick feels that sympathy so strongly that at the height of his own frenzy, with Madeline just outside the door, he twice addresses the narrator as "Madman!" (*CW*, 2:416).

Abetted by the reading of "The Mad Trist" and the special effects of the storm, Usher's death is itself a performance, with the narrator as both participant and audience. Like the phantom ship of "Ms. Found in a Bottle," destined for a secret whose attainment is destruction, the house of Usher is consumed by a vortex, but this time, not only the narrative but the narrator himself escapes—unlike the tortured romantic artist Roderick Usher, and unlike the passengers on the ship of DISCOVERY. Like Poe's readers, perhaps, the narrator becomes the double of a deranged character, but only temporarily: he enters the house of insanity and death, but he can put the book ("The Mad[eline] Trist?") down and watch the house disappear into the tarn when the story is over.[24]

"The Black Cat" . . . and Other Love Stories

Describing Poe's love stories, Daniel Hoffman wryly remarks, "What he writes on this theme will not readily be confused with the efforts of others. . . . Here, as everywhere, Edgarpoe [as Hoffman calls him] looks into the dark glass of his soul, and sees doubly" (229). Indeed, in several stories from the early 1840s Poe "doubles" his characters in various ways to dismantle conventional notions of romantic love.

The exception is "Eleonora" (1841), arguably Poe's most sentimental work of fiction. "Eleonora" at first follows the pattern set by Poe's earlier stories named for dying women: the narrator calls into question the veracity of his own story, informing us that "[m]en have called me mad" (*CW,* 2:638), and encourages us to doubt the later portion of the narrative (*CW,* 2:639); this narrator, too, watches his wife die and, in a sense, return. But the differences between "Eleonora" and the earlier trio of stories are more significant than the similarities. "Eleonora" 's narrator describes an Edenic existence in the first part of the story, a cloistered, innocent life in "the Valley of the Many-Colored Grass." (Despite the fantastic landscape he describes, he has claimed that *this* is the portion of his story that warrants belief.) The innocence ends when Eleonora is about 15 and "[l]ove entered within our hearts" (*CW,* 2:640), for soon after the blossoming of their love, and the corresponding blossoming of the magical landscape, Eleonora sees "that the finger of Death was upon her bosom," and the "manifold golden and gorgeous glories" disappear from the Valley (*CW,* 2:641, 643). Before she dies, the narrator vows never to remarry, but after mourning her for an unspecified period, and finding himself "within a strange city" (*CW,* 2:644), he suddenly has a change of heart: "What indeed was my passion for the young girl of the valley in comparison with the fervor, and the delirium, and the spirit-lifting ecstasy of adoration with which I poured out my whole soul in tears at the feet of the ethereal Ermengarde?" (*CW,* 2:644). At this point readers of the earlier tales would expect things to go very wrong. But instead, after he marries Ermengarde, a spirit visits him in the night to tell him, " 'Sleep in peace! . . . thou art absolved, for reasons which shall be made known to thee in Heaven, of thy vows unto Eleonora' " (*CW,* 2:645).

Whereas even the extraction of Berenice's teeth had carried with it some narrative logic, this abrupt ending is puzzling because Poe has done nothing to prepare us for it.[25] As in "Morella" and "Ligeia," the second woman could be said to double the first, but whereas Morella-the-daughter was a duplicate of Morella-the-wife and Rowena was the opposite of Ligeia, Ermengarde is not described in enough detail to surmise much at all about her relationship to Eleonora or the manner in which she fills the narrator's psychic needs. One might justifiably take the narrator's word that the *first* part of the story is the reliable part, and that Ermengarde is an illusion the narrator has concocted to heal his wounds—or one might regard Ermengarde as a real-world version of the spiritual or ideal Eleonora, who lives only in the imaginary realm of "the Valley of Many-Colored Grass."[26]

Since the story lacks narrative logic, it might be read more satisfactorily as a poem; it does, in fact, share with much of Poe's poetry an insistence on the reality of what must be the work of imagination or dream and an idealized portrayal of the male speaker's love and mourning.[27] The Valley of Many-Colored Grass recalls the dreamscapes of "Al Aaraaf," "Fairyland," "The Valley of Unrest," "The City in the Sea," and one of Poe's few poems from the early 1840s, "Dream-Land." Although the images of dream-work in these last three poems suggest sorrow and dread, in early poems such as "Dreams" and "Introduction," Poe also claimed dream experience to be more real and satisfying than waking life, raising the possibility that the portion of "Eleonora" set in the Valley of Many-Colored Grass is, to the narrator, believable because to him it is more vivid and coherent (being his own creation). When he finds himself "within a strange city, where all things might have served to blot from recollection the sweet dreams I had dreamed so long in the Valley of Many-Colored Grass" (*CW,* 2:644), he does not trust his ability to make sense of experience. And yet in that strange city he meets Eleonora's real-world equivalent, the spirit of a dream made flesh. In "Lenore," a poem published seven months before "Eleonora," Poe's persona commemorates the death of his beloved, but his mood is defiant, even celebratory, rather than despairing: "Avaunt!—to-night / My heart is light— / No dirge will I upraise, / But waft the angel on her flight / With a Pæan of old days!" (ll. 44–48). "Lenore," whose name is echoed by "Eleonora," does not return for the narrator, but he maintains faith in her soul's migration, "To a gold throne / Beside the King of Heaven" (ll. 58–59). Poe deleted those lines from a later version of the poem, perhaps because such hopefulness wore down as Virginia lingered on her deathbed. This affirmation of eternal life for the deceased and comfort for the mourner would be negated altogether in a later, more famous poem about a woman named Lenore, and it would never appear again in Poe's fiction.

"The Oval Portrait" (1845), a shortened version of a story Poe published under the title "Life in Death" (1842) in *Graham's* several months after "Eleonora," reverses the idealism of the earlier story. In "Eleonora" a woman who exists in a dreamworld dies but in a sense gives life to the "real" woman Ermengarde, while in "The Oval Portrait" a "real" woman dies while giving life to a man's creation, his ideal woman. Not only the portrait but the story of its creation is "framed" by a narrator who encounters both the painting and the book that contains the story of the painting. That story is a fairly simple fable: the artist has his young wife pose for him, but enamored as he is with his art, he fails to notice that she is slowly dying before his eyes. The written description and the narrator's tale both end with this suspense-building (notice the number of *and*s) sentence: "And then the brush was given, and then the tint was placed; and, for one moment, the painter stood entranced before the work which he had wrought; but in the next, while he yet gazed, he grew tremulous and very pallid, and aghast, and crying with a loud voice, 'This is indeed *Life* itself!' turned suddenly to regard his beloved:—*She was dead!*" (*CW,* 2:665–66). Because he loves art more than his wife, he loses his wife; in trying to immortalize her, he kills her. Again Poe uses a double—painting for wife—to comment on art and obsession. But the doubling does not end (or, to be precise, does not begin) there. Consider the narrator's role. His "frame" is twice as long as the tale he reads from the book—even longer in the original version of the story. He is delirious from his "desperately wounded condition" in the revised version of the story and under the influence of opium as well in the original version. In either case, his state of mind alters the "normal" perception of things and, through his narrative, conveys that new perception to the reader. In this respect he, too, is an artist, a double for the painter whose work he is "translating" for us readers: just as the artist paints the oval portrait, the narrator writes "The Oval Portrait."[28] At the same time, he is the reader's stand-in, for his main function in the story is to look at the painting and read the story about it.

And what is it about the painting that makes so great an impression on this narrator who identifies with both artist and audience? He sees, even before he reads the description, that the painting is "[l]ife itself": "I had found the spell of the picture in an absolute *life-likeliness* of expression, which, at first startling, finally confounded, subdued and appalled me" (*CW,* 2:664). The painting seems to possess the living spirit of its dead subject, but it exists primarily not as a tribute to the young bride, or a means by which *she* is kept alive; rather, because it usurped her life, the painting itself partakes of immortality. It lives by depicting her slow death, hence the original title "Life in Death": art, the bride's "rival" (*CW,* 2:665), gains what she loses. Charles May argues that "The Oval Portrait" does not warn against the "overweening pride" of the artist, as does Hawthorne's "The Birthmark," but implicitly endorses the artist's dedication "to the ideal bride, the bride who is the only possible manifestation of Supernal Beauty for Poe, that is, the art work itself."[29]

Like "Usher," this story reveals the high price paid by women whom men use as inspiration for art. If not literally killing women for the sake of melancholic beauty, male artists in both stories gain creative strength from, or "feed off of," women's suffering.[30] "The Oval Portrait" shows this vampiric relationship, but it does not lead us to condemn it: with the narrator as our stand-in, we see the male artist's triumph at the same moment and with the same emphasis as we see his tragedy, in the story's last sentence. Whereas Usher's art serves as backdrop to his relationship with Madeline, the oval portrait itself is the focal point of "The Oval Portrait." The dead woman who inspired the living work of art is reduced to background reading.

"The Spectacles," one of Poe's few comic love stories, also hinges on the disparity between an actual woman and a male narrator's artificial image of her. The plot is constructed from conventional slapstick material: one Napoleon Buonaparte Simpson, too vain to wear spectacles, falls in love with Madame Eugenie Lalonde, whom he first sees across the audience of an opera house and thereafter only at night or in dim lighting. Events and misunderstandings conspire to prevent his learning that she is 82 years old, and he soon proposes marriage. She accepts on the condition that he begin wearing spectacles on their wedding day, at which time she reveals not only her age but the fact that she is his great-grandmother. The story ends happily, though, for Grandmother Lalonde has staged a fake marriage and, having reprimanded Simpson for his stupidity, bestows on him her beautiful young heiress.

Refusing to suspend disbelief for a moment, one might wonder why Napoleon would fall in love with a blur. In one of the few genuinely funny moments in this lengthy story, he describes the object of his desire without really describing her:

> [H]ere was grace personified, incarnate, the *beau idéal* of my wildest and most enthusiastic visions. The figure, almost all of which the construction of the box permitted to be seen, was somewhat above the medium height, and nearly approached, without positively reaching, the majestic. Its perfect fulness and *tournure* were delicious. The head, of which only the back was visible, rivalled in outline that of the Greek Psyche, and was rather displayed than concealed by an elegant cap of *gaze aérienne,* which put me in mind of the *ventum textilem* [woven air] of Apuleius. (*CW,* 2:889–90)

Foreign phrases and allusions disguise a lack of meaningful detail, as Simpson praises Madame Lalonde's nearly "majestic" figure—although she is sitting and has her back to him—and the outline of her head. As the description continues, Simpson's attention is drawn to "a diamond ring, which I at once saw was of extraordinary value" (*CW*, 2:889). Since he has already revealed that he changed his name in order to inherit money, this detail hints that greed, too, might be altering his vision.[31] Without spectacles, then, he sees what he wants to see. Uncannily, he chooses a relative, as if to suggest that he is looking for—or imagining—his double, a marriage partner just like himself.

But poor eyesight, greed, and narcissism still only partially explain Simpson's attraction to his great-grandmother. Vanity seems to be a family trait, as Madame Lalonde has gone to great trouble to disguise her age: "By the aid of . . . pearl-powder, of rouge, of false hair, false teeth, and false *tournure,* as well as of the most skilful modistes of Paris, she contrived to hold a respectable footing among the beauties *un peu passées* of the French metropolis" (*CW*, 2:914). Furthermore, she gives him a miniature of herself taken when she was 27, perpetuating the misunderstanding. The story depends on comic absurdity, so there is little point in trying to rationalize Simpson's confusion, but Poe clearly directs his satire not only at the vain romantic male but at the "artificial" woman. Madame Lalonde's artificial beauty recalls an earlier Poe story, "The Man That Was Used Up" (1839), in which Brevet Brigadier General John A. B. C. Smith requires far more than false hair, teeth, and *tournure,* having been cut to pieces by Indians. But having been completely rebuilt through prosthetics, he is worshiped by the narrator of that story just as Madame Lalonde is worshiped by Simpson. Indeed, the narrator of "The Man That Was Used Up" also seems to be looking for himself by searching for the secret of General Smith, although he finds nothing real or natural. Joan Tyler Mead sees their relationship as yet another instance of doubling: not only is the narrator "restored" by General Smith's artificial reconstruction, but "both announce their presence by interrupting; the narrator claims that his memory is poor and the general has no memory; both insist pompously on their own fallacious ideas; and both make reference to a kind of pseudodeath, as the narrator does at the end of each encounter and the general does when he recounts his various tortures at the hands of the Indians."[32] The admirers of Madame Lalonde and General Smith are bumbling detectives who believe they have found the perfect woman or man. In both cases, their images of perfection reflect self-images, and these reflections can "come to life" only through artificial means.

It might seem strange to classify "The Tell-Tale Heart" and "The Black Cat," two of Poe's infamous "tales of terror," as love stories. Certainly neither treats love as a goal or an answer to its main character's problems; rather, love itself is the problem. "I loved the old man," the narrator of "The Tell-Tale Heart" explains early in the story, and yet he kills him. Does he kill him *even though* he loves him, or *because* he loves him? The narrator does not divulge his legal relationship to the old man—he could be his landlord, his uncle, a friend—but most readers seem to agree with Daniel Hoffman's claim that he is a "father figure" if not literally his father (Hoffman, 223). The narrator knows him very well, or at least believes he does, for he identifies the old man's thoughts as his own, even as he awaits his opportunity to kill him:

> Presently I heard a slight groan, and I knew it was the groan of mortal terror. . . . it was the low stifled sound that arises from the bottom of the soul when overcharged with awe. I knew the sound well. Many a night, just at midnight, when all the world slept, it has welled up from my own bosom, deepening, with its dreadful echo, the terrors that distracted me. I say I knew it well. I knew what the old man felt, and pitied him, although I chuckled at heart. (*CW,* 3:794)

The ability to duplicate the thought processes of another person becomes a valuable skill for Monsieur Dupin in Poe's detective tales, but here the narrator's knowledge of what the old man thinks and feels is not so much an ability as the inevitable result of their intimacy. Here is a rather commonplace instance of doubling: he feels the old man in himself, as sons often feel the presence of their fathers.[33]

The narrator kills the old man, he says, because of his Evil Eye. Superstitions and folklore notwithstanding, this explanation is proof of what almost every reader intuits from the story's opening: the narrator is insane. But the story invites us to find a method to the narrator's madness, to locate the logic beneath the insanity. After all, the narrator fulfills his promise to tell the story "healthily" and "calmly" (at least until the last two paragraphs), and he does have the presence of mind to engineer the perfect crime, although he lacks the self-restraint to keep quiet about it. The keys to his mad logic are two obsessions: although he names the Evil Eye as his motive, he is equally obsessed with time-keeping. He makes a point of looking in on the old man "just at twelve" and notes that "[i]t took me an hour to place my whole head within the opening," and that on the fatal eighth night, "[a] watch's minute hand moves more quickly than did mine" (*CW,* 3:793). Twice he compares the sound that haunts him—the beating of a heart—to the sound "a watch makes when enveloped in cotton" (*CW,* 3:795, 797). On the night of the murder, he believes that the old man is "listening;—just as I have done, night after night, hearkening to the death-watches in the wall" (*CW,* 3:794). This last detail is particularly ripe with implications. The "death-watch" is an insect that, as part of its mating ritual, rhythmically strikes its head against the wood to which it has attached itself (see Mabbott, *CW,* 3:798). The name emphasizes the double meaning of *watch:* both a timepiece (enveloped in cotton) and a period of watching, specifically anticipating death—precisely what the narrator, and perhaps the old man, is doing. And although love is probably not a component of the mating practices of bugs, the human association between love and mating makes the deathwatch an uncanny figure for the narrator's relationship with the old man: he loves him but wishes for his death. The term *deathwatch* explicitly relates the passage of time to the inevitable point when time runs out, suggesting the reason for the narrator's repeated references to time and timekeeping: his fear of death.[34]

And what does the narrator's obsession with time have to do with his obsession with the Eye? The narrator explains that the eye "resembled that of a vulture—a pale blue eye, with a film over it" (*CW,* 3:792), and, as Richard Wilbur points out, elsewhere (specifically "Sonnet—To Science") Poe uses the vulture as an emblem of time.[35] If the passage of time reminds him of the inevitability of death, the two symbols—vulture and eye—converge on that obsessive fear. "His rationale makes a strange kind of sense," explains J. Gerald Kennedy, "for the crime is ultimately rooted in death anxiety: the 'vulture' reference indirectly evokes the idea of carrion, while the film over the eye recalls the glassy look of the dead, the 'glaze . . . impossible to feign,' as Emily Dickinson writes."[36] Furthermore, if we consider the fact that "The Tell-Tale Heart" is purportedly a spoken rather than written narrative, along with Poe's attraction to puns and wordplay, we might see another significance in the eye, as Charles May suggests: "[W]hen the narrator says he must destroy the 'eye,' he means he must destroy the 'I.'" According to May, the narrator projects a desire for his own death onto the old man.[37] But the narrator might not be acting out of a death wish so much as attempting to destroy this constant reminder of his own mortality, for what makes "real" the inevitability of one's own death more than the death of a parent? The eye reminds him of death, and the "I" serves to underscore the fact that he sees his own reflection in the ghastly pale blue eye of his elderly and infirm father.

As if to embed this doubling of son and father (or father-figure) into his text, Poe relentlessly doubles individual words and pairs of words throughout the story. The repetition begins with the first sentence— "nervous—very, very dreadfully nervous" (*CW,* 3:792)—and continues with phrases such as "slowly—very, very slowly," "cautiously—oh, so cautiously—cautiously," "steadily, steadily" (*CW,* 3:793), "a very, very little crevice," and "stealthily, stealthily" (*CW,* 3:794). The repetitions become more frequent as the "hellish tattoo of the heart increase[s]" just before the murder: it beats "quicker and quicker, and louder and louder," again grows "louder, louder," and the old man "shriek[s] once—once only" (*CW,* 3:795). Finding the old man "stone, stone dead" (*CW,* 3:796), the killer relaxes until he hears the heartbeat in the presence of the police: "It grew louder—louder—*louder!* . . . no, no! . . . this I thought, and this I think . . . louder! louder! louder! *louder!* . . . here, here!—it is the beating of his hideous heart!" (*CW,* 3:797). Poe intensifies his rhythm and repetition to convey the narrator's nervousness and to create suspense for the reader. But at the same time, these devices reinforce the thematic elements of obsession and the narrator's seeing his life and inevitable death as a repetition of the old man's.

Like "The Tell-Tale Heart," "The Black Cat" is not so much a confession as it is a murderer's attempt to rationalize his crime. "What disease is like Alcohol!" the narrator cries, elsewhere referring to the "Fiend Intemperance" and the "demon" that "possessed me" in order to shift responsibility from himself to his illness. Temperance crusaders sought to change public opinion on alcoholism, to treat it as a disease rather than as a moral failing or vice of the alcoholic. But as T. J. Matheson makes clear, the story undercuts the narrator's insistence that the demon alcohol made him do it; readers see that his entire story is built on implausibities and lame excuses, and his crime is motivated by impulses more sinister than a weakness for drink.[38] As with "The Tell-Tale Heart," we must read against the narrator of "The Black Cat," establish which parts of his testimony should be believed and which should not, and try to discover the deeper motivations for the crime.[39]

Once again, the concept of doubling provides a means for making sense of the narrator's strange logic. The black cat that replaces Pluto is certainly a kind of doppelgänger: uncannily, he too is missing an eye, he too is loved by the wife, and he too torments the narrator. Following Daniel Hoffman, I see both cats as doubles for the wife, in the narrator's mind, at least: "Wife suggests, but husband may in truth believe, that black cat = witch. . . . [I]n the synoptic and evasive glossary of this tale, witch = wife. Ergo, black cat = wife" (Hoffman, 231).[40] Whenever the narrator mentions his wife, a black cat is close by. He physically abuses both wife and cat, he tells us, even before hanging Pluto, and when he does hang it, its image mysteriously appears, of all places, on the wall above the unhappy couple's bed.[41] Immediately after the second cat became "a great favorite with my wife," he explains, "For my own part, I soon found a dislike to it arising within me" (*CW,* 3:854): as soon he associates cat with wife, he begins to loathe the cat. It is his wife who calls his attention to the gallows shape of the white spot on the cat's breast— appropriately so, for the gallows not only reflects Pluto's fate but forecasts the narrator's punishment for killing his wife. Finally, he unknowingly walls up the living cat with the wife, so that the cat's crying leads the police to the wife and leads the narrator to the story's final image of the cat perched on the dead wife's head. Although the context makes clear that the narrator's literal reference is to the cat in the last sentence, one can imagine cat and wife converging in the narrator's mind when he says, "I had walled the monster up within the tomb!" (*CW,* 3:859).

But why would the narrator want to kill his wife? For the very reason he gives for killing Pluto: "[I] hung it *because* I knew that it had loved me" (*CW,* 3:852). He describes his wife as tender, possessing "that humanity of feeling which had once been my distinguishing trait" (*CW,* 3:855), so it is reasonable to assume she would be affectionate and loving toward him. When the cat "spring[s] upon my knees, covering me with its loathsome caresses," or follows him closely, the narrator "long[s] to destroy it with a blow" (*CW,* 3:855); this exaggerated reaction to the cat's behavior leads one to suspect that the cat's expressions of love remind him of his wife's. When he does destroy his wife with a blow, his nonchalance is chilling, in contrast with his reaction to the murder of Pluto, which he calls "a deadly sin that would so jeopardize my immortal soul as to place it—if such a thing were possible—even beyond the reach of the infinite mercy of the Most Merciful and Most Terrible God" (*CW,* 3:852). Either this guilt actually stems from his decision at that moment to kill his wife, having already killed her surrogate, or, as Susan Amper argues, he actually does kill his wife at the point when he *says* he killed Pluto, and in his confession fabricates the incident on the cellar stairs and the existence of a second cat.[42] In either case, he responds to killing the cat as he ought to respond to killing his wife, a sin that *is* deadly and unforgivable because of his wife's innocence, because she died for loving him.

Such a paradox—death as the penalty for love—seems consistent with the contradictions that make up the narrator's initial description of his story. It is "wild, yet most homely." The incidents "have presented little but Horror," yet he also refers to it as "a series of mere household events" and believes it could be perceived as "an ordinary succession of very natural causes and effects." And although he does not expect to be believed, he tries hard to explain his behavior as the result of all-too-human perverse impulses and the disease of alcoholism (*CW,* 3:849–50). One can attribute these contradictions, like the crime itself, to the narrator's madness, but again the story's network of uncanny images and plot twists warrants some consideration of how these bizarre occurrences might also be "mere household events." What the narrator does is horrible, shocking, and yet perhaps his motivations *are* common to marriages and other intimate relationships. Poe seems to have hit upon a theme associated with the twentieth-century existentialist author Jean-Paul Sartre, whose character Garcin in *No Exit* realizes, "There's no need for red-hot pokers. Hell is—other people!"[43] That can be a shocking realization, especially for someone who, like this narrator, married early, probably believing that *heaven* was another person. Not only is there a proverbial "thin line between love and hate," but there may sometimes be no line at all, and rather than try to untangle those emotions one might avoid intimacy altogether, or find himself suddenly repulsed by it. Examining the behavior of "The Black Cat" 's narrator, Christopher Benfey writes: "These fears are always with us—the fear of love and the fear of isolation. Taken to extremes, they both lead to disaster: One cat avoids us and is blinded, another cat follows us and is killed. To live life is to steer a dangerous course between these extremes and there is no point at which the current widens."[44] The narrator's hidden hatred of his wife, his unwillingness to acknowledge that hatred, his displacement of it onto the family pet, and certainly his turning to alcohol could be categorized as common "household events." His ultimate response, of course, is "wild" and "horrible"— but equally frightening is the implication that his predicament is not so uncommon, that, like the perverse impulse to do wrong for wrong's sake, the fear of intimacy is "one of the primitive impulses of the human heart—one of the indivisible primary faculties, or sentiments, which give direction to the character of Man" (*CW,* 3:852).

Unity of Effect

In his May 1842 review of Hawthorne's *Twice-Told Tales,* Poe argued for the generic superiority of the tale to the novel and established a definition for the genre now generally termed the short story. Poe's argument is simple, resting on two axioms. First, because a tale can be read at one sitting, it can be taken in by the reader as a whole, like a lyric poem or a painting, as opposed to a novel that one puts down and picks up repeatedly: "During the hour of perusal the soul of the reader is at the writer's control. There are no external or internal influences—resulting from weariness or interruption" (*ER*, 572). The "control" that the author enjoys carries some responsibility with it, however, for Poe's second axiom requires the successful tale writer to make every sentence contribute to "a certain unique or single *effect*": "If his very initial sentence tend not to the outbringing of this effect, then he has failed in his first step. In the whole composition there should be no word written, of which the tendency, direct or indirect, is not to the one pre-established design" (*ER*, 572). In an 1846 review of Hawthorne, Poe would elaborate on his contention that lyric poems and short stories require greater ingenuity than epic poems and novels, for contrary to popular opinion "perseverance is one thing and genius quite another" (*ER*, 584). Of course, part of Poe's objective is to promote the sort of writing he and Hawthorne (who at this point had written only one novel, and suppressed it) excelled at, the form he had perfected because the literary market made short magazine fiction more salable than novels or poems. But at the same time, Poe is establishing guidelines for what was then a very young literary genre—simple, practical guidelines that writers, writing teachers, and critics still apply to short fiction over a century and half later.

As is evident in his own tales, Poe's belief in the "single effect" does not preclude intricacies or multiple ways of interpreting a story. There may be many facets to a single effect, but every detail in a story, according to Poe, must have a reason for being there, giving the story's reader a sense of coherence or wholeness. While Poe was hardly the first literary critic to make artistic unity a priority, his role in the development of the short story has given his theory great currency. Specifically, his emphasis on tying every element of a story to a preconceived design has influenced generations of literary critics and teachers who have encouraged readers to seek out patterns of imagery, metaphor, and irony and forge them into a single, coherent interpretation.

Poe maintained that while the effect of beauty belongs to poetry rather than prose fiction, truth, which is *not* the aim of poetry, could be the aim of a tale. In fact, in the 1842 review of Hawthorne, he specifically mentions the sensational *Blackwood* tales—which he had lampooned a few years earlier—as "fine examples" of *tales of effect,* the type of story he believes to be superior to the novel. And as we have seen, Poe often tried to convey general human truths in his decidedly unrealistic, often dreamlike, fiction. Two tales written near the time of the 1842 Hawthorne review provide further illustration of Poe's use of sensational plots—the mode he associated with *Blackwood*—to convey a "truth": "The Pit and the Pendulum" (1842) and "A Descent into the Maelström" (1841). Both stories display Poe's authorial control as he takes his narrators to the brink of certain death—both fall into an abyss—and yet assures us from the beginning, by their very act of narration, that they will survive, indeed already have survived.

Poe begins "The Pit and the Pendulum" by mirroring the main plot of the story, as the narrator faints upon hearing his death sentence:

> [T]he angel forms [of seven white, slender candles] became meaningless spectres, with heads of flame. . . . And then there stole into my fancy, like a rich musical note, the thought of what sweet rest there must be in the grave. . . . [B]ut just as my spirit came at length properly to feel and entertain it, the figures of the judges vanished, as if magically, from before me; the tall candles sank into nothingness; their flames went out utterly; the blackness of darkness supervened; all sensations appeared swallowed up in a mad rushing descent as of the soul into Hades. Then silence, and stillness, and night were the universe. (*CW,* 2:682)

He describes his swoon as a near-death experience, but when he awakens from his mad descent into Hades he confronts the inquisitors' literalization of the eternal pit. The pseudodeath of fainting becomes agonizingly "real" as he is nearly killed by the pit, the pendulum, and the fiery furnace of the torture chamber. And yet he does not die, and his rescue at the very moment he falls suggests another sudden awakening from a dream.[45] The narrator's long discussion of dream-memories heightens this ambiguity: "[T]here have been brief, very brief periods when I have conjured up remembrances which the lucid reason of a later epoch assures me could have had reference only to that condition of seeming unconsciousness" (*CW,* 2:683). As Charles May notes, "[I]t is not clear whether the memory [of the pit and the pendulum] is of a real event or of a dream event that has been forgotten."[46] And yet, whether the narrator dreamed of the pit and the pendulum or was "really" tortured, whether he died at the moment he fell and was lifted to a better world or was "really" rescued by General Lasalle, the experience has had the effect of a real occurrence on his mind. Moreover, most interpretations do not depend on the reality status of the narrator's experience because they treat the story symbolically anyway, as a drama of spiritual or artistic redemption. Michael Clifton, for instance, equates the narrator's descent—into hell—with the poet's dangerous exploration of the unconscious; he escapes because he has not completely lost touch with the "normal" outside world. Explicating Poe's use of the book of Revelation, Jeanne Malloy sees General Lasalle's intervention as a representation of the second coming of Christ. David Ketterer regards the narrator's falls themselves as "fortunate" because they lead him toward "arabesque reality," an artistic vision that contrasts with the deceptive world (ironically, the "real world") of false appearances.[47]

Each of these readings focuses on the narrator's victory, whether it comes about by avoiding the fall or by falling. He deserves some credit for this victory, for he does help to bring about his salvation by not giving in to despair, by using the only materials he has—the meat and the rats' teeth—to free himself from the platform, buying precious time. But luck is equally responsible: he discovers the pit because he trips at exactly the right moment, and Lasalle similarly arrives in the nick of time. Given the story's apocalyptic imagery, it is logical to read the narrator's deliverance as providential: he helps himself, but ultimately God saves him. And yet such a reading rings false, not only because it is inconsistent with most of Poe's other works but because it is inconsistent with the rest of this story. As David H. Hirsch observes, "[H]is salvation is absurd in that there is no dramatic preparation for it; the narrator's 'good fortune' does not follow logically from the information the narrator has given us."[48] In other words, if the narrator is saved through some providential design, the story itself is flawed, for it violates Poe's theory of internal coherence or single effect. But when Hirsch uses the word "absurd," he is not criticizing Poe but suggesting that Poe intends for his readers to see the absurdity, the randomness, of the narrator's deliverance, suggesting that "The Pit," like "The Black Cat," anticipates twentieth-century existentialism. The key sentence in the story occurs at the moment the narrator slides out of the pendulum's path: "Free!—and in the grasp of the Inquisition!" (*CW*, 2:695). The narrator's courage and quick thinking have earned him the right to endure the next torture; his freedom at that point is meaningless, absurd. Earlier in the story, he devotes what little energy he has to calculating the size and shape of the chamber, although he recognizes the futility of his efforts: not only do they lead to false conclusions, but even accurate dimensions are useless to a man in his situation (*CW*, 2:688). Hirsch notes the resemblance between Poe's narrator and the protagonists of Kafka and Camus: he does not know what he has been charged with and yet he does not proclaim his innocence, dimly aware that his plight is simply to withstand punishment, to endure one trial to get to the next.[49] Thus his escape does not constitute a redemption or a personal triumph so much as a lucky break. The narrator's survival is an aesthetic necessity, for only he could tell the story, but the rescue itself is a random act. Paradoxically, his rescue's randomness makes it consistent with the purposelessness of his suffering, giving the story its disconcerting "unity of effect."

"A Descent into the Maelström" recalls the earlier story "Ms. Found in a Bottle" as well as *Pym* in its central action—the narrator sails into what appears to be another realm of consciousness—but in "Maelström," unlike the earlier stories, the narrator describes his escape from what would seem certain death. As a story of escape from a hellish pit, "Maelström" really has more in common with "The Pit and the Pendulum," which was published about a year and a half later. Like "The Pit" and, indeed, most of Poe's fiction from the early 1840s, "Maelström" exhibits a degree of artistic control Poe lacked with the earlier sea stories. Poe frames the Norwegian fisherman's narrative by having his listener introduce him and help establish the locale of the story—the cliff overlooking the maelström, or Moskoe-ström, into which the fisherman descended. Like "The Pit and the Pendulum," then, this story begins with a *mise en abyme,* a miniature double of the main action. Even before he sees the whirlpool, the first narrator panics upon realizing where he is, holding onto the shrubs of the cliff as if his life depends on it. He then regains composure so that he can describe the awesome Moskoe-ström as seen from above. Similarly, the fisherman panics as he first descends into ström before he collects his wits and discovers a way to survive so that he can describe the ström from a decidedly more terrifying vantage point.

Like the narrator of "The Pit and the Pendulum," the fisherman survives his ordeal through a combination of ratiocinative skill and sheer luck. He learns, through empirical evidence, that cylindrical objects sink slower than others in the maelström, so he lashes himself to the cask he is clutching. But he is lucky to be holding only to the cask already, ironically because his brother forced him away from the boat's ringbolt. Moreover, as Killis Campbell first noted, Poe's science is a fiction here, as cylinders would not descend more slowly than other objects in a vortex; Fred Madden adds to this the observation that the fisherman's weight would keep his side of the barrel under water, practically assuring that he would drown. The fisherman is indeed lucky, then, having defied the laws of gravity he claims to have discovered and used.[50] These and other inconsistencies and inaccuracies suggest to Madden that "Maelström" is a hoax, the fisherman's tall tale. But more traditional readings regard the fisherman's survival in terms similar to those of "The Pit," a spiritual regeneration, a life-changing experience that sets the fisherman apart from his fellows.[51] Poe certainly provides evidence for both providential and hoax readings, but his conclusion emphasizes the latter by raising the question of the story's truthfulness, as the fisherman describes his first efforts to tell what happened to him: "I told [my fellow-fishermen] my story. They did not believe it. I now tell it to *you*—and I can scarcely expect you to put more faith in it than did the merry fishermen of Lofoden" (*CW*, 2:594). The fisherman directs this challenge of belief to his auditor, the first narrator, but since the story ends there without further comment, the question of belief is passed on to "you" the reader. In the sentences leading up to this abrupt ending, the fisherman reveals that the experience turned his hair from black to white and changed "the whole expression of my countenance" (*CW*, 2:594). The other fishermen noticed these things, acknowledging, despite their disbelief of his story, that the narrator did indeed show the *effects* of having been through such an ordeal. Readers are likely to respond to the story similarly. When Poe, via the fisherman, raises the question of belief in the last sentences, we are startled from a trance of fiction that has had the *effect* of truth—not just on the fisherman but on readers who have suspended disbelief and become "caught up in" the fictional maelström. Despite "Maelström" 's factual errors, and despite the fact that we know it is Poe's creation, it "feels" like truth because Poe carefully employs such *fictional* devices as internal logic, dramatic momentum, and verisimilar details. Poe raises the issue of his text's truth-status in order to call attention to his ability to make readers temporarily forget to distinguish between truth and fiction in the new genre of the single sitting and the single effect.

Written in between "A Descent into the Maelström" and "The Pit and the Pendulum," "The Masque of the Red Death" (1842) inverts the movement of those stories. "Masque" can be more easily read as a parable of art and the artist's quest for transcendence than "The Pit" and "Maelström,"[52] but whereas the artist-figures in the other stories triumphed, Prospero fails. While in "The Pit" and "Maelström" a true awareness of the narrators' peril helped them achieve salvation, in "Masque" a sense of security leads to destruction. Prospero and his revelers attempt to shut out—or repress—death, but as always in Poe's tales, whatever gets shut out, buried, or walled up either refuses to stay put or draws the perpetrator to it. In this case, death cannot stay repressed because, as Joseph Patrick Roppolo reminds us in his groundbreaking interpretation, death is not the "other" that Prospero imagines it to be, but something inherent and inseparable from life: "The Red Death is not a pestilence, in the usual sense; it is unfailingly and universally fatal, as no mere disease or plague can be; and blood is its guarantee, its avatar and seal. Life itself, then, is the Red Death, the one 'affliction' shared by all mankind."[53]

Poe patterns the story's imagery to underscore the sense of death's inevitability. The seven rooms, progressing from east to west and from innocent blue to funereal black, represent the seven ages of "man," as Roppolo and others have noted.[54] Meanwhile the clock in room seven, the reminder of time's passing, stops the revelers cold, "disconcert[s]" them, makes "the giddiest gr[o]w pale," and brings about an "uneasy cessation of all things as before" (*CW*, 2:672, 674). The revelers are distraught by the passing of time much as the narrator of "The Tell-Tale Heart" had been. After each chiming of the clock they vow that the next one will not have the same chilling effect, but to no avail: "[A]nd then, after the lapse of sixty minutes, (which embrace three thousand and six hundred seconds of the Time that flies,) there came yet another chiming of the clock, and then were the same disconcert and tremulousness and meditation as before" (*CW*, 2:673). Even as he refers to the "time that flies," Poe slows time to a crawl by dwelling on the clock's chimes for a full paragraph, even reminding readers of the number of seconds in an hour, inviting us to reflect—along with Prospero's revelers—on the constant passage of time, each second bringing us a second closer to death.

Although he professed a dislike for allegory, Poe steeps "The Masque of the Red Death" in allegorical imagery and leads readers to something very much like a moral about the inevitability of death. The third-person narration, a rarity in Poe's tales, resembles the voice of Poe's allegorical poem "The Conqueror Worm," which describes another masquerade that ends with death's inevitable victory over humanity. In "The Conqueror Worm" Poe faced the problem of representing as "other" something that is within by depicting death not as a grim reaper but as a worm that consumes those who are really already dead, a killer only metaphorically. He improves on that image of death in "Masque" with this stunning revelation: "Then, summoning the wild courage of despair, a throng of the revellers at once threw themselves into the black apartment, and, seizing the mummer, whose tall figure stood erect and motionless within the shadow of the ebony clock, gasped in unutterable horror at finding the grave cerements and corpse-like mask which they handled with so violent a rudeness, *untenanted by any tangible form*" (*CW,* 2:676; my italics). Roppolo suggests that the "mummer" in the bloody mask is not death itself, but, as the title indicates, a "mask" of death, a reminder, like the clock.[55] But is fear of death enough to kill instantly not only Prospero but the entire "throng of revellers"? It might well be, but perhaps it is best not to take the suddenness of the revelers' deaths too literally. When they see that death is not tangible, that it cannot be escaped or defeated because it is not "other," they are initiated into a new awareness of death as an inevitable process or event, realizing that like everyone who lives they are already dying. They perhaps also see in the figure's lack of tangible form the state of nonbeing that boggles the human imagination and evokes much of our fear of death. Thus, in Poe's story, living in constant dread of death becomes a kind of living death.

Prospero's pursuit and unmasking of the "enemy" within his own skin is reminiscent of the first story discussed in this chapter, "William Wilson." Prospero, like Wilson, finally confronts the double he has been avoiding, thinking he could not live with it—only to find a part of himself he cannot live without. But neither Wilson nor Prospero profits from his encounter with his double, for both misinterpret their doubles and try to kill them rather than accept them. From the moment he stabs Wilson II, Wilson I is "forever dead" to the earth's "honors, to its flowers, to its golden aspirations" (*CW,* 2:426). For his part, Prospero tries to murder death but finds that he has murdered himself. Prospero and his revelers—like the human race itself, if we treat the story as allegory—cannot truly live in defiance of death and should not treat death as an enemy to be defeated. But the revelers are in a no-win situation, for to acknowledge death as an absence, a state of nonexistence, is equally terrifying, as Poe makes clear in the final paragraph, which begins, "And now was acknowledged the presence of the Red Death" (*CW,* 2:676).[56] Ironically, their awareness of death-as-absence makes death undeniably present in the psychic landscape of Poe's story, a place where, finally, "Darkness and Decay and the Red Death held illimitable dominion over all" (*CW,* 2:677).

Chapter Five

Betting Your Head, Getting Ahead

Poe's comic satires, hoaxes, detective stories, and reviews from the early 1840s reveal a growing preoccupation with competition and rivalry. His tales on these subjects would take a grim, violent turn later in the decade, but during his Philadelphia period (which I extend to the end of 1844 to include his first months in New York), his characters' game-playing and confidence schemes are usually more amusing than disturbing. And only two stories, both published after his move to New York, take up the subject of revenge ("The Purloined Letter" and "Thou Art the Man"). In this chapter I focus first on tales *about* games, betting, and rivalry, and then on some reviews as well as stories that reflect Poe's growing obsession with "getting ahead" in the literary marketplace or the larger business world. The next section deals with a group of hoaxes and other fictions in which Poe assumes a bantering or competitive relationship with his readers, hinging on the question of belief in "the odd" or the implausible. The chapter culminates in a discussion of Poe's tales of ratiocination or detection, in which his characters Dupin and Legrand, formidable competitors who rely on the same skills Poe prided himself on, serve as successful surrogates for an author who remained woefully unable to make a decent living from his own creative and resolvent skills.

"One Vast Perambulating Humbug"

"Never Bet the Devil Your Head" ("Never Bet Your Head" in its original 1841 version in *Graham's*) may well be Poe's funniest story for modern readers, not only because it is less dependent on contemporary references than his earlier comic tales but because it begins with Poe making fun of his own reputation as an amoral writer while taunting literary critics, who find profundity in inferior popular literature and children's rhymes: "Our more modern Scholiasts . . . demonstrate a hidden meaning in 'The Antediluvians,' a parable in 'Powhatan,' new views in 'Cock Robin,' and transcendentalism in 'Hop O' My Thumb.' In short, it has been shown that no man can sit down to write without a very profound

design. Thus to authors in general much trouble is spared" (*CW,* 2:621).
Poe proceeds to refute those who claim he has "never written a moral
tale" on the grounds that critics simply have not found his morals yet.
To make it easy for them, he announces his moral in the story's title, but
he undoes that moral by literalizing it, playing it strictly for laughs.
Although Poe's narrator describes Toby Dammitt as a hopeless "villain"
(*CW,* 2:623), Toby's only real crime is mild swearing: being too poor to
make any real wagers, he backs his claims and challenges by saying "I'll
bet the devil my head that . . ." The devil collects, however, when Toby
bets his head that he not only can clear but "cut a pigeon-wing over" a
turnstile at the end of a covered bridge. When he attempts the stunt,
Toby's neck hits a horizontal brace hidden in the darkness of the tunnel,
and the devil, who has appeared on the scene as "a little lame old gentleman," carries his payment off as Toby's headless body hits the ground.

The story's humor takes the form of absurd understatement and
exaggeration. After Toby has been decapitated, the narrator "hurried up
to him and found that he had received what might be termed a serious
injury" (*CW,* 2:631). Earlier passages indulge in slapstick and absurdist
humor reminiscent of "Loss of Breath." Toby's vices, we are told, result
from parental mismanagement, his being beaten in the wrong direction:
"The world revolves from right to left. It will not do to whip a baby
from left to right. If each blow in the proper direction drives an evil
propensity out, it follows that every thump in an opposite one knocks its
quota of wickedness in" (*CW,* 2:622). In his attempts to cure Toby of
swearing, the narrator also resorts to violence: "I threatened—he swore.
I kicked him—he called for the police. I pulled his nose—he blew it,
and offered to bet the Devil his head that I would not venture to try
that experiment again" (*CW,* 2:624).[1] As usual, Poe's humor is brutal
and cartoonish—the story ends with the narrator having Toby's corpse
dug up and sold for dog meat—but it serves his satirical purposes, however slight or petty they may be. "Never Bet the Devil Your Head" jabs
not only at critics and moralistic readers but at one of Poe's perennial
targets, the transcendentalists. He specifically mentions *The Dial,* Emerson, Coleridge, Carlyle, and Kant, ridiculing their supposed enthusiasm
and pretention by describing "the transcendentals" as a disease caught
by Toby, the symptoms of which are "wriggling and skipping about
under and over everything that came in his way; now shouting out, and
now lisping out, all manner of odd little and big words, yet preserving
the gravest face in the world all the time" (*CW,* 2:627). Moreover, he
sells Toby's body because the transcendentalists refuse to pay for the

funeral and accept responsibility for a fellow enthusiast losing his head. Still, despite its violence and its satiric edge, the story, by virtue of its thoroughgoing absurdity, retains a spirit of mildly satiric, freewheeling comedy.

Three less successful comedies—"Three Sundays in a Week" (1841), "Why the Little Frenchman Wears His Hand in a Sling" (1840), and "The Devil in the Belfry" (1839)—all focus on some act of one-upmanship, just as "Never Bet" pits a clever Devil against an unsuspecting "free spirit." In "Three Sundays" a suitor wins his cousin-bride by answering the challenge of his uncle, the fiancée's father, who says they may marry *"when three Sundays come together in a week"* (*CW*, 2:651). One Sunday the couple introduces to Uncle Rumgudgeon two friends who have just traveled around the world in opposite directions. Because of incremental time changes created by crossing datelines, one traveler experienced Sunday the previous day, while the other is anticipating the next day to be Sunday. The cleverness is really neither the narrator's nor Poe's, however: the narrator reveals that Kate, his fiancée, masterminded the plan, while Poe borrowed the plot from a pair of articles published earlier in 1841 in the Philadelphia *Public Ledger*, one of which even bore the title "Three Thursdays in One Week" (Mabbott, *CW*, 2:648). "The Little Frenchman" is also borrowed, though to a lesser extent. George Pope Morris had introduced a popular character called "The Little Frenchman" in 1836 (Mabbott, *CW*, 2:462); Poe's narrator, however, is not the story's stereotyped comic Frenchman but a stereotyped comic Irishman, Sir Pathrick O'Grandison. The rivalry between Frenchman and Irishman over Lady Tracle (suggesting *treacle*) leads to their mutual embarrassment when, each thinking he is rubbing hands with the lady behind her back, they discover they have been caressing each other. Stuart Levine and Susan F. Levine correctly label the story "essentially a dialect joke,"[2] but the dialects are so overdone that the result is offensive and difficult to read.

Similarly, "The Devil in the Belfry" offers little more than ethnic humor, although in this story Poe fuses it with political satire. The parodically named town of Vondervotteimittiss is populated by provincial Dutchmen concerned only with timepieces and cabbages. The shape of the town itself resembles a clock, with 60 houses forming a circle around a belfry, while other images of time fill the residents' houses and gardens.[3] Their perfectly ordered society is disrupted by a "foreign-looking young man" of dark complexion, dressed in black and carrying an over-sized fiddle. This "devil" dances (without "the remotest idea [of] *keeping time* in his steps" [*CW,* 2:371]) into the center of the village, attacks the belfry-man just before noon, and then sounds the bell 13 times to the shock and dismay of the citizens and cabbages. William Whipple persuasively argues that Poe's devil is a caricature of Martin Van Buren, his fiddling the tunes "Judy O'Flannagan" and "Paddy O'Rafferty" a reference to Van Buren's pandering to Irish immigrants for votes, to the dismay of the "traditional" Dutch and German constituency.[4] Since the "devil" is himself foreign-looking to the Dutch, he could represent the "invading" Irish rather than Van Buren. Either way, Poe's chauvinism in this story recalls his caricature of the Dutch in "Hans Pfall" as well as the dialect humor in "The Little Frenchman" and the anti-Semitism of "A Tale of Jerusalem." In short, "The Devil in the Belfry" evokes the Poe-esque theme of chaos or irrationality winning out in its contest with the rationality, but here the political and ethnic jokes drown out any message that might transcend the story's topicality.

Poe's own competitiveness was still evident in his reviews; although by 1840 he had published a novel as well as the collection *Tales of the Grotesque and Arabesque,* he was still best known as a critic. Indeed, he continued to advertise himself in his reviews, as he did in May 1841 by successfully predicting the as-yet-unrevealed identity of the murderer in Dickens's serialized novel *Barnaby Rudge* when only the first chapters had been published (he guessed incorrectly at other plot developments, however). Poe explicitly claimed to know better than Dickens himself how the novel would unfold. When he reviewed the completed novel the following year in *Graham's,* Poe balanced his praise of Dickens by detailing what he saw as flaws caused mainly by serialization. Poe prefaced this second review with another version of the argument he had made in "Letter to B——," that the popularity of a literary work is no indication of its merit, implying that because of Dickens's popularity, his novels were simply assumed to be great. Poe's criticism of Dickens was hardly the sort of "tomahawking" he was notorious for, but challenging the most popular English prose writer of the day was itself a power play.

Poe praised many writers in print, including Dickens, whose *Old Curiosity Shop* he had reviewed more enthusiastically than *Barnaby Rudge,* but he almost never allowed such praise to go unqualified, as if that might imply that someone out there was a better writer than Poe. His second review of Hawthorne's *Twice-Told Tales,* in addition to setting forth Poe's theory of the short story, makes great claims for Hawthorne's ability as a fiction writer. And yet he concludes his review by pointing out a suspicious "resemblance" between Hawthorne's story "Howe's

Masquerade" and his own "William Wilson." While the charge was clearly ridiculous—the resemblance is rather slight, and Hawthorne's story was published first—Poe quoted passages from "Howe's Masquerade" that bore a more noticeable similarity to "The Masque of the Red Death," a tale he was publishing for the first time in the very same issue of *Graham's*.[5] Since Poe regards Hawthorne's originality as his great virtue, the suggestion that, in one case at least, he is the original from which Hawthorne copies can be seen as an attempt to place himself "one up" on the American fiction writer he admires most. If Poe did in fact borrow from "Howe's Masquerade," we might attribute his calling attention to it as a veiled confession brought about by his own imp of the perverse.

Meanwhile, Poe continued to crusade against corrupt practices among writers, editors, and publishers, here, too, jockeying for position, trying to "one-up" even critics with whom he agreed. In an 1841 review of Lambert A. Wilmer's literary satire *The Quacks of Helicon*, he allies himself with Wilmer, whom he claims is courageously risking his livelihood in taking on the New York literary coteries: "For this reason, and because it is the truth which he has spoken, do we say to him from the bottom of our hearts, 'God speed!' " (*ER*, 1006). Poe's sermonic tone—rhetorical questions, biblical reference, pronouncement of total depravity—continues into the next paragraph:

> We repeat it:—*it is* the truth which he has spoken, and who shall contradict us? He has said unscrupulously what every reasonable man among us has long known to be "as true as the Pentateuch"—that, as a literary people, we are one vast perambulating humbug. He has asserted that we are *clique*-ridden, and who does not smile at the obvious truism of that assertion? He maintains that chicanery is, with us, a far surer road than talent to distinction in letters. Who gainsays this? (*ER*, 1006)

For most of the review Poe neglects Wilmer but continues to testify against literary corruption. He imagines that "some twenty or thirty so-called literary personages . . . will now blush, in the perusal of these words, through consciousness of the shadowy nature of that purchased pedestal upon which they stand—will now tremble in thinking of the feebleness of the breath which will be adequate to the blowing it from beneath their feet" (*ER*, 1011). Poe's imagery recalls the "puffs" that elevated those pretenders to their current status: his godlike task is to blow down—or deflate—the reputations that have been inflated.

When Poe returns to Wilmer's satire in the final three paragraphs, he directs the language of judgment toward *The Quacks of Helicon* itself, although his real targets are still writers more popular than himself. In charging Wilmer with "the sin of indiscriminate censure" (a complaint that was repeatedly leveled against Poe and one that certainly applies to the passage quoted above), Poe arrogantly damns a few of his rivals with faint praise: "Mr. Morris *has* written good songs. Mr. Willis is not *quite* an ass. Mr. Bryant is not *all* a fool. Mr. Longfellow *will* steal, but perhaps he cannot help it, (for we have heard of such things,)" (*ER*, 1013). If these comments were not enough to cast some doubt upon the serious intent of Poe's criticism of Wilmer, he adds, "neither are we *all* brainless, nor is the devil himself so black as he is painted" (*ER*, 1013). Poe doubles back finally to applaud Wilmer's satire, proclaiming that it will survive earthly judgment: "[T]he talent, the fearlessness, and especially the *design* of this book, will suffice to save it even from that dreadful damnation of 'silent contempt' to which editors throughout the country, if we are not very much mistaken, will endeavor, one and all, to consign it" (*ER*, 1013). As he had done in his earlier *Messenger* reviews, Poe is blending criticism and metacriticism, using a review to attack other critics and indeed the entire corrupt network of writers, reviewers, and editors. At the same time, he positions his own judgment above that of the "puffed up" literati he condemns.

In two comic stories from this period, Poe fictionalized his criticism of the business of literature, as he had done previously with such tales as "Lionizing" and "How to Write a Blackwood Article." In "The Man That Was Used Up," Brevet Brigadier General John A. B. C. Smith, a seemingly perfect man who is universally admired, is revealed to be completely artificial, having been butchered by Indians in a recent campaign. The naive narrator eventually discovers that Smith (whose title, appropriately, is twice as long as his name) is not even a man, but rather a reputation, a legend, built into the shape of a man. Critics have identified several possible political figures whom Poe might have targeted in his portrayal of Smith, the most convincing of which is then Vice President Richard M. Johnson.[6] But given the fact that the term "used up" and the metaphor of scalping were conventional and frequently employed by Poe (the leading "tomahawking" critic of his day) to describe writers who were harshly and thoroughly criticized in print, it is reasonable to read this story in terms of literary success and failure as well.[7] The narrator, like an imperceptive reader, cannot see through the general's advance publicity. A "kind friend" has told him that Smith "was a *remarkable* man—a *very* remarkable man—indeed one of the most remarkable men of the age" (*CW,* 2:380), and the narrator adopts not only the same opinion but the same words: "There was something, as it were, remarkable—yes, *remarkable,* although this is but a feeble term to express my full admiration" (*CW,* 2:378). Not only does the repetition and italicization of remarkable suggest remakeable, but also rewritable (re-mark-able), for he has been "written up" by secondhand reports as thoroughly as he had been "used up." Indeed, a few years later Poe would explicitly place the phenomenon of being "used up" by one's enemies only to come back more impressive than ever in the context of the publishing world: "Newspaper editors seem to have constitutions closely similar to those of the Deities of 'Walhalla,' who cut each other to pieces every day, and yet got up perfectly sound and fresh every morning" (*ER,* 1299).

Poe attacks the methods by which literary reputations are made more directly in "The Literary Life of Thingum Bob, Esq." (1844). Thingum's first attempt at composition, a pasting together of Dante, Shakespeare, Homer, and Milton, is "used up" not because it is detected as plagiarism but because its reviewers do not understand the works he has copied. He soon finds success, however, playing "Thomas Hawk" as a literary critic, employing the same plagiaristic system Poe had attributed to Blackwood in "How to Write a Blackwood Article" (see chapter 2). Even Thingum's larger plan for success in publishing is based on avoiding writing and instead establishing power over competitors in the field. Poe's point is that literature in the 1840s is a business like any other; Thingum simply relies on "systems" to create his product and on trickery and puffs, which in this story are literally paid advertisements, to sell it. When, in the last paragraph, he declares over and over that he *wrote* ("Ye Gods, did I *not* write? ... Through joy and through sorrow, I—*wrote*" [*CW,* 3:1145]), the irony is clear. "The Literary Life," Poe suggests, has nothing to do with writing. Of course, this story about gaining power in the republic of letters was itself a power play. Mabbott suggests a range of Poe's satiric targets, including Graham and Lewis Gaylord Clark, editor of the *Knickerbocker* (*CW,* 3:1124).[8] At the same time, as Timothy Scherman points out, the story contains autobiographical elements, suggesting that Poe was once again implicating himself in his satire.[9] As if he were winking at the identification between Thingum and himself, Poe concludes the story with this self-reflexive statement referring to his character's "whizz!—fizz!" writing style: "I am giving you a specimen of it right now" (*CW,* 3:1145).

Poe's satirical vision of the publishing industry reflects a larger cultural anxiety over the moral implications of modern business practices at a time when the confidence man had come to represent the dangers of an increasingly anonymous, urbanized, capital-driven America.[10] Advice literature and sensation novels such as George Lippard's *The Quaker City* warned readers to beware attractive appearances and assurances of sincerity. Contemporary commentators recognized the implicit element of confidence game in modern institutions. David Reese, in his book *Humbugs of New York* (1838), focused not on small-time swindlers but on any system that "is found to 'steal away men's brains,' in ingenious sophisms and false logic." Reese describes New York as "the theatre of humbugs; the chosen area of itinerating mountebanks, whether they figure in philosophy, philanthropy, or religion."[11] The *New York Herald* in 1849 observed that the stock market was "The Confidence Man on a Large Scale."[12] At the same time, though, the popularity of folkloric trickster figures such as the "Yankee peddler" and Davy Crockett, associated not with modern urban life but with an American knack for "getting ahead," suggests that while Americans feared confidence men, they were willing to endorse certain forms of duplicity for financial gain.[13]

Poe denounced shortcuts to success as "villainy" in his reviews and satires of the literary scene, but when he wrote explicitly about con artists outside his profession, his position was less consistent. In both "The Business Man" and "Diddling Considered as One of the Exact Sciences," he depicts business itself as humbug, but in the first story he treats his subject with the same disdain he shows for Thingum Bob, whereas in the latter he reveals some admiration for the diddler's ability to succeed by his own wits. "The Business Man" satirizes the early-nineteenth-century worship of "self-made" millionaires, reducing their achievements to swindles or extortion.[14] Poe's self-proclaimed businessman Peter Proffit ("Peter Pendulum" in the first published version) distinguishes himself from more conventional entrepreneurs by ironically referring to them as "geniuses" who embark on "fantastic" or "eccentric" pursuits such as merchandising or manufacturing. Those respectable professions that Proffit ironically considers "out of the usual way" involve some risk taking, whereas his jobs depend only on *method* or *system* for their success; in short, Proffit represents new, innovative ways of making money. His "method" consists of creating problems people will pay him to eliminate (or discontinue) rather than offering his services to a market he cannot control. The "Eye-Sore trade," "mud-dabbling," and organ-grinding amount to extortion, as Proffit is paid not to be a nuisance. His other businesses also involve either setting traps for customers or otherwise circumventing the laws of supply and demand; for example, when the legislature, in an effort to reduce the cat population, offers a premium for cattails, Proffit begins breeding cats for the purpose of cutting their tails off. Poe's businessman, in this sense, utilizes the sort of "method" that would come to define consumer capitalism: he creates demand or in some way ensures that his product will be needed, leaving nothing to chance. By the 1830s and 1840s name-brand advertising was coming into use to control the price of manufactured goods; rather than continuing to let the consumer dictate prices by forcing competitors to undersell each other, producers used brand advertising to affix a standard of quality to a product or company name and put a price on the name representing that standard. Like Peter Proffit, sellers of goods and services could now "create" demand; by the time Poe wrote "The Business Man" the first advertising agents were facilitating this process.[15] Not surprisingly, the first business Proffit goes into is advertising: he shows off suits tailored by his employers, Messrs. Cut & Comeagain, and brings potential customers to the shop. For all his pride in being a "made man" (an expression that recalls General John A. B. C. Smith), Poe's businessman is clearly pathetic, willing to get beaten up or to cut off cats' tails for money. But such is the state of modern business, according to Poe: as in the field of literature, "genius" (here represented by such "out of the usual way" occupations as dry-goods dealing or blacksmithing) is being replaced by "method" or "system." Just as Thingum Bob and Mr. Blackwood systematize reviewing and tale-writing, Proffit systematizes other forms of commerce.

Like "The Business Man," "Diddling Considered as One of the Exact Sciences" (originally "Raising the Wind") suggests that swindles represent normal business practices rather than aberrations.[16] "Man," writes Poe, "is an animal that diddles" (*CW*, 3:869). In fact, Poe links diddling to standard business practices even more explicitly here than in "The Business Man":

> His [the diddler's] business is retail, for cash, or approved paper at sight. Should he ever be tempted into magnificent speculation, he then, at once, loses his distinctive features, and becomes what we term "financier." This latter word conveys the diddling idea in every respect except that of magnitude. A diddler may thus be regarded as a banker *in petto*—a "financial operation," as a diddle at Brobdingnag. (*CW*, 3:870)

Writing not from the perspective of the diddler but in the voice of an objective magazine essayist, Poe again assumes the role of exposer-of-fraud, which he had perfected as literary editor of the *Messenger*. Thus the satire, for a change, focuses not on the speaker, nor even on the putative subject; instead, Poe aims his derision at the gullible "honest citizens" who fall prey to the diddler's tricks.

In "Diddling," Poe seems genuinely to admire the work he describes. He introduces his examples with phrases such as "[a] very good diddle is this" (*CW*, 3:871) or "quite a respectable diddle is this" (*CW*, 3:872). Others are "bold," "neat" (*CW*, 3:874), "very minute" (*CW*, 3:875), "very clever" (*CW*, 3:876), "small, but . . . scientific" (*CW*, 3:875), and "rather elaborate" (*CW*, 3:877). Indeed, while some of the diddles are barely worthy of Peter Proffit (such as posing as a bill- or toll-collector), others demonstrate the intellectual sophistication of the diddler who succeeds by knowing how other people think. For instance, he knows, as most confidence men do, that a shop owner or landlady will trust a "gentleman" and that most people become vulnerable at the appearance of easy money. Accordingly, Poe's diddlers are introduced, respectively, as "a polite and voluble individual" (*CW*, 3:871), "a well-dressed individual" (*CW*, 3:872), "an official looking person," and "a traveller, portmanteau in hand" (*CW*, 3:873), and nearly all beguile their victims with unusual financial incentives. Furthermore, Poe praises the personal qualities of the diddler—perseverance, ingenuity, nonchalance, originality—even as he exposes him. Under "Perseverance," for example, Poe remarks, "He steadily pursues his end, and *Ut canis a corio nunquam absterrebitur uncto* ["as a dog is never driven from a greasy hide"], so he never lets go of his game" (*CW*, 3:870). And under "Nonchalance" he notes approvingly that the diddler "is not at all nervous. He never *had* any nerves" (*CW*, 3:870–71). In some respects the diddler's personality is paradoxical: he is motivated by personal gain, yet he places such importance on originality that he would "return a purse . . . upon discovering that he had obtained it by an unoriginal diddle" (*CW*, 3:871).[17] While the "ingredients" are for the most part admirable, the "compound" is a con man—a significant paradox in light of Poe's contention that "man is an animal that diddles."

Perhaps because in this story the diddler, unlike Peter Proffit, is not merely a representative "Business Man" but a representative "man," Poe's depiction of him is ambivalent. The final quality Poe attributes to the diddler suggests a strictly personal satisfaction that one can imagine Poe knew well:

Grin:—Your *true* diddler winds up all with a grin. But this nobody sees but himself. He grins when his daily work is done—when his allotted

labors are accomplished—at night in his own closet, and altogether for
his own private entertainment. He goes home. He locks his door. He
divests himself of his clothes. He puts out his candle. He gets into bed.
He places his head upon the pillow. All this done, and your diddler *grins.*
This is no hypothesis. It is a matter of course. I reason *à priori,* and a diddle would be *no* diddle without a grin. (*CW,* 3:871)

Whether or not we attribute this *à priori* reasoning to Poe himself, the
passage points to an identification between the exposer (Poe's persona)
and the perpetrator.[18] Implicit in Poe's ability to reveal the secrets of the
magazine business is the fact that he is, after all, an insider. Poe is
divided between, on the one hand, condemning the practices that allow
"the quacks of Helicon" to succeed while he fails, and, on the other,
accepting the world of commerce, inside the publishing industry and
outside it, as part of an amoral universe in which someone with his analytical powers should ultimately triumph.

Toward Science Fiction

Some of Poe's literary diddling required little or no skill, however. In
1839 he put his name to a textbook on seashells, *The Conchologist's First
Book,* although he had written only the preface and introduction. The
main text was an abridgment of a manual by scientist Thomas Wyatt,
who, because his publishers owned the copyright of the original, could
not publish the abridgment under his own name. Since Poe worked in
accord with Wyatt, who paid him for the use of his name, the deception
was harmless to its true author, though not to its original publisher.[19]
Poe committed another borderline plagiarism with the unfinished *Journal of Julius Rodman,* which *Burton's* issued serially throughout the first
half of 1840 (before Poe's departure). Poe borrowed heavily from the
journals of Lewis and Clark, Washington Irving's *Astoria,* and other
works, making *Rodman,* as Burton R. Pollin notes, "more nearly . . . a
verbal collage than any other work by Poe."[20] What makes *Rodman* a
"borderline" case is that Poe did not explicitly take credit for the work
when he published it in *Burton's;* indeed, he tried to pass it off as an
authentic narrative of "the first passage across the Rocky Mountains of
North America ever achieved by civilized man" (*IV,* 507). From a diddler's point of view *Rodman* is an interesting experiment: a pastiche of
previous accounts presented as a newly discovered journal that predates
the works it plagiarizes. Poe tips his hand, as if wanting to expose his

own hoax, by referring, in an editorial introduction, to the expeditions whose accounts he plunders. Unfortunately, the concept of this playful experiment is more intriguing than Poe's execution of it. While a few critics have examined *Rodman* in light of *Pym* and Poe's approach to landscape and individual perception,[21] it remains primarily an example of Poe's complicity in the amoral system of literary production.

Although few of Poe's contemporaries noticed *The Journal of Julius Rodman* when it appeared in *Burton's*, it succeeded as a hoax nonetheless, being cited by the librarian to the State Department in the U.S. Senate Documents of 1839 and 1840. Poe created a more immediate stir with a clever hoax published as an "extra" to the *New York Sun*, a fake news article now known as "The Balloon Hoax" (1844). Incorporating the same verisimilar, journalistic style (as well as some of the details) he had used in "Hans Pfaall," Poe described a balloon voyage from England to the United States, landing at Sullivan's Island, South Carolina (where he had been stationed during his stint in the army). Obviously, an aerial voyage across the ocean was more plausible than a trip to the moon; moreover, Poe did not frame "The Balloon Hoax" with satire or banter. As a result, with the possible exception of *Rodman*, "The Balloon Hoax" is Poe's most "sincere" effort to fool his readers. It attracted a good deal of attention but apparently few believers, largely because readers remembered that the *Sun* had perpetrated its own infamous "moon hoax" nine years earlier. Poe was even reported to have revealed the hoax himself to a crowd outside the publisher's door on the day of its distribution.[22] That report jibes with Poe's self-exposure in his plagiarism charge against Hawthorne and with his fictional criminals' perverse impulses to confess. As he put it in an 1844 "Marginalia" entry, "a certain order of mind" is never satisfied with knowing how to do a thing or even with doing it: "It must both know and show how it was done."[23]

Poe's attempt to make plausible the seemingly impossible and to use fiction to predict future technological innovations places "The Balloon Hoax," along with "Hans Pfaall" and several other stories, squarely within the tradition of science fiction. Actually fooling the public seems to have been a low priority in most of his hoaxes; rather, like many modern science-fiction writers, Poe sought to suspend his readers' disbelief even though those readers knew that what they were reading was not "real." The same applies in some sense to all fiction, in that it creates a "fake" reality, but, particularly in his science fiction, Poe explored ways in which those fictional worlds might impinge upon the material world, ways in which the boundary between fiction and truth might be blurred. A hoax can be a warning not to believe everything one reads, but it is also an invitation to believe, either because today's fiction could be tomorrow's headline, or because clinging too closely to observable fact limits one's perception, or even because believing is more fun than doubting.

Subtitled "An Extravaganza," "The Angel of the Odd" (1844) urges the suspension of disbelief necessary for appreciating science fiction. The title character believes in believing and converts the narrator to a position of belief by subjecting him to a series of incredible mishaps and coincidences. At the beginning of the story, the narrator, sated with rich food, alcohol, and dull reading material, turns to the newspaper, where he finds an improbable story of a man who accidentally killed himself playing a game in which a dart is blown through a tube: "He placed the needle at the wrong end of the tube, and drawing his breath strongly to puff the dart forward with force, drew the needle into his throat. It entered his lungs, and in a few days killed him" (CW, 3:1101). The narrator's vow never to believe such odd stories again summons the Angel, a creature made out of various wine and liquor receptacles, who chastises him in a (presumably) German dialect: "[Y]ou mos pe pigger vool as de goose, vor to dispelief vat iz print in de print. 'Tiz de troof—dat it iz—eberry vord ob it" (CW, 3:1103). The Angel proceeds with his violent, comic therapy, which culminates in dangling the narrator from a rope while riding in (of all things) a balloon, asking the crucial questions of belief—in the possibility of the odd, and in the Angel of the Odd. Having converted the narrator, the Angel drops him, leaving him where he started (the dining-room hearth). This ending suggests that the narrator has dreamed or hallucinated his adventures with the Angel—yet he cannot afford to admit that he dreamed it, for he has sworn his belief. Poe, through the Angel, dares readers to believe in the odd, the improbable, the very material from which his fiction is made. A good fiction writer, like the Angel of the Odd, leaves his readers no choice.

Accordingly, when Poe writes a hoax based on the idea that through mesmerism one can report back to the living his experiences in the hereafter, he begins by asserting that those who doubt the legitimacy of mesmerism "are your mere doubters by profession—an unprofitable and disreputable tribe" (CW, 3:1029). "Mesmeric Revelation" (1844) did fool some journalists, although here Poe seems less concerned with the hoax-frame than with the theory of physics the story's narrator sets forth, particularly the "metamorphosis" of the human body after death (an idea he would later develop in *Eureka*). A pseudoscientific precursor of modern hypnosis, mesmerism excited the popular imagination in the early nineteenth century. It is not clear whether Poe believed in it or not, but the concept naturally appealed to his interest in alternate states of consciousness and the possibility of knowing, while alive, what it is like to be dead. As Charles May explains, "Poe uses mesmerism as a means of exploring his own metaphysical views about the nature of reality, for, like a hoax, mesmerism is a fiction posing as reality; in its similitude of death it can be mistaken for the real state."[24] One can read "Mesmeric Revelation" simply as a hoax aimed at believers in mesmerism, but most likely the editor of the *Universalist Watchman,* who commented on the story after reprinting it in 1845, took the right approach: "We do not take the following article as an historical account, nor, as a burlesque on mesmerism; but, as a presentation of the writer's philosophical theory which he wished to commend to the attention of his readers" (quoted in *CW,* 3:1027).

Poe uses mesmerism to add interpretive possibilities to his underappreciated science-fiction story "A Tale of the Ragged Mountains" (1844). "Ragged Mountains" might be termed a hoax since the narrator asserts its veracity—"It is only now, in the year 1845, when similar miracles are witnessed daily by thousands, that I dare venture to record this apparent impossibility as a matter of serious fact" (*CW,* 3:941–42)—but Poe makes little effort to authenticate the "facts" of the story; the plot and style share more with "Ligeia" than with "The Balloon Hoax" or even "Mesmeric Revelation." Bedloe, a mysterious young gentleman of indeterminate age, has come under the influence of Templeton, a doctor who practices mesmerism. While walking in the woods one day, Bedloe believes he is transported to a Middle Eastern battlefield, where he is killed by a "poisoned barb" that pierces his right temple—and yet he is found, alive, by a search party that includes the narrator. (Thus yet another Poe character "dies" but returns to describe the death experience.) When he relates this story to a group that includes both the narrator and Templeton, the doctor produces a portrait of Oldeb, a man nearly identical in appearance to Bedloe, who had been killed in a battle that took place in India in 1780. Templeton, who claims to have been Oldeb's friend, was writing his account of Oldeb's death at the same time that Bedloe experienced the battle. Stricken with fever, Bedloe dies soon afterward when Templeton, purportedly by mistake, bleeds him with a "venomous vermicular sangsue" (a poison leech, Poe's invention) placed above the right temple. Not only is Bedloe fatally wounded in precisely the same spot as Oldeb, but the wounds are inflicted by oddly similar instruments. The poisoned leech, the narrator tells us in the postscript, differs from other leeches in part by virtue of its snakelike motions, while the poisoned arrow that killed Oldeb was "made to imitate the body of a creeping serpent" (*CW,* 3:947).

It all sounds a little silly, but like some of Poe's most celebrated stories, "Ragged Mountains" is designed to raise interpretive questions that put the reader in the detective role, and the clues Poe provides hardly lead to definitve solutions.[25] Even more than Ligeia, Bedloe looks suspiciously like a living corpse or skeleton—limbs "exceedingly long and emaciated," "complexion . . . absolutely bloodless," pronounced mouth and teeth forming a smile with "no variation whatever," eyes "abnormally large . . . so totally vapid, filmy and dull, as to convey the idea of the eyes of a long-interred corpse" (*CW,* 3:940). He takes morphine every morning. He and Templeton have a kind of symbiotic rapport— another instance of doubling—although the mesmerist clearly has control over this symbiosis. Was Bedloe's dreamlike experience brought on by his drug use? Is Bedloe Oldeb reincarnated, fated to die as his counterpart did? Did Templeton unintentionally suggest the death fantasy in Bedloe's mind by writing about Oldeb's death? Or did Templeton attempt to murder Bedloe through the power of suggestion, and then follow through by killing him with the poisoned leech? Poe's most important clues are linguistic: because of a typographical error in his obituary, the newspaper misprints "Bedloe" without the final "e," making his name "Oldeb" spelled backwards; also, *Temple*ton's name indicates where both Oldeb and Bedloe received their fatal wounds. The anagrammatic names suggest a supernatural design in having Oldeb return as Bedloe only to die in an uncannily similar manner, and yet the fact that Templeton applies the leech above the patient's temple points to his guilt, hinting that he has left his "signature" on the victim.[26]

As part of a larger pattern, these instances of wordplay point not only toward Templeton's responsibility for Bedloe's death but toward a metafictional element of the story, for as verbal clues the anagram and the pun constitute evidence only for readers of the story—they are either unnoticed or dismissed as coincidence by the narrator. It stands to reason that a story so preoccupied with names, words, and writing should be resolved, as May claims, "in the only way it can be resolved: aesthetically."[27] Templeton is Poe's proxy in the story, controlling his reader/patient's mind through mesmerism, but also through the act of writing that transports Bedloe to another place and time. Bedloe believes his dream to be real because, as in Poe's theory of the well-constructed tale, "[a]ll was rigorously self-consistent" (*CW*, 3:946). Moreover, the act of mesmerism shares a basic principle with the writer-reader relationship as Poe imagined it: the two are in complete sympathy, but one has total control over the other as long as the spell or story lasts. In this strikingly self-referential tale, every bit as modern as Poe's detective stories, the clues ultimately lead back to the writer, who "plays God" with his reader.[28]

Though not exactly a hoax, "A Tale of the Ragged Mountains" challenges readers by engaging them in a detective-like game. This playful approach is even more evident in "The Premature Burial," another story that manipulates readers by undermining the expectations the story itself sets. It begins like a journalistic report on the phenomenon of premature burial, which did concern enough people of Poe's time that a "life-preserving coffin" equipped to fly open upon the least movement from within was exhibited in New York in 1843, and a subgenre of "buried alive" literature flourished.[29] Poe's narrator recounts several occurrences of live burial over 20 paragraphs (about half the story) before shifting his attention to his own phobia. Suddenly the journalistic report begins to read like one of Poe's Gothic tales. The narrator reveals more about his catalepsy and consequent fear of premature burial, describing a nightmare in which he sees all the graves of the world laid bare: "[T]he real sleepers were fewer, by many millions, than those who slumbered not at all; and there was a feeble struggling; and there was a general sad unrest; and from out the depths of the countless pits there came a melancholy rustling from the garments of the buried" (*CW*, 3:964). He takes extreme precautions to guard against his own premature burial but makes it clear that he will fall victim to it nonetheless: "But, alas! what avails the vigilance against the Destiny of man? Not even these well contrived securities sufficed to save from the uttermost agonies of living inhumation, a wretch to these agonies foredoomed!" (*CW*, 3:966). As promised, the story concludes with an episode in which the narrator wakes up inside a box, surrounded by complete darkness, with none of his provisions for escape at hand. But in the manner of *Pym*, the narrator's crisis turns out to be only a pseudocrisis: he had forgotten that he had spent the night in a narrow berth on board a ship and had not, in fact, been buried. Twice, then, "The Premature Burial" proves to be something other than what it pretends, first going from journalistic report to "tale of sensation" and then deflating the sensation by not delivering a "real" premature burial.

Poe's conclusion deflates what he had treated as serious subject matter throughout the story, turning premature burial into a kind of joke.

To heighten this effect, the narrator pronounces himself cured of both his catalepsy and his phobia, having replaced his precautions against premature burial with precautions against fear of it: "I read no 'Night Thoughts'—no fustian about church-yards—no bugaboo tales—*such as this*" (*CW,* 3:969). At this moment the narrator steps back from his text as he writes it to point out that we readers have been humbugged, that we have been reading *his* bugaboo tale all along. As J. Gerald Kennedy observes, Poe "implicitly deconstructs his account, dismisses the genre which it represents, trivializes the idea of living inhumation, and leaves the reader holding the shroud." But Kennedy also notes that, despite the narrator's assertions of good health and clear mind, he is still sufficiently obsessed with the "one sepultural Idea" to review case after case of living interment, to keep writing about his fear even after he has supposedly conquered it.[30] Poe has set us up, insisting on the truth of his story while building slowly toward the premature burial that isn't—and yet the story is not pure hoax or satire. At one point the narrator describes the fear of premature burial as universal: "We know of nothing so agonizing upon Earth—we can dream of nothing half so hideous in the realms of the nethermost Hell. And thus all narratives upon this topic have an interest profound; an interest, nevertheless, which, through the sacred awe of the topic itself, very properly and very peculiarly depends upon our conviction of the *truth* of the matter narrated" (*CW,* 3:961–62). Even though the story ends by depriving us of that conviction, the fear "we" have, which Poe has skillfully summoned up, cannot be completely deflated, just as the narrator cannot quite laugh it off. Notice, too, that Poe does not claim that our interest depends on the *truth* of the matter, but on our *conviction* of it. The distinction is important, for the purpose of a hoax—again, like the purpose of fiction generally—is to convince readers that the (con) artist's creation is real. Thus, like his own diddler, and like the Imp of the Perverse, Poe in his hoaxes and science fiction keeps readers off balance by asking them to believe and take seriously the seemingly impossible—a balloon trip across the Atlantic, a mesmerized patient speaking from the hereafter, metempsychosis, premature burial—all the while winking at us, reminding us that we are, after all, being taken for a ride.

Detective Fiction

While the claim that Poe "invented" the detective story seems somewhat exaggerated—David Van Leer, for one, reminds us to remember *Oedipus*

Rex, Hamlet, and *Macbeth* as well as Voltaire's *Zadig* and earlier Gothic fiction by Ann Radcliffe, William Godwin, and E. T. A. Hoffmann—two of the most renowned writers of detective fiction, Sir Arthur Conan Doyle and Dorothy L. Sayers, have placed Poe at the beginning of the tradition, and scholars have traced to Poe numerous conventions of the genre, notably the "armchair detective" and the sidekick/narrator who serves as an intermediary between detective and reader.[31] But Poe's "tales of ratiocination," all written between 1840 and 1844, raise many issues beyond the question of their originary status, addressing problems such as "reading" the urban world of strangers, fathoming the workings of the human mind, and collecting the rewards for intellectual effort.

The plots of several Poe stories from this period hinge on detective work without emphasizing the character of the detective and the ratiocinative method as Poe does in the Dupin trilogy and "The Gold Bug." "The Man That Was Used Up," "The Spectacles," and "The Oblong Box" all feature bumbling protagonists who "play detective" in their mystery-solving quests, but each allows his own desires to shape his interpretation of physical clues, leading to embarrassing false conclusions.[32] The narrator of "The Man of the Crowd" (1840) also fails in his quest, concluding that his man is a book that will not permit itself to be read, and yet this story more fully anticipates the Dupin tales in its concern with vice and crime in the modern city and in Poe's doubling of pursuer and pursued. Students who read it alongside other frequently anthologized Poe stories often remark that it doesn't sound like a Poe story: the narrator does not begin by ranting about his sanity, nor does he discourse upon his opium use or his tendency to confuse fantasy with reality; he merely explains that he "had been ill in health, but was now convalescent" and that he feels intellectually energized by his recovery (*CW,* 2:507). "The Man of the Crowd" defies our expectations not only of a Poe story but of any kind of story, for Poe presents this fiction as a personal essay, less formal but similar in tone to "The Premature Burial." Rather than insist on the veracity of incredible events, this narrator employs a rational, conversational style and relates nothing that could be confused with the supernatural. And yet, for all this normalcy, the story's premise is rather odd: a lone people watcher, entranced by the "idiosyncracy" of expression on an old man's face, follows him through the streets of London for an entire night and the following day, never speaking to him and never seeing him do anything extraordinary, other than to keep moving among the crowd.

Because the narrator sounds rational and intelligent, readers tend to focus on the strange appearance and behavior of the "man of the crowd," but if one imagines how the action of the story would look, one sees two men wandering interminably through crowds, one following the other in a sort of low-speed chase. The man in front, according to the narrator, is in his late sixties, "decrepid," "short . . . very thin, and apparently very feeble," while the pursuer (probably younger, given his emphasis on the older man's age) has a handkerchief tied around his face and is trying not to be noticed by the other (*CW,* 2:511). If the scene appears anything other than absurd, it would probably look as if the old man has at least as much reason to fear the disguised stranger who is following him (and surely he would know he was being followed after the first few hours) as the narrator has to fear him, despite the old man's fiendish looks and the dagger beneath his cloak.[33] If the narrator is not the more sinister figure, he is at least, as Patrick Quinn suggests, the old man's double, at least for a day, for judging by appearances, he, too, fits his own description of "the man of the crowd": He is "the type and the genius of deep crime. He refuses to be alone" (*CW,* 2:515).[34]

The narrator is attracted to the old man initially because of the paradoxical ideas he forms while looking at him, "ideas of vast mental power, of caution, of penuriousness, of avarice, of coolness, of malice, of blood-thirstiness, of triumph, of merriment, of excessive terror, of intense—of supreme despair" (*CW,* 2:511). Before spotting the mystery man, the narrator had been amusing himself by classifying groups of people who pass by the window of his hotel's coffeehouse. In his lengthy discussion of the various groups, he reveals his preoccupation with creating order out of the chaos of an urban crowd, trying to impose a hierarchical classification system on a fluid, widely diverse mass of people. The man of the crowd deconstructs this classification system, reflecting the chaos of the mob he represents, evoking in the narrator contradictory responses: triumph and despair, coolness and terror. Ultimately, the crowd also defies the narrator's efforts to classify it, for no stable hierarchy emerges and it remains unknowable.[35] The man never leaves the crowd because he *is* the crowd of which the narrator, too, has now become a part. Dressed in the filthy rags of what had been fine clothing, riding the flow of foot traffic from a respectable hotel to a gin shop in the slums, the old man embodies contradiction but ultimately represents qualities of the metropolis that frightened the genteel middle class of the nineteenth century just as they frighten so many people today: anonymity, rootlessness, vice, poverty, lack of personal space, and, most of all, the threat of violence.

In the first two Dupin tales, urban violence is more than a threat: in "The Murders in the Rue Morgue" (1841) two women are brutally murdered, and in "The Mystery of Marie Rogêt" (1842–43), a young sales-girl's corpse is found in the Seine. Although the Dupin trilogy is set in Paris, the stories, like "The Man of the Crowd," evoke the big city as a kind of abstraction more than they utilize detail specific to any single metropolis. As Amy Gilman observes, Poe's "urban settings are more imaginary and metaphoric than real" because he chose cities unfamiliar to him: London, which he knew only from childhood memories, and Paris, where he had never been.[36] Still, Poe's urban vision reflects real fears of his contemporaries, who produced a steady stream of novels and pamphlets exposing the hidden dangers of the city.[37] The penny news-papers certainly contributed to the city's violent image; in fact, the New York dailies sensationalized the case on which "Marie Rogêt" is based, the mysterious death of one Mary Rogers. Accordingly, Poe has Dupin work on the mystery by reviewing newspaper accounts, devoting most of the story to a dialogue between the detective and the papers. Simi-larly, much of Dupin's evidence comes from the "Gazette des Tri-bunaux," and he lures the owner of the ape to his apartment by means of a newspaper advertisement. Even before she became a headline, Mary Rogers had been part of an urban phenomenon as a young, single work-ing woman, specifically a "cigar girl" whose good looks attracted cus-tomers to the shop; Poe has her double, Marie, selling perfume. As Gilman points out, even the confusion over the "language" of the orang-utan in "Rue Morgue" arises from the urban phenomenon of ethnic diversity within a small district, as people of various backgrounds hear the voices in the L'Espanayes's apartment and make guesses at the unfa-miliar accent of the killer.[38]

Particularly in this modern urban setting, where one encounters the new and anomalous on an almost daily basis, the ability to detect the truth behind the headlines, behind the facades of great buildings and men of the crowd, becomes a valuable skill, a way to get ahead. So it is with Dupin, who rarely leaves his apartment during the day but likes to walk the streets at night, who can make himself an unreadable text by donning green spectacles. An urban enigma himself, Dupin is expert at reading others, unlike the narrator of "The Man of the Crowd," and he is rewarded with the admiration of his peers, the self-satisfaction of defeating the Prefect of Police, and, in the case of "The Purloined Let-ter" (1844), 50,000 francs.

Dupin's methods can be summarized in the terms the prefect uses to describe the case of the purloined letter: simple and odd. Dupin explains his reasoning so that his conclusions appear inevitable, the result of common sense as opposed to the scientifically precise but procrustean methods of the police. At the same time, Dupin clearly has intuitive skills everyone else in the story lacks, for he alone solves the locked-room mystery of Rue Morgue and the purloined letter case. Dupin explains his uncanny ability to the narrator early in "Rue Morgue," as he retraces the narrator's long, unspoken thought process that leads inevitably from the fruit vendor to the inadequacy of the actor Chantilly, and again through analogy with the boy who wins all the marbles playing the even-and-odd game with his schoolmates. The boy can predict his opponent's strategy by doubling the other's intellect, even reading his thoughts:

> When I wish to find out how wise, or how stupid, or how good, or how wicked is any one, or what are his thoughts at the moment, I fashion the expression of my face, as accurately as possible, in accordance with the expression of his, and then wait to see what thoughts or sentiments arise in my mind or heart, as if to match or correspond with the expression. (*CW,* 3:984–85)

In each case, Dupin's explanation is absurd; no rational method can account for this sort of mind-reading ability. As Stephen Rachman observes, "Poe's detective stories promise the reader solutions, even the origin of all solutions, but the solutions they deliver invariably invite the reader to question the assumptions that underlie the process of detection itself."[39] In a letter to his friend Philip Pendleton Cooke, Poe acknowledged the mystification that makes the reasoning of Dupin—and hence the reasoning of his creator—appear more incredible than it is:

> [P]eople think [the tales of ratiocination] are more ingenious than they are—on account of their method and *air* of method. In the "Murders in the Rue Morgue," for instance, where is the ingenuity of unravelling a web which you yourself (the author) have woven for the express purpose of unravelling? The reader is made to confound the ingenuity of the supposititious Dupin with that of the writer of the story. (*Letters,* 2:328)

Dupin's methods work only within the world of Poe's creation; it is no coincidence that in "The Mystery of Marie Rogêt," the only tale based on an actual unsolved case, Dupin fails to solve the mystery and Poe fails to write a compelling story.[40]

Poe's comments on his own creations hold true for most detective fiction insofar as the author/detective simply "solves" mysteries of his or her own creation; nonetheless, creating challenging puzzles generally requires at least as much ingenuity as solving them, provided the puzzler or detective writer plays fair with her or his audience. Poe, for one, does not play fair, as he withholds key evidence until Dupin explains his solutions in "Rue Morgue" and "The Purloined Letter." But with most detective stories, readers take up the challenge of trying to solve the mystery before the detective does, essentially making a game of it, which ought to make detective fiction by definition "disposable," not worth rereading because the suspense, the basic challenge, cannot be re-created. John T. Irwin begins his study of Poe and Jorge Luis Borges by raising that issue: "[I]f the point of an analytic detective story is the deductive solution of a mystery, how does the writer keep that solution from exhausting the reader's interest in the story? How does he write a work that can be reread by people other than those with poor memories?"[41] Irwin suggests many answers, but as his analysis and others' demonstrate, the solution to the mystery—Who killed Madame and Mademoiselle L'Espanaye, or Marie Rogêt? Where was the Minister hiding the letter?—is not Poe's only "hook." Irwin finds far more intrigue in Poe's allusions to mythology and other writers' works and his use of puns to challenge his readers. For example, Irwin links the locked-room mystery of "Rue Morgue" to labyrinth mythology through Dupin's explanation of how the broken nail in the back window "terminated the clew" (i.e., the thread of deduction), a clew fastened to a nail at the entrance being Theseus's method for negotiating the Minotaur's labyrinth. Irwin presses on: "And, of course, the French word for *nail,* the word Dupin would have used repeatedly, is *clou.* Which is simply Poe's way of giving the reader a linguistic clue (hint) that the clew (thread) will ultimately terminate at a *clou* (nail)—although even the most attentive reader will probably experience this pun as a clue only retrospectively, so that Poe remains one up."[42] The fact that "even the most attentive reader" will not notice this verbal game on first reading—or twentieth—suggests why such a mystery story withstands multiple readings, but more significantly, it shows Poe bantering with his readers in the detective stories just as he does in his hoaxes.

Indeed, the same thirst for competition drives Dupin, giving readers another reason to conflate author and detective. Like Poe the "tomahawking" critic, Dupin promotes his skill largely by emphasizing the shortcomings of his competitors. While he never identifies the murderer of Marie Rogêt, he seems satisfied with disproving a few theories newspaper writers have suggested. He concludes "Rue Morgue" by commenting on the limits of the prefect's intellect, devotes much of his talk in "The Purloined Letter" to the same topic, and concludes that story with his taunting message to the Minister D——. In this relationship between the cool criminal and the equally cool armchair detective we see a William Wilson-like rivalry based not on oppositions between the two but on uncanny similarities. As Liahna Klenman Babener has demonstrated, Poe builds "The Purloined Letter" around pairings and reflections to suggest a psychic identification between Dupin and the Minister D——.[43] The most significant instances of doubling include the fact that both Dupin and D—— are able to baffle the prefect because they defy his systematic approach to detection; both substitute another letter for the one they take; both want their victims to know who stole the letter from them; and both are able to steal the letter while it lies in plain sight because they can properly "read" the holder of the letter. More to the point, Dupin can read D—— not because he contorts his face to match his opponent's but because he already knows how this particular opponent's mind works—very much like his own. The fact that Poe identifies the minister only by the letter D——, concealing the rest of his name, invites speculation that D——'s full name is Dupin, or might as well be. In trying to place the minister, the narrator asks Dupin if he is really a poet:

> "There are two brothers, I know; and both have attained reputation in letters. The Minister I believe has written learnedly on the Differential Calculus. He is a mathematician, and no poet."
> "You are mistaken; I know him well; he is both. As poet *and* mathematician, he would reason well . . ." (*CW,* 3:986)

Not only does Dupin reveal here that he knows the minister well, but he affirms another link to himself, for he, too, is both poet *and* mathematician, having earlier declared himself guilty of "certain doggrel" (*CW,* 3:979).

Are the two men brothers, then, or even a single person? Babener provides evidence for such a conclusion, notably the fact that D—— is present in the story only at second hand, discussed by other characters but never appearing himself.[44] In "Rue Morgue" the narrator, referring to Dupin's "mental excitement," meditates on "the old philosophy of the Bi-Part Soul," amusing himself "with the fancy of a double Dupin— the creative and the resolvent" (*CW,* 2:533). Since Poe makes clear that in a detective story the resolvent and the creative are virtually identical, one can easily imagine these two poet/mathematicians as components of one mind: what D—— creates (a mystery), Dupin resolves, like the web that an author weaves simply to unravel. But Poe's portrayal of Dupin and D—— is not merely self-reflexive, for, as Babener concludes, "the tale is, in its deepest implications, a study in the oneness of pursuer and pursued."[45] Since Dupin—in this story more a thief for hire than a fighter for justice—can claim no moral superiority to D——, and since the game of one-upmanship will presumably continue when D—— finds a way to strike back, this high-stakes battle between virtually identical combatants presents an image of rivalry similar in its irony to Antonio Prohias's "Spy vs. Spy" comics, in which the two spies (crows in detective/spy garb) are differentiated only by the fact that one is dressed in black and the other in white, and their efforts to destroy each other never end.[46]

Given its geometrically structured plot, its use of repetition, and the fact that the contents of the story's letter are never revealed, it is not surprising that "The Purloined Letter" has become a lightning rod for innovative poststructuralist readings. Whatever qualms early- and mid-twentieth-century scholars might have had about Poe's significance as a "serious" writer have all but disappeared in the wake of a series of essays launched by the eminent psychoanalyst and language theorist Jacques Lacan in his 1956 "Seminar on the Purloined Letter," which was translated from French to English in 1972. Jacques Derrida, the enormously influential deconstructionist philosopher, challenged Lacan's reading in his essay "The Purveyor of Truth" (1975; English translation 1987), generating an extended response from literary critic Barbara Johnson and significant additional commentary by other critics, notably Shoshana Felman and John T. Irwin. Because Lacan's and Derrida's essays defy concise summary, and because this continuing discussion has more to do with theories of language and writing in general than with "The Purloined Letter" specifically, I will not attempt to summarize their arguments, although I recommend John P. Muller and William J. Richardson's collection *The Purloined Poe* (1988), which includes Lacan, Derrida, Johnson, Felman, as well as Babener and others.

For our purposes, it should be sufficient to know that Lacan sees the relationships in the parallel theft scenes as triangular: one party (first the king, then the police) is blind to the nature or presence of the letter; another party (the queen, then D——) believes her/himself safe because of the first party's blindness; and a third party (D——, then Dupin) sees the blindness of the first party, the second party's awareness of the first party's blindness, *and* the second party's lack of awareness of the third party's total insight. Derrida argues that because each of these "primal" scenes is narrated by Dupin's sidekick, they are quadrangular rather than triangular, the fourth party accounting for the writing of the story. In his commentary on Lacan, Derrida, and Johnson, Irwin deconstructs the deconstructionists, observing that Derrida has "gone one up" on Lacan in playing the number four to Lacan's three:

> And playing that game means endlessly repeating the structure of "The Purloined Letter" in which being one up inevitably leads to being one down. For if the structure created by the repeated scenes in the tale involves doubling the thought processes of one's opponent in order to use his own methods against him—as Dupin does with the minister, as Derrida does with Lacan, and as Johnson does with Derrida [by refusing to "take a *numerical* position"]—then the very method by which one outwits one's opponent is the same method that will be used against oneself by the next player in the game, the next interpreter in the series, in order to leave the preceding interpreter one down.[47]

Although these theorists do not go back and forth but rather build on each other's insights, their competitiveness does reflect the rivalry depicted in the story, and Irwin's commentary is reminiscent of Poe's own acute sense of the competitiveness of the literary publishing environment he was immersed in when he wrote "The Purloined Letter."

As if to "one up" himself, within two months of "The Purloined Letter" Poe also published what is probably the first parody of detective fiction, "Thou Art the Man" (1844). Mabbott also credits the story with originating the "least-likely-person theme" and, citing Howard Haycraft, the "scattering of false clues by the real criminal" (*CW,* 3:1042). Here the narrator is the detective himself, who, suspecting that the murderer is the victim's best friend, packs the victim's corpse into a wine crate and has it delivered to the suspect to prompt a confession. Poe's tone, his comic names (the villain is named Charley Goodfellow, the victim Barnabus Shuttleworthy), his short-circuiting suspense through rather obvious ironic clues, and the absurdity of the conclusion, in which the ventriloquist narrator has the corpse cry "Thou art the man!" as he pops up from the crate, all put an absurd, comic spin on the genre Poe was developing in the Dupin stories.

Even in the comic mode of "Thou Art the Man," Poe does not make the detective/narrator the butt of a joke or an object of satire: like Dupin, the narrator reads physical evidence and human behavior well enough to solve the mystery and extract the confession. But nowhere is the image of detective-as-expert-reader more explicit than in "The Gold Bug" (1843), Poe's most popular story during his lifetime. The story's plot—the pursuit of riches by carefully decoding and interpreting a text—had a particular resonance for Poe, who had repeatedly demonstrated and boasted of his skill at solving cryptograms and whose best work as a literary critic relied on his "close reading" ability.[48] Terence Whalen clarifies Poe's motivations in writing "The Gold Bug," pointing out the popularity of fiction about money amid public debates surrounding the "Bank War" and the depression that followed the Panic of 1837. Whalen argues that Poe wanted to depict cryptography as "a rare and commercially valuable expression of genius" and at the same time longed for a way to prevent his writing from remaining a mere commodity, sold by Poe for four or five dollars a page to a publisher who in turn sold it to the public. Legrand acts out Poe's fantasy by turning his intellectual labor directly into gold. The fact that Captain Kidd's map is written on parchment not only makes literal sense for the plot but, according to Whalen, comments obliquely on the debate over paper money: "Poe deliberately avoids paper and instead uses a kidskin note by Captain Kidd to capitalize on the demand for pecuniary themes, laughing—or kidding—all the way to the bank. . . . The treasure chest, which contains 'no American money' (*CW,* 3:827), further indicates the central exchange of the story: not paper for paper, but code for gold."[49] Poe's "The Gold Bug" proved far less valuable than Legrand's, but it did increase his renown as a fiction writer while earning the more tangible reward of a $100 prize in a contest sponsored by the appropriately named *Dollar Magazine.*

Like Dupin, Legrand is a purely intellectual hero, succeeding not through courage or physical strength but through his remarkable reading ability. Kidd's text is particularly difficult, requiring Legrand first to recognize the fact that it *is* a text (it is written in disappearing ink), then to crack the code, and then to interpret correctly Kidd's language, which includes obscure phrases like "good glass," "bishop's hostel," and "devil's seat."[50] As Michael Williams demonstrates, Poe emphasizes Legrand's ability to meet the "requirements of the interpretive act" by contrasting his versatility in reading signs with the narrator's and Jupiter's repeated misreadings. Poe depicts Jupiter in the manner of a minstrel-show "darkie," whose ignorance of left and right forestalls the discovery of the treasure chest and whose dialect and limited vocabulary create comic misunderstandings.[51] Although it hardly mitigates his racist portrayal of Jupiter, Poe makes it clear that the educated, white narrator is also limited in his understanding of the complexity and instability of language and therefore is just as confused by the textual clues Legrand deciphers, much like the narrator of the Dupin tales.

Finally, like Dupin, Legrand has been "reduced" financially but has an aristocratic background, suggesting that Poe imaginatively conflated himself with these two detectives much as he believed his readers would. Poe must have identified particularly with Legrand, the eccentric Southerner whose cryptographic skills lead to fortune. But Legrand, for all his ratiocinative skill, meets with incredible luck, something Poe himself almost never had. Within a short span of years, Poe had made important contributions to the detective story and science fiction, published an enduring theory of the short story, and demonstrated that theory in a dozen or so classic tales, but he never cracked the "code for gold" or discovered anything that looked like a treasure map. Such a map remained for him what the parchment was for the narrator of "The Gold Bug" and what the old man was for the narrator of "The Man of the Crowd": a text that did not permit itself to be read.

Chapter Six

"*At Length* I Would Be Avenged": 1845–1849

In the Shadow of "The Raven"

On January 29, 1845, the *New York Evening Mirror* published a new poem that N. P. Willis, the *Mirror*'s editor, claimed was "unsurpassed in English poetry for subtle conception, masterly ingenuity of versification, and consistent, sustaining of imaginative lift and 'pokerishness' " [i.e., spookiness]; he concluded his introduction by promising, "It will stick to the memory of everybody who reads it" (quoted in *CW,* 1:361). The poem Willis referred to was "The Raven," and if he overstated its artistic merits somewhat, he accurately assessed its impact on readers, for the poem transformed Poe from a respected but somewhat shady intellectual/literary figure to a true celebrity, at least for a while. It remains the one work by Poe that most Americans can quote or at least recognize when quoted. Poe must have known "The Raven" would be a hit, for although he had sold it to the *American Review* for their February 1845 issue, he had Willis publish the poem in advance, and he also sent it to the *Southern Literary Messenger,* which published it in March. Almost immediately it was widely reprinted, discussed, and parodied, so that by May Poe could boast that " 'The Raven' has had a great run . . . but I wrote it for the express purpose of running—just as I did 'The Gold Bug' . . . the bird beat the bug, though, all hollow" (*Letters,* 2:287).

Kenneth Silverman's comparison of the immediate reception of "The Raven" to "that of some uproariously successful hit song today" also applies to the poem itself.[1] Like most hit songs, "The Raven" is rather light on ideas; painstaking analysis seems inappropriate to a work whose appeal relies so much on its catchy sound. But "The Raven" succeeds on its own terms, which are the terms of the popular song (or poem); it works largely *because* it is clever rather than ponderous or obscure. Poe relies on such conventions as sentimental grief (arising from idealized love) and obvious symbolism, as well as persistent rhyme and refrain and strict adherence to rhythm, but he shapes them into something original enough to demand the public's attention. One can easily fault Poe for straining his rhythm and rhyme—for instance, rhyming "that is," "lattice," and "thereat is" in stanza 6; or the ludicrous "Followed fast and followed faster" in line 64—but the fact remains that, as in many of his stories, he manages to weld the spare parts of popular literature into a surprisingly powerful reading experience.

In fact, Poe tried to convince his readers that he had done something more like welding than inspired writing in his own essay on "The Raven," "The Philosophy of Composition" (1846):

> Most writers—poets in especial—prefer having it understood that they compose by a species of fine frenzy—an ecstatic intuition—and would positively shudder at letting the public take a peep behind the scenes, at the elaborate and vacillating crudities of thought—at the true purposes seized only at the last moment—at the innumerable glimpses of idea that arrived not at the maturity of full view—at the fully matured fancies discarded in despair as unmanageable. . . . (ER, 14)

Had Edison's famous quotation been available to him for paraphrase, Poe might have declared poetic genius 1 percent inspiration and 99 percent perspiration (in "The Rationale of Verse" [1848], in fact, he would reduce poetry to a similar formula: 10 percent ethical and 90 percent mathematical [ER, 26]). The difference, he claims, between "most writers" and himself is his willingness to admit that writing poetry is a workmanlike process; building on the theatrical metaphor, he promises his readers the unprecedented peep behind the scenes at the mundane tools and machinery of art, "at the wheels and pinions—the tackle for scene-shifting—the step-ladders and demon-traps—the cock's feathers, the red paint and the black patches, which, in ninety-nine cases out of the hundred, constitute the properties of the literary *histrio*" (ER, 14). Either Poe's attitude toward poetry had changed drastically since the early 1830s, when he had presented himself as an inspired Byronic genius, or "The Philosophy of Composition" must be read ironically, as more mystification than revelation.[2] Or perhaps, as is often the case with Poe, we must read the essay as both sincere and ironic, for although Poe sets out to represent poetry as the result of hard work and trial and error rather than some sort of divine madness, he carries the point to such an extreme that it is impossible to take the essay entirely seriously.

From the opening reference to the "mechanism" of Dickens's *Barnaby Rudge*, Poe emphasizes systematization and mechanical construction, to the extent that the poem becomes a product created by a series of repeatable steps. Claiming that no accident or intuition enters the creation of the poem, Poe guides his readers "step by step" through a composition that proceeds "with the precision and rigid consequence of a mathematical problem," invoking formulas and proportions, citing *r* as the most "producible consonant," insisting on the inevitability of the word "nevermore," and so on (*ER*, 15, 18). The description of his determining the proper length of "The Raven" (which amounts to the same commonsense point he had made about the length of a literary work in his second review of Hawthorne) reads like a parody of someone trying to find the mathematical formula for poetry:

> [T]he extent of a poem may be made to bear mathematical relation to its merit—in other words, to the degree of the true poetical effect which it is capable of inducing; for it is clear that the brevity must be in direct ratio of the intensity of the intended effect:—this, with one proviso—that a certain degree of duration is absolutely requisite for the production of any effect at all.
>
> Holding in view these considerations, as well as that degree of excitement which I deemed not above the popular, while not below the critical, taste, I reached at once what I conceived the proper *length* for my intended poem—a length of about one hundred lines. It is, in fact, a hundred and eight. (*ER*, 15–16)

In earlier satires—"How to Write a Blackwood Article" and "The Literary Life of Thingum Bob, Esq."—Poe had mocked writers whose "genius" was nothing more than "diligence" (as Thingum himself admits), but here he presents his own composition process in those very terms, claiming that his most famous poem is as much a mechanical contrivance as General John A. B. C. Smith of "The Man That Was Used Up."[3] In the late twentieth century many people lament the decline of reading tastes as reflected by airport novelettes and formulaic romances, meanwhile suspecting that computers could and soon will write them. Similarly, more than a century before the computer age, Poe sensed that the systematization and assembly-line methods that were beginning to transform other facets of everyday life might transform literature, too. Although it is hard to imagine Poe writing "The Raven" in the manner he claims, "The Philosophy of Composition" entertains the notion that "a poem that should suit at once the popular and the critical taste" (*ER*, 15) *could be* built on an assembly line, or perhaps by using a kit that comes with complete instructions. The essay contains equal parts self-directed satire and braggadocio, as Poe disclaims his own poetic genius while boasting of his ability to *manufacture* literary masterpieces.

The fact that Poe was able to place "The Philosophy of Composition" in the widely circulated *Graham's,* which reportedly had rejected "The Raven," attests to the boost the poem gave to his reputation. Within months of "The Raven" 's publication, Poe became a desirable guest at New York literary salons, and in the summer of 1845 he formed a partnership that gave him a one-third financial interest in a weekly magazine, the *Broadway Journal.* He also published another collection of tales and his first volume of poetry in 14 years, *The Raven and Other Poems.* But once again bad luck and self-destructive impulses overwhelmed Poe's hopes for lasting success. In the same letter in which he boasted of "The Raven" 's "great run," he complained: "I have made no money. I am as poor now as ever I was in my life—except in hope, which is by no means bankable" (*Letters,* 2:286). His financial bind would tighten, in fact, as the *Broadway Journal* soon turned into a money pit rather than a source of profit, folding just two months after he gained sole ownership. Meanwhile, *Tales,* although well reviewed, earned him only $120, and he apparently made little or nothing from *The Raven and Other Poems.*[4]

Had Poe maintained the creative energy that had seen him through hard times in Philadelphia—or had he really been able to manufacture popular literature as he claimed in "The Philosophy of Composition"— he might have built something "bankable" on the fame he won with "The Raven." But the combination of Virginia's worsening condition, the demise of the *Journal,* bouts of paranoia, and a counterproductive streak of professional jealousy overwhelmed him, triggering more debilitating drinking binges. During a lucid interval in November 1845, he told his friend Evert Duyckinck, "I really believe that I have been mad."[5] Until the *Journal* collapsed altogether in January 1846, Poe devoted most of the energy he did have to filling its pages with whatever he could reprint (more than half of his already-published tales appeared in the *Journal*) or write hurriedly. Impressive as "The Cask of Amontillado," *Eureka,* and such late poems as "To Helen" and "Annabel Lee" may be, Poe's literary output for the last five years of his life pales alongside that of the previous five. From 1845 on, Poe seemed to take more interest in writing about other writers than in composing new stories or poems. His reputation as a tough literary critic dated back to his tenure with the *Southern Literary Messenger,* but in the mid-to-late 1840s his responsible, well-reasoned criticism was overshadowed by pointless attacks on Henry Wadsworth Longfellow and petty wars with other writers and editors. The thirst for publicity still motivated him, but the desire to raise the country's literary taste was now far less evident in his criticism than was his jealousy of wealthier, more acclaimed writers.

A few incidents illustrate Poe's tendency during this period to alienate associates and worsen his personal reputation. In 1845 the Boston Lyceum, which organized popular public lectures, invited Poe to lead off their series in October. Poe accepted but, in the midst of writer's block and bouts of drinking and illness, found himself unable to compose a new poem. Rather than cancel or simply admit at the performance that he was reading already-published poems, he tried to pawn off his early long poem "Al Aaraaf" as a new work, now titled "The Messenger Star." Poe's audience, which had already heard a long speech before he came onstage, apparently responded unenthusiastically, and the crowd thinned before Poe closed with a reading of "The Raven." The performance received unfavorable reviews from the Boston press, not surprising since Poe had already declared himself hostile to the New England literary establishment in print and had repeatedly insulted Longfellow, the city's most celebrated poet. But rather than cut his losses, Poe continued to bait his Bostonian audience and the city's editors. He not only revealed his deception but falsely claimed that he had written the poem before the age of 12, and that he had read a poem he acknowledged as inferior, inscrutable work to show his disdain for Bostonians. Once back in New York, he described the episode in the pages of the *Broadway Journal* as an ingenious hoax, but his attempts to save face or turn what should have been a small embarrassment into a triumph seem merely pathetic, symptomatic of his increasing combativeness and loss of perspective.

Earlier that year, while he was still the toast of the New York literary salons, Poe became acquainted with, and apparently charmed, a number of literary women, among them the popular poet Frances Osgood. Although it is unlikely that their relationship was sexual, Poe and Osgood flirted openly at literary gatherings and also visited and wrote each other frequently. When some of Osgood's friends persuaded her to reclaim her "indiscreet" letters, Poe reportedly told one of her emissaries, Elizabeth Ellet, that she should "look after her *own* letters," by implication letters to Poe himself.[6] At that point Ellet's brother, William H. Lummis, demanded the return of Ellet's letters, which Poe claimed he had already given back. In his fear of Lummis, Poe sought the help of Thomas Dunn English, more often his enemy than his friend, asking English to lend him a pistol. English refused, Poe became irate, and the two men scuffled. Both later claimed victory, but youth, good health, and physical size were all on English's side.[7] While recovering from this brawl, Poe avoided more serious violence by smoothing the matter over with a letter to Lummis in which he denied having referred to an indiscreet correspondence with Ellet and pleaded temporary insanity in case he *had* made such an accusation.[8] Nevertheless, Poe had offended the polite society of literary New York, and he was now excluded from the salons where other influential writers and patrons of the arts mingled and made contacts.

The incident also provided English with more motivation and material with which to satirize Poe when Poe insulted him in the "Literati of New York City" series the following year. English, who had already parodied Poe in his novel *The Doom of the Drinker,* countered with a savage sketch— in the manner of Poe's own "Literati" profiles—in the *New York Mirror.* He referred to Poe's cowardly behavior during the Osgood/Ellet affair and accused him of forgery and of obtaining money from him under false pretenses. Poe knew he could disprove those two charges, so he sued the *Mirror* for libel and was awarded $225.06 in damages and $101.42 in court costs. But as much as Poe needed the money, the impression he made by bringing the suit worsened his already battered reputation, suggesting that he could dish out insults but couldn't take them.[9] Moreover, English got the best of Poe in print. Before the libel suit was decided, he caricatured Poe in his serialized novel *1844, or The Power of the S. F.,* in which a pedantic critic and author of a poem called "The Black Crow," one Marmaduke Hammerhead, sinks from literary renown to destitution and madness exacerbated by drinking. English continued to take potshots at Poe after the trial in his own satirical magazine, the *John-Donkey,* repeatedly claiming that Poe had been committed to an asylum.

For the most part, Poe brought scandal on himself, but personal misery seemed to prey upon him at the same time. Five years after her first dramatic signs of tuberculosis, Virginia died in February of 1847. Poe, too, fell ill in late 1846 and early 1847, suffering from what more than one friend called a "brain fever"; he was probably malnourished and, along with Muddy and Virginia, had little protection against the harsh winter weather.[10] At least partly to avoid the unhealthy environment of the city, Poe had moved the family to a small cottage in Fordham, about 13 miles from Manhattan, in May of 1846. But neither Virginia's health nor Poe's improved, and after her death his grief weakened him even more. With the help of a family friend, Marie Louise Shew, Poe tried to regain his health and restart his career in mid-1847 and again in early 1848, when he composed what he believed would be his most important work, the cosmological "prose poem" *Eureka*. But for the rest of his life Poe's physical and mental health remained unstable. He and Muddy continued to live in the Fordham cottage, although during his last year Poe was away more than he was home, lecturing, trying again to raise subscriptions for a magazine that would never appear, and trying desperately to find a wife.

After Virginia's long illness and death, Poe felt an emotional void; despite (or because of) his erratic behavior, he seems to have longed for stability and for more emotional support than his aunt could provide. Marie Louise Shew had seen Poe through Virginia's death and the months that followed, but by mid-1848 she had retreated from Poe's side, probably bothered by his drinking as well as the impious ideas he advanced in *Eureka*.[11] In July 1848 Poe visited Jane Locke, a poet with whom he had exchanged several letters, in Lowell, Massachusetts, but discovered there that she was married. While in Lowell, Poe met Nancy Richmond, another married woman, whom he found much more appealing than Jane Locke. Poe and "Annie," as he called Mrs. Richmond, maintained a close friendship until his death, but Poe's letters to her make it clear that he wished they could marry (*Letters*, 2:400–403, 414–15).[12] In November of 1848, driven at least partly by despair over Annie, Poe attempted suicide by taking an overdose of laudanum (opium dissolved in alcohol, legal and widely used in the nineteenth century). After swallowing an ounce (30 times the average dose), he wrote Annie asking her to come to him, with the plan of taking another ounce when she arrived, but in his stupor he failed to mail the letter and probably came close to dying over the next two days.[13]

Although Poe never abandoned his dream of a marriage to Annie, by the time he attempted suicide he was in the midst of another ill-fated romance. Sarah Helen Whitman, a poet from a well-to-do Providence family, greatly admired Poe and seriously considered marrying him. But Whitman's mother disapproved, and friends warned her of Poe's instability. Worried by Poe's reputation and his drinking, she hesitated and placed conditions on their engagement; angered and hurt, Poe wrote her letters that were at once reprimands and pleas for love, similar in this regard to the letters he had written John Allan 20 years earlier.[14] His behavior as well as his letters betrayed his instability, and by the time the newspapers announced their upcoming marriage in January 1849, Poe and Helen Whitman had broken off the engagement.[15]

While Poe was desperately seeking a replacement for Virginia, he was also chasing another dream, that of controlling his own magazine. He had entered into a partnership with a prosperous and admiring young editor and publisher, E. H. N. Patterson, who agreed to help finance the magazine while giving Poe editorial control.[16] Poe planned to tour the South and West, raising money with lectures and enlisting 1,000 subscribers, although as usual he would fall far short of his expectations. Poe began his "tour" on June 29, 1849, traveling first to Philadelphia. A cholera epidemic had broken out there, and Poe, if his account can be believed, became sick and took calomel, which contains mercury, to fight the disease. As a result of either mercury poisoning or a drinking binge—perhaps both—Poe became "deranged" for "more than ten days," according to his own report.[17] He suffered hallucinations and became paranoid, but two friends, the engraver and magazine publisher John Sartin and novelist George Lippard, saw him through it and raised enough money to send him farther south.[18]

Poe traveled on to Richmond, where he resumed his search for a wife, in this case the former Elmira Royster, whom he had courted as a teenager. Elmira's husband, Alexander Shelton, a successful businessman, had passed away five years earlier. Mrs. Shelton was impressed with Poe's literary accomplishments, and she was lonely since her husband's death; nostalgia and the promise of stability—emotional and financial—undoubtedly attracted Poe to her.[19] But, like Helen Whitman, Elmira was wary of Poe's declarations of love, especially after so many years of estrangement, and she almost certainly knew that he had a drinking problem. Their marriage would have presented other difficulties as well: Elmira had two children, a responsibility for which Poe was unprepared, and she would lose much of her inheritance (to her 10-year-old son) once she married, in accordance with her husband's will.[20] Mrs. Shelton later claimed that they had never really been engaged; for his part, Poe seems to have pursued the engagement although he harbored serious doubts. He wrote to Muddy that he believed the wedding would take place but also confessed to her "that my heart sinks at the idea of this marriage."[21] Anticipating a marriage he did not really want, and still hoping that Patterson would finance his magazine, Poe left Richmond on the morning of September 27 on a steamship bound for Baltimore, the first scheduled stop on his journey home. He died there under mysterious circumstances 10 days later.

Late Criticism

Although the bulk of Poe's writing over the last five years of his life consists of nonfictional prose (especially if one includes *Eureka* in that category), he wrote relatively few book reviews during this period. Compared to his work in Richmond and Philadelphia, his critical writings from New York tend to be fragmentary and often trivial. His "Marginalia" series, begun in late 1844, was fairly standard magazine journalism, items that would normally be used as "filler" strung together to create a total of 17 article-length installments. (He had written a similar, single-installment article, "Pinakidia," for the *Southern Literary Messenger* in 1836.) Poe described his other series, the popular "Literati of New York City," as "critical *gossip*," not to be confused with the "elaborate criticisms" readers had come to expect from him (*Letters*, 2:332).

Poe could still write courageous and insightful criticism, however. He covered the theater for the *Broadway Journal*, reviewing plays and criticizing the general state of English and American drama. In the first of two notices of Anna Cora Mowatt's popular comedy *Fashion*, Poe moves from the play's flaws—the plot and characters lack verisimilitude and originality—to a blanket condemnation of "modern" drama, which he believes has failed to respond to the revolutionary changes in other literary forms since the mid-eighteenth century: "The drama has not declined as many suppose: it has only been left out of sight by every thing else. We must discard all models. The Elizabethan theatre should be abandoned. We need thought of our own—principles of dramatic action drawn not from the 'old dramatists' but from the fountain of a Nature that can never grow old."[22] Here Poe borrows a page (as he often does) from his perceived enemies the transcendentalists, claiming that drama, particularly American drama, can move forward by simplifying. He concludes his review by putting *Fashion* in stark perspective: "Compared with the generality of modern dramas, it is a good play—compared with most American dramas it is a *very* good one—estimated by the natural principles of dramatic art, it is altogether unworthy of notice" (*BJ*, 69).

Such a striking combination of praise and condemnation is typical of Poe in the late 1840s. In the *Fashion* review this tactic is effective, for it helps make his ultimate position clear; moreover, he proceeds from that conclusion in a later notice of the play to envision a new, reformed drama that breaks traditional boundaries of tragedy, comedy, farce, opera, and so on (*BJ*, 78). But in other reviews Poe's habit of mixing praise and scorn is merely confusing. Elizabeth Barrett Browning was justifiably baffled by Poe's lengthy 1845 review of her collection *The Drama of Exile, and Other Poems*.[23] Early in the review Poe doubts that anyone admires her more than he does, and near the conclusion he ranks her second only to Tennyson among contemporary poets: "That Miss Barrett has done more, in poetry, than any woman, living or dead, will scarcely be questioned:—that she has surpassed all her poetical contemporaries of either sex (with a single exception) is our deliberate opinion—not idly entertained, we think, nor founded on any visionary basis" (*BJ*, 14). He makes a few similar claims in between but spends nearly all the review finding what he presents as major flaws: he criticizes her portrayal of Eve in the title poem; condemns her use of allegory (and allegory in general; *BJ*, 5); refers to the "utter indefensibility of 'The Drama of Exile,' considered uniquely, as a work of art" (*BJ*, 5); dismisses the volume's sonnets, along with a long list of other poems (*BJ*, 7); accuses her of imitating Tennyson (which for Poe insinuated plagiarism; *BJ*, 8); refers to her "inexcusable" affectations (*BJ*, 10); criticizes a number of specific phrases in her poems, as well as occasional "*far-fetchedness* of imagery, which is reprehensible in the extreme" (*BJ*, 10); points out her tendency to repeat herself (*BJ*, 11); and refers to her "deficiencies of *rhythm*" (*BJ*, 12). Twice Poe focuses on Barrett's lack of "constructive ability," highlighting one of his most important artistic criteria (*BJ*, 5, 9). As in fiction, unity of effect is essential to a successful poem, which makes a long poem such as "The Drama of Exile" a near-certain failure in Poe's view. Similarly, any hint of didacticism in poetry generally roused Poe's ire, as it does in the Barrett review (*BJ*, 6). Poe proudly distinguished himself from critics who either "puff" a work with unqualified praise or condemn it just as thoroughly; one could also defend his fault-finding as a way of showing his respect for Barrett, reading her poetry more carefully than any other reviewer. But Poe gets so carried away with his criticisms that the review becomes self-contradictory. The disdain with which he criticizes so many qualities of her work overwhelms any sense of qualified praise, so that one cannot imagine how a writer whose work he finds so seriously flawed could also be his second favorite contemporary poet.

Compared to his baffling assessment of Barrett, Poe's mixed feelings toward Hawthorne are fairly clear in his third review (1847) of *Twice-Told Tales* (this time together with *Mosses from an Old Manse*). In addition to reiterating (essentially reprinting) his theory of the short story's superiority to the novel, Poe reevaluates Hawthorne. Five years earlier he had declared Hawthorne "original at *all* points," in tone as well as matter, and he begins the later review reasserting his belief in Hawthorne's "extraordinary genius," still claiming he is generally underrated. But as the essay unfolds, it becomes clear Hawthorne is being demoted, and in the final paragraph Poe decrees that "[h]e is peculiar and *not* original" (*ER,* 587). Ostensibly justifying this turnabout, Poe constructs an overly subtle definition of originality, which he claims requires both (apparent) novelty and profundity: "[T]rue originality . . . is that which, in bringing out the half-formed, the reluctant, or the unexpressed fancies of mankind, or in exciting the more delicate pulses of the heart's passion, or in giving birth to some universal sentiment or instinct in embryo, thus combines with the pleasurable effect of *apparent* novelty, a real egotistic delight" (*ER,* 581). In an original work, then, something the reader regards as new entices him or her while evoking a strong, very personal response that until then had lain dormant. But if the response is less personal, causing the reader to feel an affinity not with the author alone but with all other readers, Poe terms it "natural" writing (*ER,* 581). Apparently Hawthorne falls into this lower category because of his fondness for allegory, which is never subtle enough to create the intimacy between reader and writer Poe associates with "true originality." Poe failed to recognize Hawthorne's ability to undermine the conventions of allegory, to shape them into new forms of expression. But beyond his hatred of allegory, Poe was also prejudiced by his hostility toward Hawthorne's fellow New Englanders, as he reveals in the final sentence by urging him to "come out from the Old Manse, cut Mr. Alcott, hang (if possible) the editor of 'The Dial,' and throw out of the window to the pigs all his odd numbers of 'The North American Review' " (*ER,* 587–88).

Throughout most of 1845 Poe concentrated the hostility he felt for New England writers and intellectuals, as well as his continuing sense of personal insult at not being wealthy and respected, on one enemy, Henry Wadsworth Longfellow. The four reviews of Longfellow Poe had written before 1845 were for the most part evenhanded: general praise mixed with legitimate criticism of Longfellow's didacticism and imitativeness. But with his 1845 review of *The Waif,* an anthology edited by Longfellow, Poe made the provocative claim that the book was "infected with a *moral taint*": "[T]here *does* appear, in this exquisite little volume, a very careful avoidance of all American poets who may be supposed especially to interfere with the claims of Mr. Longfellow. These men Mr. Longfellow can continuously *imitate* (*is* that the word?) and yet never even incidentally commend" (*ER,* 702). Poe continued to make those two basic claims throughout the "Longfellow War": that Longfellow used his influence (in this case his editorship) to promote himself at the expense of his competitors, and that his imitation of those same writers amounted to plagiarism. Friends of Longfellow rose to his defense, and Poe relished the print war that ensued, reminiscent as it was of the attention he had attracted with his *Southern Literary Messenger* reviews in the mid-1830s. He fueled the debate first in Willis's *Evening Mirror* and then in the *Broadway Journal*. Longfellow himself did not respond in print to Poe or others who joined the fracas, but one of his defenders, a writer who identified himself as "Outis" (Greek for "nobody"), constructed a counterargument that Poe returned to obsessively, writing five responses to Outis's single letter. Some scholars, notably Burton R. Pollin and Kenneth Silverman, believe Poe wrote the Outis letter himself, mainly to control the terms of the debate and to enliven the controversy, while others have made cases for other authors or at least questioned Poe's authorship.[24] Whether or not he wrote the Outis letter, however, Poe could not get away from it for the simple reason that Outis demonstrated that the kinds of similarities Poe was trying to classify as plagiarism or deliberate imitation most often resulted from coincidence, influence, and poetic convention. With his fourth reply to Outis Poe became overly defensive, shifting the ground from the issue of plagiarism to his own reputation as a critic, claiming that he had never "descended . . . to that personal abuse which, upon one or two occasions, has indeed been levelled at myself" and arguing that a critic's job is primarily to censure rather than to praise (*ER*, 742). Then, writing anonymously in the *Aristidean*, Poe launched his most vicious attack on Longfellow, calling him "the GREAT MOGUL of the Imitators" (*ER*, 761) and accusing him of one plagiarism after another, including himself among the victims. His examples, however, tend to support Outis's explanation of poetic similarities better than they support Poe's charges.

   With his fifth reply in the *Journal*, Poe conceded to Outis without admitting he was doing so. Ignoring his accusation of a "moral taint" and his anonymous plagiarism charges, Poe claims that "[i]t will be seen by any one who shall take the trouble to read what I have written, that I make *no* charge of moral delinquency against . . . Mr. Longfellow" (*ER*, 758). He then settles the debate by making a "point of defence . . . unaccountably neglected by Outis" that is in fact quite similar to Outis's argument: because poets possess "a peculiarly, perhaps an abnormally keen appreciation of the beautiful . . . [w]hat the poet intensely admires, becomes thus, in very fact, although only partially, a portion of his own intellect. . . . [H]e thoroughly feels it as *his own*" (*ER*, 758–59). Therefore, the "most eminent poets" are the ones who most frequently plagiarize, but under this new definition of plagiarism, no crime has been committed—in other words, Poe finally admits that what he has been calling plagiarism is usually a matter of influence or poetic convention. This turnabout, which Poe does not acknowledge as such, typifies the inconsistency of his late criticism, while the controversy as a whole reveals a growing sense of personal injustice and thirst for revenge.

Poe's jealousy arose partly from Longfellow's being singled out in a much-discussed 1844 survey of American poetry in the London *Foreign Quarterly Review*, which claimed that all other American poets were either imitators or plagiarists; Poe, in fact, was mentioned as an imitator of Tennyson. But he seems to have been equally galled by Longfellow's wealth, much of which had come through marriage. Poe's former employer George Rex Graham told Longfellow that it was probably his "more widely established reputation" that offended Poe, then added: "Or if you have wealth—which I suppose you *have*—that is sufficient to settle your damnation so far as Mr. Poe may be presumed capable of effecting it."[25] Poe saw the issue of plagiarism in terms of class, opposing "men of genius," who "are proverbially poor," to the established authors, "men of wealth and leisure," whom he claimed commit most plagiarisms.[26] The lack of international copyright, which Poe addressed frequently in the mid-to-late 1840s, also had the effect of making the rich richer and the "poor devil authors," as he called them, poorer.

Poe's essay-story "Some Secrets of the Magazine Prison-House" (1845) illustrates this point with the case of a young author who is promised handsome pay for an article. He and his family starve for a month while he writes it, and after another four months, despite his reminders to the editor, the article has not appeared and the writer has not been paid. Six months later he demands the article: "No—he can't have it—(the truth is, it was too good to be given up so easily)— 'it is in print,' and 'contributions of this character are never paid for (it is a *rule* we have) under six months after publication. Call in six months after the issue of your affair, and your money is ready for you—for we are business men, ourselves— prompt' " (*CW,* 3:1208). The author waits, "but Death in the meantime would not" (*CW,* 3:1208). The "business man" on whom the author depends "is fatter henceforward and for ever to the amount of five and twenty dollars, very cleverly saved, to be spent generously in canvasbacks and champagne" (*CW,* 3:1209). Despite the title's metaphor, Poe does not refer to authors as prisoners; instead he compares them to "silk worms" or "caterpillars": congressional demagogues argue against the "absurdity . . . that a man has any right and title either to his own brains or the flimsy material that he chooses to spin out of them, like a confounded caterpillar as he is" (*CW,* 3:1207). Harmless and tiny, in contrast with the fattened publisher, the author-as-worm does not own even what is "naturally" his. Poe's metaphors portray writers as helpless victims in the power of publishers, and his paranoid tone conveys his fear of never having control over his own career.

While Poe had sought a kind of revenge for these injustices in his attempt to tarnish Longfellow's reputation, a wider opportunity presented itself when he began the "Literati of New York City" series in *Godey's Lady's Book* in May 1846. As the most widely circulated periodical of the 1840s, *Godey's* ensured Poe a large audience for his candid opinions of New York writers and editors. Most of Poe's sketches generated little controversy, as they merely described in fairly objective terms the writing, background, and appearance of their subjects, but Poe did not miss the opportunity to "use up" his enemies, including his former *Broadway Journal* partner, Charles F. Briggs, his longtime rival from the *Knickerbocker,* Lewis Gaylord Clark, and, of course, Thomas Dunn English. Poe introduced the series by promising more than he would in fact deliver, once again offering readers a glimpse "behind the scenes," exposing to view what others in his position would keep hidden, in this case, the fact that "[t]he most 'popular,' the most 'successful' writers among us, (for a brief period, at least,) are, ninety-nine times out of a hundred . . . busy-bodies, toadies, quacks" (*ER,* 1118).

And yet by 1846 Poe must have suspected that he himself numbered among those 99. His "Philosophy of Composition" had cast his most celebrated poem as a mathematical calculation rather than a work of genius. In the "Longfellow War" he had either defeated himself by assuming the role of Outis or perversely played out a belabored losing argument against a real antagonist; moreover, he had tried to advance his own career by making flimsy accusations against another writer who could just as easily have accused him of plagiarism. Poe's comments in "A Chapter of Suggestions" (1845) apply equally well to his sense that he was preyed upon by his enemies and his sense that he, too, preyed upon eminent writers: "[U]ndoubtedly, of all despicable things, your habitual sneerer at real greatness, is the most despicable. . . . [T]here will always exist a set of *homunculi,* eager to grow notorious by the pertinacity of their yelpings at the heels of the distinguished" (*Brevities,* 470–71).

As if to get revenge on himself for his own "quackery," in 1846 Poe began an essay entitled "A Reviewer Reviewed, by Walter G. Bowen" (first published in 1896). Poe had intended it for *Graham's,* but for some reason—perhaps lack of nerve—he never submitted or even completed it. While Poe might have been acting on the old principle that there is no such thing as bad publicity (he often said as much), "Bowen"'s observations are too accurate and too incisive not to have damaged (had the article been published) what was left of Poe's reputation. Following Poe's usual method, Bowen compliments Poe's writing at the outset of the essay and then begins criticizing him—for his severity, sarcasm, "sneers," and, more specifically, his habit of damning with faint praise, conventional criticisms Poe had alluded to elsewhere and probably would not have minded printing. But Poe/Bowen goes further, claiming that Poe is incapable of "honest, heartfelt praise" even when he is trying to compliment "some of his *lady* friends" (*CW,* 3:1381), and then that Poe is guilty of the very transgressions he relishes pointing out in other writers' work: scientific inaccuracies ("A Descent into the Maelström"), grammatical errors, and plagiarism (several poems, "Hans Pfaall"). In short, "A Reviewer Reviewed" reads like an attempted confession in the only meaningful form Poe knew: a publishable review of himself.

Last Jests

Poe's impulse to reveal his own literary crimes is consistent with his tales' adherence to justice. Although businessmen and diddlers might get away clean, the killers of "William Wilson," "The Black Cat," "The Tell-Tale Heart," and "Thou Art the Man," the blackmailing thief of "The Purloined Letter," and the owner of the killer ape in "Rue Morgue" all either confess or are found out and held accountable for their crimes. Like the first three of those stories, "The Imp of the Perverse" (1845) takes the form of a killer's confession. The story's central concept should be familiar to readers of "The Black Cat" and *Pym,* not to mention Poe biography: "I am not more certain that I breathe, than that the assurance of the wrong or error of any action is often the one unconquerable *force* which impels us, and alone impels us to its prosecution" (*CW,* 3:1220–21). Like "The Premature Burial," "The Imp of the Perverse" begins as an analytic essay but ends as a story, as we learn that the clinical, intellectual voice that has been theorizing on the implications of perverseness for phrenology is also the voice of a condemned killer. This narrator states explicitly the irony beneath "The Black Cat" and "The Tell-Tale Heart": the murders were carried out through the use of reason, while a perverse "madness" prompted the confession, thwarting otherwise "perfect" crimes. While not explicitly a revenge tale, "Imp" casts the perverse confession as a revenge enacted on the self, simultaneously bringing about justice and self-destruction. Thus Poe did not completely abandon the doubling motif in the late 1840s, as revenge always suggests doubling one's opponent or, if the revenge is self-directed, splitting oneself in two.

In "The Cask of Amontillado" (1846), one of Poe's most tightly constructed tales, the narrator takes revenge on both his adversarial double and on himself. Many critics have noted the story's biographical resonance for a writer who believed himself beset by a "thousand injuries" at the hands of various enemies and, at the very time he was writing the story, the insults of Thomas Dunn English.[27] But along with the story's wish-fulfillment of silencing one's nemesis once and for all is Poe's continued awareness of the "circularity of revenge."[28]

Irony pervades, even structures, the story. Although Poe immerses us in the perspective of the avenger Montresor, he discourages sympathy with him. Montresor claims to have been injured and insulted by Fortunato, but he never names Fortunato's specific offense. Moreover, the victim seems unaware of having offended Montresor. Even though Fortunato is drunk and wishes to prove his wine-tasting expertise, his lighthearted willingness to visit the catacombs of Montresor's mansion would be impossible if he had knowingly insulted his host "with impunity." The closest thing to a motive that emerges throughout their conversation is simple jealousy, for, as Montresor feigns concern for his victim's health, he tells him: "You are rich, respected, admired, beloved; you are happy, as once I was. You are a man to be missed. For me it is no matter" (*CW,* 3:1259). Montresor proves himself adept at duping other people, but he seems to have fooled himself into thinking he had a legitimate score to settle with Fortunato; more likely, he has "created" an enemy on whom he can blame his disappointments and failures.

More particular instances of irony fill Montresor's narrative; his use of language and psychology is so playful that if one does not take the story too seriously one can easily find him a likable murderer. He uses the same reverse psychology on his servants that he is using on Fortunato; to ensure their absence, he "told them that I should not return until the morning, and had given them explicit orders not to stir from the house" (*CW,* 3:1258). Conversely, while repeatedly urging Fortunato to leave, he ensures that he will stay simply by invoking the name of Luchesi, Fortunato's rival in wine connoisseurship. When Fortunato insists that they go on because, after all, he "shall not die of a cough," the man who knows precisely how he will die replies, "True—true" (*CW,* 3:1259). Not long afterward, Montresor answers Fortunato's toast "to the buried that repose around us" by drinking "to your long life" (*CW*, 3:1259). Even the choice of wine he offers Fortunato, "De Grave," puns on their destination, which will prove to be Fortunato's grave. As Kennedy suggests, Montresor seems to be giving clues to his victim, knowing Fortunato's "ineptitude as a reader of signs."[29] This exercise in taunting his unsuspecting victim (appropriately dressed in motley) peaks when Montresor shows Fortunato the trowel with which he will entomb him. Having tested Montresor by using a secret sign, Fortunato concludes that his friend is "not of the brotherhood." Montresor replies:

> "How?"
> "You are not of the masons."
> "Yes, yes," I said, "yes, yes."
> "You? Impossible! A mason?"
> "A mason," I replied.
> "A sign," he said.
> "It is this," I answered, producing a trowel from beneath the folds of my *roquelaire*. (*CW*, 3:1260)

At this point one might expect Fortunato to ask why his friend is carrying around a trowel, but he is only shrewd enough to recognize the pun: " 'You jest,' he exclaimed, recoiling a few paces. 'But let us proceed to the Amontillado' " (*CW*, 3:1260).

Fortunato proceeds, of course, to a slow and torturous death at the story's end, which brings us, as it so often does with Poe, back to the beginning, to Montresor's criteria for revenge: "*At length* I would be avenged; this was a point definitively settled—but the very definitiveness with which it was resolved precluded the idea of risk. I must not only punish, but punish with impunity. A wrong is unredressed when retribution overtakes its redresser. It is equally unredressed when the avenger fails to make himself felt as such to him who has done the wrong" (*CW*, 3:1256). At first glance Montresor would seem to have fulfilled both requirements: Fortunato cannot strike back, and he knows who has killed him. And yet Fortunato still does not seem to know that this is an act of revenge; Montresor apparently has "fail[ed] to make himself felt as such," that is, as an avenger. Furthermore, as most (though not all) commentators on this story assert, Montresor fails to fulfill the other criterion for true revenge, for the narrative itself is subtle evidence that retribution has overtaken him in the form of guilt.[30] Fifty years later, he still remembers his heart's "growing sick—on account of the dampness of the catacombs," but this heartsickness likely arises from empathy with the man he is leaving to die amid that dampness.[31] Montresor addresses his narrative to "[y]ou, who so well know the nature of my soul" (*CW,* 3:1256)—certainly not the reader, but, given Montresor's advanced age, very likely a priest or other confidante to whom he is making a deathbed confession.

Ironically, then, Montresor has failed to exact revenge on the terms he set down in order to demonstrate the perfection of his plot. He has conceived revenge as something that can end with the destruction of only one adversary, but, as Kennedy explains: "Like William Wilson, he discovers in the killing of his hated double the price which retribution— even the most flawlessly conceived—exacts from the perpetrator. The victim of revenge is invariably the self."[32] Montresor's coat of arms—"A huge human foot d'or, in a field azure; the foot crushes a serpent rampant whose fangs are imbedded in the heel" (*CW,* 3:1259)—emblematizes this "circularity of revenge." The Montresor family could be represented by the foot, which crushes its enemies, or the snake, which sinks its fangs into the heel of its adversary, bringing to mind the flag used by American Revolutionaries reading "Don't Tread on Me."[33] In either case, both the foot and the snake are injured, perhaps fatally (if the snake is poisonous); neither wins.

If Montresor, for all his cunning, has failed to commit the perfect crime, then the perfect crime cannot be committed—which is precisely Poe's contention. Particularly in a revenge scenario (which Montresor, at least, believes this is), the criminal will be undone by empathy for the victim if nothing else. David Ketterer makes the case for regarding the two wine connoisseurs as doubles, concluding that Fortunato is Montresor's image of his "happier self": "The relationship between the two of them is like that between Amontillado and sherry, between which Luchresi cannot distinguish for the very good reason that Amontillado is a sherry."[34] Poe emphasizes the likeness of the two men by having Montresor mimic Fortunato as he walls him up. The suddenly chained, "astonished" Fortunato yells, "The Amontillado!" "True," Montresor replies, "the Amontillado" (*CW,* 3:1262). When his victim begins to scream, Montresor replies with screams: "I re-echoed—I aided—I surpassed them in volume and in strength" (*CW,* 3:1262). Then Montresor simply repeats Fortunato's last utterances:

". . . Let us be gone."
"Yes," I said, "let us be gone."

"For the love of God, Montresor!"
"Yes," I said, "for the love of God!" (*CW,* 3:1263)

By trying to rid himself of this unfortunate-fortunate rival, Montresor has become one with him, as these repetitions suggest, for he will be haunted by Fortunato until he dies. Montresor's last words—of the story, but perhaps of his life as well—are a hopeful wish not only for his victim, but for himself, now that he has confessed: *"In páce requiescat!"* (May he rest in peace; *CW,* 3:1263).

"The Cask of Amontillado" plays out one last time themes Poe had been exploring since "William Wilson": the close identification between adversaries and self-inflicted punishment for the crime of killing off one's double/rival. But in "Hop-Frog" (1849), one of his last tales, Poe subverts the notion of the cyclical, self-defeating nature of revenge by finally creating an avenger who triumphs without a hint of remorse or a suggestion that he will meet his comeuppance. In this fractured fairy tale, the hunchbacked dwarf and court jester Hop-Frog is driven to rage by the king's and his ministers' abuse, which extends, in a particular instance, to his friend Tripetta, "a young girl very little less dwarfish than himself" (*CW,* 3:1346). When the king and his ministers demand that Hop-Frog furnish them with costumes for a ball, Hop-Frog persuades them to appear as eight escaped orangutans, chained closely together; at the ball, he hoists them off the floor with the ballroom's chandelier chain and sets their tar-and-flax-covered bodies on fire before escaping through the skylight. As Ketterer notes, Poe employs a subtle doubling in establishing the relationship between Hop-Frog and the king: Hop-Frog is treated as if he were subhuman by the king and his ministers, so he literalizes *their* inhumanity by persuading them to dress as orangutans, using the flammability of their costumes to enact his revenge.[35] Following Shakespearean tradition, the court's "fool" exposes his master as fool, but in stark contrast to, for instance, Lear's fool, Hop-Frog does not preserve the king with this table-turning exposure but destroys him with it.

Like "The Cask of Amontillado," "Hop-Frog" can be read as Poe's fictional wish-fulfillment, for until the end of his life he continued to feel victimized by his enemies. The fact that the king forces Hop-Frog to drink, knowing that wine "excited the poor cripple almost to madness; and madness is no comfortable feeling" (*CW,* 3:1347), furthers the identification between Hop-Frog and Poe. Poe's resentment toward the rich, whom he described as growing fat off the labor of poor devil authors in

"Some Secrets of the Magazine Prison House," surfaces here, too, as he repeatedly refers to the fatness of the king and his ministers. Moreover, these privileged but unimaginative men demand of Hop-Frog the same type of work publishers demanded of writers: "We want characters— *characters*, man—something novel—out of the way. We are wearied with this everlasting sameness" (*CW,* 3:1347). Poe, who had reveled in the role of exposer of fraud throughout his career, casts Hop-Frog's revenge as exposure of the beastly nature of men in high places: just before setting his nemeses on fire, Hop-Frog repeatedly shouts to the company that he will tell them or show them who they really are:

> "Ah, ha!" said at length the infuriated jester. "Ah, ha! I begin to see who these people *are,* now!" Here, pretending to scrutinize the king more closely, he held the flambeau to the flaxen coat which enveloped him, and which instantly burst into a sheet of vivid flame . . .
>   "I now see *distinctly,*" he said, "what manner of people these maskers are." (*CW,* 3:1353–54)

Although Poe would publish three more stories before his death, there is an element of autobiographical prophecy in the avenger's last words: "As for myself, I am simply Hop-Frog, the jester—and *this is my last jest*" (*CW,* 3:1354).

Hop-Frog, who announces his victims' offenses as he torches them and escapes never to be seen again, achieves revenge on the terms set down by Montresor. However much "Hop-Frog" might represent Poe's thirst for revenge, however, Poe does not glorify his protagonist: Hop-Frog grinds his fanglike teeth, foams at the mouth, and wears an "expression of maniacal rage" at the moment of his triumph. Even as he makes his escape, the third-person narrator refers to him as the king saw him, as a "dwarf" and a "cripple" (*CW,* 3:1354). But the hideousness of his vigilante justice, more than anything else, forces most readers to dwell on Hop-Frog's insanity rather than on his sense of an underdog's vindication. Noting that Hop-Frog is a slave from (in Poe's words) "some barbarous region . . . that no person ever heard of" (*CW,* 3:1346), Joan Dayan suggests that Hop-Frog's revenge reverses the master-slave relationship by blackening and chaining the "master race."[36] Perhaps "Hop-Frog" does betray Poe's fears of slave rebellion, which almost certainly underlay his depiction of the Tsalalians in *Pym* and may well have influenced his portrayal of ape-as-razor-wielding-killer in "Rue Morgue."[37] Read in the context of antebellum slavery and whites' fear of uprisings,

"Hop-Frog" makes clear the sort of justice masters could expect from their slaves while recognizing the masters' responsibility for instilling rage and provoking rebellion. Read in any context, however, "Hop-Frog" depicts an amoral world where barbarity prevails; Poe seemingly endorses cruel and disproportionate punishment and yet makes the punisher as much a monster as the tyrant he slays. For these reasons, this "last jest" may well be Poe's most disturbing tale.

Poe treated revenge comically in another of his last tales, "X-ing a Paragrab." Although the plot is a conventional anecdote, one can easily see why Poe would be drawn to it, given his acute sense of the written—and even more, the printed—word's power to mystify readers. An editor from New England named Touch-and-go Bullet-head starts up a newspaper in the Western town of Alexander-the-Great-o-nopolis, or Nopolis ("no city") for short. When John Smith, the town's other newspaper editor, ridicules Bullet-head for his overuse of the letter *o*, Bullethead responds with a diatribe against Smith in which nearly every word contains an *o*. Anticipating this move Smith steals the *o*s from the printer's font, knowing that the printer will use *x*s in their place and that the "X-ed" version will be virtually unreadable. Once again Poe suggests that tricks are the most expedient way to overcome competition, particularly in publishing, but more telling is the reaction of the townspeople to the mysterious X-ed paragraph: they assume that it conceals some "diabolical treason," and consequently would have ridden Bullet-head on a rail had he not already skipped town (*CW,* 3:1374). As the story dissolves into a series of puns on the letter *x*, Poe satirizes the confusion and irrationality of the mass reading audience: "That Bullet-head had been driven to an extremity, was clear to all; and in fact, since *that* editor could not be found, there was some talk about lynching the other one" (*CW,* 3:1375).

Poe's mistrust of the reading audience is transposed onto a single auditor in another lighthearted story, "The Thousand-and-Second Tale of Scheherazade" (1845). Having kept herself and a thousand other women alive by making up stories, Scheherazade suddenly switches to nonfiction, transporting Sinbad to Poe's times in order to describe natural phenomena and technological innovations through the eyes of someone completely unfamiliar with them. Her narrative, explained with Poe's editorial footnotes, introduces the king to a steam-driven battleship, hot-air balloons, a printing press, and the telegraph in terms that defamiliarize and reassess these modern tools for Poe's readers. The printing press, for instance, is "neither man nor beast": "[It] had brains of lead, intermixed with a black matter like pitch, and fingers that it employed with such incredible speed and dexterity that it would have had no trouble in writing out twenty thousand copies of the Koran in an hour. . . . This thing was of prodigious strength, so that it erected or overthrew the mightiest empires at a breath; but its powers were exercised equally for evil and for good" (*CW,* 3:1166–67). Ironically, the king disbelieves the entire story, with the exception of one phenomenon not based on scientific fact but on the Koran: a continent "supported entirely upon the back of a sky-blue cow that had no fewer than four hundred horns." The king believes it, he says, because he had "read something of the kind before, in a book" (*CW,* 3:1165). When Scheherazade tells the king about the practice of women wearing bustles—Sinbad visits a country where ladies believe that "personal beauty . . . consists altogether in the protuberance of the region which lies not very far below the small of the back" (*CW,* 3:1169)—the king can stand no more and has her killed. Although Scheherazade has made her truths sound as fantastic as Arabian Nights tales, the fact remains that her audience of one rejects them and, like the citizens of Nopolis, reacts violently to what he does not understand. To make her task all the more daunting, her stories lack the endorsement granted by books, which by Poe's time were produced by a certain amoral creature with brains of lead.[38]

Ever aware of the power of the press to give credence to incredible stories, Poe perpetrated two more hoaxes over the last five years of his life. He claimed not to have intended "The Facts in the Case of M. Valdemar"—in which a patient's death and decay are arrested through mesmerism—for a hoax, but he reveled in reports of readers and mesmerists being taken in by it. Poe apparently did expect readers to be taken in by "Von Kempelen and His Discovery" (1849), which was aimed at dampening the excitement surrounding the California gold rush. Despite bantering references to the *New York Sun*'s moon hoax and Maelzel's chess player (see chapters 5 and 2), Poe sustains the illusion of an earnest report, using his old trick of pretending that readers should have already read about the case in other periodicals. The discovery of a process for turning lead into gold was perhaps too much for the public to swallow, particularly since it came from Poe, with his history of hoaxes, and since it was reported in so minor a paper as the *Flag of Our Union,* where Poe consigned his last few tales. And yet Poe claimed that "nine persons out of ten (even among the best-informed) will *believe* the quiz (provided the design does not leak out before publication) and that thus, acting as a sudden, although of course a very temporary, *check* to the gold-fever, it will create a *stir* to some purpose" (*Letters,* 2:433). The fact that Poe believed his story could have such an effect indicates his faith in the periodical press's ability to "create" truth, for although his hoaxes vary greatly in conception and purpose, from "Hans Pfaall" to "Von Kempelen" they all suggest that modern newspapers and magazines have the ability to make truth more a matter of negotiation or persuasion and less a condition of absolute factuality.

A pair of wide-ranging satires, "Some Words with a Mummy" (1845) and "Mellonta Tauta" (1849), make a similar point, as Poe insists that historians fictionalize what they attempt to re-create. In the earlier story, the revivified mummy describes the (mis)interpretation of primary-source texts as "a kind of literary arena for the conflicting guesses, riddles, and personal squabbles of whole herds of exasperated commentators" (*CW,* 3:1189). He explains that once the ancient Egyptians' advanced embalming methods made it possible for them to live "in instalments," contemporary historians would lie dormant for several hundred years so that they could return to set the record straight (*CW,* 3:1189). "Mellonta Tauta" critiques textual (mis)representation of history by looking at eighteenth- and nineteenth-century America from the perspective of the year 2848. Having learned of the excavation of a cornerstone for a monument to Washington's defeat of Cornwallis, the twenty-ninth-century writer Pundita (an ironic name she shares with her husband "Pundit") concludes from its inscription and other "historical" knowledge that the "Amriccans," who were cannibals, intended Cornwallis for a sausage. Pundita also notes that "from a hasty inspection of the fac-similes of newspapers, &c. &c., I find that *the* great men in those days among the Amriccans, were one John, a smith, and one Zacchary, a tailor" (*CW,* 3:1305), alluding to the "common man" and the president.

Along with this playful satire of historical inaccuracy, "Mummy" and "Mellonta Tauta" also feature deeply cynical assessments of democracy and progress. Poe's thinking—on literature as well as broader cultural matters—had always been hierarchical; for instance, his plan for marketing the *Stylus* was to appeal first to wealthy, well-educated men of refined taste, assuming that the masses would then emulate their social and cultural superiors by subscribing also.[39] David Long argues that "[a]lthough he generally avoided national politics, Poe co-opted what has been called the 'moral and cultural posture' of American Whiggery—cosmopolitan in taste, protectionist in policy, non-partisan in principle—and expounded its literary ramifications."⁴⁰ By the mid-to-late 1840s Poe clearly equated democracy and democrats with "mobocracy" and chaos. When the scientists in "Some Words with a Mummy" boast "of the great beauty and importance of Democracy," the mummy dismisses their claims with a historical analogy, explaining that "[t]hirteen Egyptian provinces determined all at once to be free," but the experiment ended in "the most odious and insupportable despotism that ever was heard of upon the face of the Earth." The tyrant's name, he says, was "*Mob*" (*CW,* 3:1193–94).

In "Mellonta Tauta" Poe expands on the theory that democracy, which initially promotes individualism, leads to mob rule. Pundita is aghast at the idea of "Amriccans *govern{ing} themselves!—*"

> [D]id ever anybody hear of such an absurdity?—that they existed in a sort of every-man-for-himself confederacy, after the fashion of the "prairie dogs" that we read of in fable. [Pundit, her husband] says that they started with the queerest idea conceivable, viz: that all men are born free and equal—this in the very teeth of the laws of *gradation* so visibly impressed upon all things both in the moral and physical universe. (*CW,* 3:1299)

She continues to describe the failed experiment and the eventual despotism of Mob ("a foreigner, by the by"), concluding that "democracy is a very admirable form of government—for dogs" (*CW,* 3:1300). One might wonder whether Poe intends us to take these views seriously. He does undermine Pundita's assertions elsewhere, when she misinterprets the surrender of Cornwallis, and earlier when she applauds letting a ship's passenger drown when he is knocked overboard: "I rejoice . . . that we live in an age so enlightened that no such a thing as an individual is supposed to exist. It is the mass for which the true Humanity cares" (*CW,* 3:1293). The contradiction is clear, for the trampling of individual rights (the right to life, in this case) for the sake of "the mass" is part of what conservatives such as Poe feared from "Mob."⁴¹ Perhaps Pundita's inconsistency reveals that her own society has fallen prey to mobocracy without realizing it, or that individuality is "gradually merg[ing] in the general consciousness," as Poe predicts in *Eureka* (*PT,* 1358); but, more likely, Poe wrote the story in a hurry and was inconsistent himself, first planning to make Pundita's society a reflection of his own and then turning the satire directly on the "Amriccans." Pundita's description of their descent into mob rule is exaggerated but not ironic, and her antidemocratic views are consistent with those expressed by Poe elsewhere.

Poe similarly ridiculed Americans' faith in other forms of "progress," such as reform movements and technological advances. Although he seems to admire certain technological breakthroughs in "Scheherazade," throughout the story Poe emphasizes the wonders of natural phenomena that had been discovered or newly understood in the eighteenth and nineteenth centuries far more than recent mechanical inventions, and he describes such innovations as the steamship and the printing press in less than flattering terms. "Mummy" and "Mellonta Tauta" also challenge his contemporaries' assumption that mid-nineteenth-century Western civilization—the United States in particular—was the pinnacle of human achievement. Both stories poke fun at the worship of fashion and wealth, and "Mummy" 's plot consists mainly of patriotic Americans trying desperately to name one advance their society had made over that of the ancient Egyptians. They finally believe they have vanquished the mummy by naming two patent medicines, "Ponnoner's lozenges" (named for one of the characters in the story) and "Brandeth's pills," a laxative. The mummy's name, Count Allamistakeo (all a mistake, oh) is likely a commentary on American society's efforts to progress and its smug sense of accomplishment.

Poe's cynical attitude toward "progress" and his fear of revolt surface in yet another late satire, "The System of Doctor Tarr and Professor Fether" (1845). The story's narrator tours an insane asylum that he has learned is run on modern principles known as the "soothing system," under which patients are generally indulged and allowed to move freely about the premises. Thus at first he is uncertain as to the status (sane or insane) of people he encounters, but the superintendent, Monsieur Maillard, informs him that he has abandoned the "soothing system" for the system of "the learned Doctor Tarr" and "the celebrated Professor Fether" (*CW,* 3:1017). The true state of affairs becomes clear when, at a lavish banquet that night, the people Maillard claims are staff members dwell obsessively on the odd behaviors of specific inmates, some "imitating" the patients' "crotchets" (crowing like a rooster, undressing in public). Meanwhile, Maillard explains that the danger of the former system became clear when the patients revolted:

> ["]A lunatic may be 'soothed,' as it is called, for a time, but, in the end, he is very apt to become obstreperous. His cunning, too, is proverbial, and great. . . . When a madman appears *thoroughly* sane, indeed, it is

high time to put him in a straight jacket. . . . [S]ure enough, one fine
morning the keepers found themselves pinioned hand and foot, and
thrown into the cells, where they were attended, as if *they* were the
lunatics, by the lunatics themselves, who had usurped the offices of the
keepers." (*CW,* 3:1018)

The narrator fails to realize that Maillard is describing his own revolt
and that the "lunatics" are still running the asylum. The story ends
when the tarred-and-feathered staff, which the narrator at first takes for
an "army" of "Chimpanzees, Ourang-Outangs, or big black baboons,"
break out of their cells and restore order.

The story clearly mocks attempts to reform treatment of the mentally
ill; the innovative "soothing system" was widely discussed in the 1830s
and 1840s, but Poe, despite writing some of his best stories from the perspective of deranged individuals, apparently had no sympathy with this
brand of "progress." Moreover, the plot device of lunatics taking over the
asylum suggests other sorts of rebellion. As with "Hop-Frog," the reference to victims of rebellion looking like apes might have put Poe's contemporaries in mind of slave revolt: in both stories the "tables are turned"
as masters are transformed by their former subjects/patients into a conventional nineteenth-century caricature of Africans (an image often
endorsed by racist pseudoscience). Maillard also refers to the "cunning"
of seemingly innocent, gentle lunatics, echoing another stock image of
African slaves. But, more likely, in a decade that would eventually wit-
ness revolutions throughout Europe and, in 1848, the publication of
Marx's *Communist Manifesto,* Poe apparently had in mind "mob" uprisings
of any sort. Maillard describes the revolt in terms of political movements:
"[A] lunatic [Maillard himself]—who, by some means, had taken it into
his head that he had invented a better system of government than any
ever heard of before—of lunatic government, I mean . . . and so he persuaded the rest of the patients to join him in a conspiracy for the overthrow of the reigning powers" (*CW,* 3:1018). The story also contains allusions to the two great revolutions of the previous century: "Maillard," the
name of the lunatic who led the revolt and devised the tar-and-feather
"system," recalls a leader in the storming of the Bastille, Stanislas-Marie
Maillard (Mabbott, *CW,* 3:1022); and, at the height of the banquet's
chaos, an orchestra of inmates strikes up "Yankee Doodle," a tune closely
associated with the American Revolution.

Maillard had actually been the asylum's superintendent before he
"grew crazy himself"; as a former "reigning power," he knew the expe-

diency of a "better system of government" consisting of tar, feathers, bread, and water "pumped on [the prisoners] daily" (*CW,* 3:1021). Despite Maillard's insanity, the narrator expresses approval of this "treatment," presumably when it is applied to the "proper" inmates and not to the "legitimate" authorities. Thus, if we regard the lunatic mob as a metaphor for groups of people whose lives must be managed by others (whether those others be called "master," "lord," or "boss"), Maillard's "system" represents the sort of social control needed to punish, or perhaps prevent, the overthrow of the "natural order." Although this story's tone is comic, it is decidedly dark comedy, and its topical references reveal Poe's reactionary social views. Like "Some Words with a Mummy" and "Mellonta Tauta," "Doctor Tarr and Professor Fether" is at best a curmudgeonly antidote to mid-nineteenth-century American optimism and at worst a cynical refutation of democracy and social progress. Along with his last tales of revenge, Poe's last satires are marked by a profoundly grim vision of human nature.

Chapter Seven

The Universe of Art

Eureka

Even as Poe's outlook on his own culture grew darker, he produced a work that affirmed his faith in the power of art and the artist, and in the rejuvenation not just of individual souls but of the entire cosmos. Although *Eureka* is seldom read by anyone other than those Daniel Hoffman calls "Poefessors," Poe seems to have regarded it as his most important work. A year after its publication he wrote to Maria Clemm, "I have no desire to live since I have done 'Eureka.' I could accomplish nothing more" (*Letters,* 2:452).[1] Naturally, a number of scholars seeking a coherent worldview in the Poe canon have anchored their arguments with *Eureka,* since it is here that Poe purportedly explains how the universe was created and how it works.[2]

However unconvincing Poe's cosmology may be, it does bring together a number of threads woven throughout Poe's criticism, fiction, and poetry. For instance, its entropic conclusion recalls "The Fall of the House of Usher" and "A Descent into the Maelström." More broadly, Poe had devoted numerous poems and stories to imagining postmortem consciousness and the possibility of rejuvenation, from the burlesque "Loss of Breath" (1832) to the philosophical "Colloquy of Monos and Una" (1841). In "Monos and Una" one spirit describes for another his sensations after death and during his burial, while in "The Conversation of Eiros and Charmion" (1839) two spirits recall the destruction of the earth by fire. *Eureka*'s pantheistic strains echo two earlier works: "Mesmeric Revelation," which identifies God as the "universal mind" manifested in "unparticled matter" and claims that human beings are individualized "portions of the divine mind" (*CW,* 3:1036); and the plate article "The Island of the Fay" (1841), whose narrator imagines all of nature as "one vast animate and sentient whole," then contemplates a vast universe, "cycle within cycle without end—yet all revolving around one far-distant centre which is the Godhead" (*CW,* 2:600–601). In "The Power of Words" (1845)— like "Eiros and Charmion" a postapocalyptic dialogue—the spirits Oinos and Agathos describe God as the "source of all thought," the creator

160

whose word literally became not only flesh but all other matter in the universe. Finally, "Mellonta Tauta" (which was written before Poe published *Eureka* but did not appear in print until 1849 [Mabbott, *CW,* 3:1022]) provides the basis for *Eureka*'s "remarkable letter" that satirizes science's and philosophy's reliance on induction and deduction.

While portions of *Eureka* build on Poe's earlier writings, the whole is nonetheless a stylistic departure. Originally presented as a lecture, Poe expanded it into a book of about 150 pages with no chapter divisions, a far cry from the concise magazine stories and articles to which he devoted most of his career. Moreover, *Eureka* challenges generic boundaries even more boldly than *Pym.* Although I follow other critics in terming it a "cosmology," Poe refers to it in his subtitles and preface as an "essay," a "Book of Truths," an "Art-Product," a "Romance," a "Poem," and, on the book's title page, "A Prose Poem." Such a label is surprising considering Poe's career-long insistence on a clear distinction between poetry and prose, along with his contention that "the phrase, 'a long poem,' is simply a flat contradiction in terms" (*ER,* 71). And yet, if we recall how often Poe's poetry attempts to break through ordinary experience to another mode of consciousness, we can see how *Eureka* functions as a poem for Poe, who uses an analogy early on to suggest a revolution (in both senses of the word) in perception: "He who from the top of Aetna casts his eyes leisurely around, is affected chiefly by the *extent* and *diversity* of the scene. Only by a rapid whirling on his heel could he hope to comprehend the panorama in the sublimity of its *oneness*" (*PT,* 1261). Poe goes on to explain that in order to achieve an *"individuality* of impression" when writing about the universe, "we require something like a mental gyration on the heel. We need so rapid a revolution of all things about the central point of sight that, while the minutiae vanish altogether, even the more conspicuous objects become blended into one" (*PT,* 1262). The fact that Poe was suggesting a gyration atop an active volcano suggests another complication in classifying *Eureka,* for Poe injects the work with irony and satire even though his tone is predominately sincere. Ultimately, all of Poe's labels suit *Eureka,* but it makes most sense to me as a "romance," specifically a story about the story of the universe, as "plotted" by God.[3]

However, Poe's romance does not lend itself to plot summary. Poe offered an outline in a letter to George Eveleth, but clearer and more careful synopses have been written by, among others, Edward Davidson, Michael Williams, and Kenneth Silverman. Robert Jacobs's straightforward description of Poe's shifts in tone is particularly helpful in presenting an overview of the text: "[T]he beginning is satirical, the middle is scientifically objective, and the end is ecstatic."[4] The satirical letter that serves as a kind of introduction concerns the problem of pursuing truth through conventional methods. From the perspective of the year 2848, the letter writer finds it hard to imagine "that it is scarcely more than eight or nine hundred years ago since the metaphysicians first consented to relieve the people of the singular fancy that there exist *but two practicable roads to Truth*" (1263), specifically the deductive method of Aries Tottle (Aristotle) and the inductive method of Hog (Francis Bacon). The letter writer proposes as an alternative method intuition, which seemingly combines induction and deduction but transcends their limitations. To solve the mysteries of the universe it takes a Dupin-like thinker who not only pays attention to details but comprehends "the big picture," as if by spinning on his heel atop a mountain.[5] But although Poe, like Dupin, approaches the cosmos as both poet and mathematician, it is ultimately the poet or artist whose vision prevails in constructing *Eureka*. In the guise of the correspondent from 2848, Poe stakes his claim to truth on his theory's consistency—the aesthetic principle that guided his best fiction and poetry—rather than on verifiable fact:

> By the bye, my dear friend, is it not an evidence of the mental slavery entailed upon those bigoted people by their Hogs and Rams [an allusion to *Aries* Tottle], that in spite of the eternal prating of their savans about *roads* to Truth, none of them fell, even by accident, into what we now so distinctly perceive to be the broadest, the straightest and most available of all mere roads—the great thoroughfare—the majestic highway of the Consistent? (*PT,* 1269)

Furthermore, citing Kepler, the correspondent claims that the truths arrived at by intuition on the road of consistency are borne out by later scientific observation. Thus the imaginative "theorist" gets a kind of posthumous revenge on the age that scorned him. The correspondent adopts a strangely combative tone toward philosophers who supposedly had been discredited for centuries, paraphrasing Kepler but clearly speaking for Poe at the end of the letter: "*I care not whether my work be read now or by posterity. I can afford to wait a century for readers when God himself has waited six thousand years for an observer. I triumph. I have stolen the golden secret of the Egyptians. I will indulge my sacred fury*" (*PT,* 1270).

Having closed the satirical letter, Poe promises that "distinctness—intelligibility, at all points, is a primary feature in my general design"

(*PT,* 1271), a comment that must be taken as either ironic or disingenuous. The 75 or so pages that follow combine often-circular logic, hairsplitting distinctions, and geometric ratios into what David Ketterer calls a "hit-and-miss hodgepodge" of science.[6] As Joan Dayan argues, "Poe believes in the limitations of our mind, and he proves this belief by luring us with concord and giving us chaos."[7] Poe's science is not altogether a humbug: drawing on contemporary astronomy and physics, he advances some valid, although unoriginal, hypotheses.[8] But the real problem for readers, as Dayan suggests, is that *Eureka* lacks intelligibility and consistency. For example, in his critique of deductive reasoning, Poe dismisses axioms altogether but replaces them with intuitive assumptions about the nature of God and matter, assumptions that are hard to distinguish from axioms. He argues against infinity and yet uses words like "interminable" and "limitless" to describe the succession of universes he imagines. Daniel Hoffman sums up another feature of Poe's logical sleight of hand, pointing out that, for much of his argument, "Poe has marshalled all the evidence he can from his scientific confrères to buttress the plinth upon which his demonstrations rest. He has worked out his line of argument with such cunning totality that the plinth is supported by the arguments and theories of which it is itself the supporting assumption" (Hoffman, 282). Throughout the text one senses (though we can never be sure) that it all made sense to Poe, but he either neglected to revise for clarity or concluded that he would rather dazzle and mystify readers than persuade them with coherent logic.[9] At one point he follows a formula for the degree of attraction among atoms with this statement: "Here, indeed, a flood of suggestion bursts upon the mind" (*PT,* 1284). What makes *Eureka* uncharacteristic of Poe is that so much of it reads not like a carefully contructed analysis or a unified story or poem but rather like a "flood of suggestion."

And yet, toward the end of this cosmological romance, Poe's enthusiastic "flood" does become an artistic strength, making the work "strangely compelling," as Ketterer observes. Beverly Hume has suggested that we read against *Eureka*'s narrator (a persona I and most other critics identify as Poe himself) as we do the unreliable narrators of "The Black Cat" and "The Tell-Tale Heart."[10] While I doubt that this was Poe's intention, *Eureka* does close with the same intensity and insistence on a dubious explanation that characterizes the insane narrators of Poe's fiction. Throughout the text Poe has emphasized the principle of unity, arguing that God created a simple but expanding universe (or system of universes) that will eventually "collapse." His breathtaking conclusion is that the universe will finally contract into nothingness. Because "Matter *exists* only as Attraction and Repulsion," once the work of attraction is complete matter will no longer exist: "In sinking into Unity, it will sink at once into that Nothingness which, to all finite perception, Unity must be—into that Material Nihility from which alone we can conceive it to have been evoked—to have been *created* by the Volition of God" (*PT,* 1355). But Poe's vision of the universe is ultimately hopeful, for a succeeding universe will "swell into existence" as a manifestation of God's heartbeat.

How does Poe know this? Through intuition, or "deep tranquility of self-inspection" (*PT,* 1356). Although the re-creation of the universe by the divine heartbeat is only a "justified belief" or a "hope," Poe proceeds to treat it as truth, much like the murderers and mourners of his tales and poems who become convinced that the dead, one way or another, return. All people, he assumes, have "memories of a Destiny more vast" than our "world-existence," particularly during youth—an idea reminiscent of Poe's early poetry. In imagining the rebirth of the universe, then, Poe projects onto the cosmos his career-long concern with some spiritual essence surviving physical death:[11] "Existence—self-existence—existence from all Time and to all Eternity—seems, up to the epoch of Manhood, a normal and unquestionable condition:—*seems, because it is*" (*PT,* 1356–57).

Not only are human souls eternal, according to Poe, but they are, as Emerson had famously put it, "part or parcel of God."[12] Poe takes his customary swipes at transcendentalists early in *Eureka,* but, particularly toward the end, his terms are similar to theirs: "[E]ach soul is, in part, its own God—its own Creator. . . . God—the material *and* spiritual God—*now* exists solely in the diffused Matter and Spirit of the Universe" (*PT,* 1357). In a rare democratic gesture, he asserts that "no one soul *is* inferior to another" (*PT,* 1357), but for Poe equality of souls apparently does not imply an equality among flesh-and-blood human beings. In contrast to Emerson and Thoreau, Poe's pantheism and his belief in the equality of souls had apparently no implications for how people should live their lives, much less try to change their society. Poe had made clear in "Mellonta Tauta" his belief that meaningful human progress is a delusion, and nothing in *Eureka* suggests otherwise.

Of course, by calling his work an "Art-Product," a "Romance," and a "Poem," Poe disclaims not only a responsibility to use scientific methods but also the kind of practical "truth" that science seeks to provide; instead, those labels suggest that the work be read for its beauty of design or unity of effect. In this sense *Eureka* reflects the universe it describes, or perhaps the universe reflects *Eureka.* Poe may be referring to both his text and the subject of his text in the preface when he writes, "*What I here propound is true:*—therefore it cannot die:—or if by any means it be now trodden down so that it die, it will 'rise again to Life Everlasting' " (*PT,* 1259). Poe's writing, then, like human beings and the universe itself, will die only to be reborn. *Eureka*'s truth, according to Poe, is the eternal truth of art, which springs from the imagination and proves itself by its consistency. God is the consummate artist—a writer, in fact: "The plots of God are perfect. The Universe is a plot of God" (*PT,* 1342). But since Poe's story contains God's design, the universe of *Eureka* is finally not so much a plot of God as a plot of Poe, as Ketterer suggests: "Poe creates a vital universe in which deduction, induction, and intuition; past, present, and future; radiation, repulsion, and attraction exist in a web of tensions created by their mutual dependence."[13] In *Eureka,* art neither imitates life nor creates what Robert Frost would call a "momentary stay against confusion";[14] instead, art demands that the "real world" conform to *its* rules, as written by Poe, insisting that life—indeed, the life of the entire cosmos—imitate art.

Return to the Poetic Principle

In light of *Eureka*'s artistic vision, it should come as no surprise that in his last two years Poe all but abandoned serious fiction and returned to poetry, the medium through which a writer could best "struggle, by multiform combinations among the things and thoughts of Time, to attain a portion of that Loveliness whose very elements, perhaps, appertain to eternity alone," as he described it in "The Poetic Principle" (*ER,* 77). Not only did Poe write about half of his most famous poems within the last two years of his life, but the aesthetic values he tried to maintain in his poetry became the subjects of his serious prose works: two late works of fiction, "The Domain of Arnheim" (1847) and "Landor's Cottage: A Pendant to 'The Domain of Arnheim' " (1849), apply his poetic vision to the art of landscape gardening, while his theoretical essays concerned "The Poetic Principle" (published in 1850) and "The Rationale of Verse" (1848).

"The Domain of Arnheim," an expanded version of "The Landscape Garden" (1842), can be described as a poet's dream of what he would do with $450 million. Ellison, a young man with a poetic temperament and an inheritance of that very amount, creates an earthly paradise by manipulating not words but trees, plants, water, and everything else in his "domain." Poe makes the connection between poetry and landscape clear when his narrator explains that "[i]n the widest and noblest sense [Ellison] was a poet. He comprehended, moreover, the true character, the august aims, the supreme majesty and dignity of the poetic sentiment" (*CW,* 3:1271). The combination of wealth and poetic sentiment makes Ellison a true anomaly in Poe's fiction—a happy man.[15] He uses his wealth primarily to fulfill "the august purposes for which the Deity had implanted the poetic sentiment in man"—not the improvement of "the general condition of man," for which he has no more faith than Poe, but the perfecting of nature (*CW,* 3:1271–72). Ellison can make real the dreamscapes that otherwise exist only in verse or on canvas. In fact, Poe borrows from Thomas Cole's popular *Voyage of Life* paintings (1839–1840) to describe Ellison's paradise.[16] One apparent reference to Cole concludes the story: "[U]pspringing confusedly from amid all, a mass of semi-Gothic, semi-Saracenic architecture, sustaining itself as if by a miracle in mid air . . . seeming the phantom handiwork, conjointly, of the Sylphs, of the Fairies, of the Genii, and of the Gnomes" (*CW,* 3:1283). While not a precise transcription, this description of a majestic, floating palace corresponds to the second painting in Cole's series: *Youth,* the time of life Poe associates in *Eureka* with being in touch with one's eternal existence (and the time of life during which Poe wrote most of his poetry). Moreover, Ellison imposes on the landscape the kind of order that Poe requires for poetry and short fiction and that he imagines for the universe in *Eureka*—a "weird symmetry" (*CW,* 3:1279), a logic that life outside the domains of art and Arnheim lacks.

Modern readers tend to be put off by Ellison's heavy-handed "perfection" of the landscape, which Andrew Horn likens to Disney World, where concealed machinery replaces the natural world with a magical, man-made version in which "[e]ach element in it is calculated, shaped, and controlled."[17] As if to modify the poetic vision of "Arnheim," which depends so heavily on the artificial, in "Landor's Cottage" Poe describes a paradise created apparently without wealth and without great changes in the land. Here, too, the narrator considers the landscape a work of art, likening it to poetry and observing that "[i]ts marvellous *effect* lay altogether in its artistic arrangement *as a picture*" (*CW,* 3:1335). But where Ellison had declared himself a proponent of the "artificial style" of landscape gardening, Landor seems to have adopted the alternative method described by Ellison, "seek[ing] to recall the original beauty of the country . . . detecting and bringing into practice those nice relations of size, proportion and color which, hid from the common observer, are revealed everywhere to the experienced student of nature" (*CW,* 3:1274). Or Landor may have had nothing to do with the scenery: he is the owner of a cottage, after all, not a domain, and the narrator never attributes the poetic effect of the landscape to him. Instead, more deliberately and more often than in "Arnheim," the "experienced student of nature" refers to his own creative act of merely perceiving and describing the unity and perfection of the landscape, even concluding the story with a reference to his role as a translator, both writer and painter, of the scene: "It is not the purpose of this work to do more than give, in detail, a picture of Mr. Landor's residence—*as I found it*" (*CW,* 3:1340). In both stories art is created by an interplay among artist, nature, and perceiver, but in "Landor's Cottage" Poe shifts his emphasis: experiencing the landscape as an artist—rather than altering it—constitutes the creative act.

Poe gave his most minute accounting of the work performed by the literary artist in "The Rationale of Verse," which appeared in the magazine in which he had made his name as a critic, the *Southern Literary Messenger.* This long essay seems to bear out James Russell Lowell's caricature of Poe in "A Fable for Critics" (1846) as talking "like a book of iambs and pentameters, / In a way to make people of common sense damn metres."[18] Poe assumes his old combative critical posture, insisting on the inadequacy of modern prosodists, who cling to tradition rather than using common sense. As with *Eureka,* Poe claims to have discovered a new approach to his subject; he tells a story of how poetry evolved that is similar to his story of how the universe evolved—expanding from simplicity and unity, from spondees to "bastard trochees." As Silverman notes, "Not much can be said in defense of Poe's thinking, according to which the same principles and devices of versification that arose in English should also have arisen in Tagalog, Turkish, and all other human tongues as well."[19] And yet Poe does make a legitimate point, that modern scansion does not adequately account for the variety of rhythm in verse. His system for denoting the rhythm of a line, although overly restrictive and mathematical, acknowledges that syllables in verse often have a range of time values similar to those given to musical notes: not merely short or long, syllables vary in their shortness in relation to the length of the long syllable.[20]

While "The Rationale of Verse" exemplifies Poe's preoccupation with systematizing poetry, playing up its mathematical properties, "The Poetic Principle," a lecture Poe delivered first in December 1848, emphasizes once again the poet's inspiration and quest for heavenly beauty. Perhaps because so much of the essay is recycled from earlier essays and criticism, "The Poetic Principle" may well be Poe's best summation of his poetic theory. A poem should be neither too short to create a "profound or enduring effect" (*ER,* 73) nor too long to preserve its unity and coherence

(*ER,* 71). Having been briefly equated with each other in *Eureka,* beauty
and truth are once again divorced as Poe inveighs against "the heresy of
The Didactic," the mistaken belief that "the ultimate object of all Poetry is
Truth" (*ER,* 75). Finally, Poe neatly summarizes his theory that the
"Human Aspiration for Supernal Beauty" is the poetic principle, and "the
manifestation of the Principle is always found in *an elevating excitement of
the Soul*" (*ER,* 92–93). The poems by other writers that Poe inserts
throughout the lecture convey the musical qualities of metered verse,
which Poe, even in his first theoretical essay, the "Letter to [B]———,"
claimed were vital to the success of a poem. In "The Poetic Principle," he
speculates that "[i]t is in Music, perhaps, that the soul most nearly
attains the great end for which, when inspired with the Poetic Sentiment,
it struggles—the creation of supernal Beauty" (*ER,* 78) before defining
poetry as *"The Rhythmical Creation of Beauty."*

It is not surprising, then, that a strong sense of rhythm and musical-
ity pervades Poe's late poetry, which is generally more daring than his
early work in its use of sound effects. In the most extreme example,
"The Bells," various types of repetition—rhyme, alliteration, refrain, as
well as the mantra of "bells, bells, bells"—create a nearly hypnotic
effect. But such repetitions characterize nearly all of Poe's significant
late poems. One early-twentieth-century commentator claimed that
because of its "monotonous reiterations . . . 'Ulalume' properly intoned
would produce something like the same effect upon a listener knowing
no word of English that it produces upon us."[21] Even in the second "To
Helen," written in blank verse—which usually creates a "natural" or
conversational voice—Poe uses assonance, alliteration, and repeated
words and phrases to emphasize the obsessiveness of the speaker, the
slowness of his thoughts as he dwells upon Helen's beauty:

> the very roses' odors
> Died in the arms of the adoring airs.
> All—all expired save thee—save less than thou:
> Save only the divine light in thine eyes—
> Save but the soul in thine uplifted eyes.
> I saw but them—they were the world to me.
> I saw but them—saw only them for hours—
> Saw only them until the moon went down.
>
> (ll. 34–41)

Indeed, such repetition nearly always suggests obsession in Poe's late poetry, which centers on Poe's own obsessive themes—mourning, the power of romantic devotion, and the possibility of postmortem consciousness.

Even in late poems not primarily concerned with mourning, love and death are suggestively intertwined. In "The Bells" two sets of bells are associated with churches: the wedding bells of stanza 2 and the funeral bells "that dwell up in the steeple" in stanza 4. The speaker of "A Dream within a Dream," whose title and refrain ("All that we see or seem / Is but a dream within a dream" [ll. 10–11]) recall Poe's early poetry,[22] contemplates his death as a parting from his lover, to whom he addresses the poem: "Take this kiss upon the brow! / And, in parting from you now, / Thus much let me avow . . ." (ll. 1–3). In other poems Poe more explicitly combined love, mourning, and life after death into a general motif or masterplot. Mourning is an expression of devotion, which in Poe's poetry is always grounded in romantic love. And as we have seen in "Ligeia," "Lenore," and "The Raven," this devotion can keep the dead alive, although it is never clear whether the dead live only in the memory or imagination of their mourners or, as spirits, continue to be aware of others' devotion.[23] Mourning may be life-sustaining, Poe suggests, but keeping the dead alive through memory can torture the mourner even as it sustains his relationship with the deceased.

"Ulalume" picks up where "The Raven" left off: the grief-stricken speaker believes he has forgotten the lost Ulalume, and yet he finds himself walking unwittingly toward his beloved's tomb on the anniversary of her death, accompanied by Psyche, a personification of his soul or mind. As he did in "The Raven," Poe creates an atmosphere appropriate for Halloween recitations, setting the poem on an October night when "The skies they were ashen and sober; / The leaves they were crispéd and sere" (ll. 1–2), and makes dramatic use of rhythm, rhyme, and repeated words. Unlike the earlier poem, however, "Ulalume" is rather difficult to follow, for its symbolism and the logic of its plot are not as clear as "The Raven" 's. The speaker, along with his more reflective, less impulsive other self, is led by "Astarte's bediamonded crescent" (l. 37), either the planet Venus or a star associated with the goddess of love. Psyche mistrusts Venus's guardianship, but the speaker sees Hope in the "crystalline light" of the star or planet. In following Astarte the narrator places hope in love, but on finding himself at the tomb of Ulalume he learns that love is inextricable from grief.

The distraught speaker asks, "[W]hat demon hath tempted me here?" (l. 90), but when he and Psyche attempt an answer, they describe Astarte's appearance as a blessing, despite its Hellish nature:

> Said we, then—the two, then—"Ah, can it
>   Have been that the woodlandish ghouls—
>   The pitiful, the merciful ghouls,
> To bar up our way and to ban it
>   From the secret that lies in these wolds—
>   From the thing that lies hidden in these wolds—
> Have drawn up the spectre of a planet
>   From the limbo of lunary souls—
> This sinfully scintillant planet
>   From the Hell of the planetary souls?"
>
> (ll. 95 – 104)

Why would "merciful" or sympathetic ghouls call up something that shines in order to keep hidden the "secret" of Ulalume's tomb? The name "Ulalume" suggests one explanation: if, as Mabbott suggests, the name combines the Latin *ululare*, to wail, with *lumen*, a light, to create "a light of sorrow" (*CW*, 1:419), then the appearance of Astarte's "spectre" is a reminder, a warning to stay away, for the light of sorrow and the star of love are, in Poe's dreamscape, one and the same. Of course, such a warning defeats itself, for one cannot be reminded to forget something—Love's warning against remembrance is therefore also an invitation to remember. Accordingly, the inseparability of love and sorrow causes the speaker and his soul to join voices in those final, paradoxical lines, for he will continue to fear the memory of Ulalume (as Psyche did) even as he clings to that memory. In summoning the spirit of the dead lover, the "woodlandish ghouls" are both sympathetic and threatening to the speaker, for Ulalume, although consigned to a "limbo of lunary souls," will not allow herself to be forgotten.[24]

The grief-striken lover of "Annabel Lee" expresses his compulsion more directly, but again love takes the form of an intense mourning. As with "Ulalume," the speaker reveals almost nothing about who Annabel Lee was, what she looked like, how she lived, only that she thought of nothing but him, that she was "a child," and that she lived "[i]n this kingdom by the sea" (l. 8). Otherwise she is present to him only as an absence, as if Annabel Lee is his name for love and grief. The inextricability of those emotions is heightened by the speaker's insistence that her death resulted not from random misfortune but from their love, for he tells us that the "wingéd seraphs," her "high-born kinsmen," were jealous of him and took her away. In an early poem, "Introduction," Poe's speaker confessed that he "could not love except where Death / Was mingling his with Beauty's breath" (ll. 31–32); the same apparently is true of this speaker of Poe's last poem, who concludes by confessing to lying "all the night-tide" not near, but *in* "her sepulchre there by the sea— / In her tomb by the side of the sea" (ll. 38, 40–41).

Sarah Helen Whitman, Elmira Shelton, and Sarah Anna Lewis (a poet whose career Poe more or less managed toward the end of his life) all claimed to have been the inspiration for "Annabel Lee," while Francis Osgood unselfishly (and more logically) argued on behalf of Virginia. But no such confusion surrounds the second "To Helen" or "For Annie," written for Whitman and Nancy Richmond, respectively. In addition to their biographical significance—they are a good indication of how different Poe's feelings were for the two women—these poems recast the interlocking themes of devotion, mourning, and postmortem consciousness. Although Helen still lives, the poem focuses on her absence and suggests that she remains forcefully present in his memory years after the one time he saw her: "[Your eyes] have not left me (as my hopes have) since. / They follow me—they lead me through the years" (ll. 54–55). Through Poe's romantic hyperbole, the speaker, too, is sustained—not kept alive, but given a reason to live—by that memory of a brief glimpse into Helen's eyes:

> They are my ministers—yet I their slave.
> Their office is to illumine and enkindle—
> My duty, *to be saved* by their bright light,
> And purified in their electric fire,
> And sanctified in their elysian fire.
>
> (ll. 56–60)

As in "Ligeia," the eyes of a beautiful woman suggest a strength of will that subjugates the speaker and (in "Ligeia") is capable of overcoming death.

Although this Helen is distinct from the Helen of Poe's early poem, a comparison of the two suggests a continuity in Poe's representation of women in poetry. Even when Poe writes to a specific, real Helen, he presents her as an idea or an emotion: although he devotes half of the poem to Helen's eyes, he describes not so much the eyes themselves or what they reveal about her but rather what those eyes do to him. Like Ulalume and Annabel Lee, both Helens are essentially projections of the male speakers' longings—certainly not lust, but longings for perfection, security, and immortality.

Whereas the male speakers' devotion kept alive Lenore, Ulalume, and Annabel Lee, in "For Annie" the female subject keeps the speaker alive after his death. Poe had experimented in his fiction with characters speaking from "the other side," but usually through some gimmick such as mesmerism or a comic "loss of breath." "The Colloquy of Monos and Una" is "For Annie"'s fictional corollary, for in both works men who are physically dead describe their sensations calmly, for the benefit of their lovers.[25] "You," the auditor of the poem, believe that the speaker is dead, for good reason: his "lingering illness / Is over at last— / And the fever called 'Living' / Is conquered at last" (ll. 3–6); he does not move a muscle (l. 9); he lies in a narrow bed (l. 48); and he refers to the light having been extinguished (l. 79). Physically, the speaker *is* dead, lying "at full length" (l. 10) in a coffin. Only he and Annie know that their mutual love sustains his spirit, which "lies happily, / Bathing in many / A dream of the truth / And the beauty of Annie—" (ll. 67–70). As in all of these late poems, repetition underscores theme, as the speaker invokes "Annie" and "light" at the ends of the last five lines:

> [My heart] sparkles with Annie—
> It glows with the light
> Of the love of my Annie—
> With the thought of the light
> Of the eyes of my Annie.
>   (ll. 98–102)

Another of Poe's last poems, "Eldorado" (1849), is anomalous in that it does not concern romantic love or mourning—yet it provides a fitting close to a discussion of Poe's career. Poe's contemporaries would have seen in the title a reference to California, where gold seekers were flocking in 1849, but the parable applies to any quest for happiness. The "gallant knight" spends his life seeking Eldorado, but as his strength gives out and he faces death, he learns from a "pilgrim shadow," probably a spirit who ushers him into the next realm of consciousness, that his quest was in vain. Eldorado can be sought only through the imagination—"Over the Mountains / Of the Moon"—or through death—"Down the Valley of the Shadow" (ll. 19–21). Whether or not Poe sensed that his own death was imminent, the biographical resonance is clear: his life consisted largely of personal tragedies, professional frustrations, and unrelenting poverty, throughout which he pursued a higher realm of consciousness through art and speculated on art's connection with the eternal. But the poem need not be limited to biographical interpretation, for "Eldorado" reflects not just his own life but human life in general, as Poe found it. Especially in the late 1840s, skepticism toward human endeavor (other than art) coupled with faith in reincarnation—both personal and universal—pervades Poe's fiction and poetry as well as *Eureka,* so that toward the end Poe presented something close to a coherent worldview. With the possible, rare exception of an Ellison, who possesses both a poetic temperament and limitless wealth, no one in this life is really content, but poetry and other forms of art hold out the promise of Eldorado, where earthly chaos is replaced by unity and order, and where estrangement—from one's own psyche as well as others'—is transformed into self-knowledge and a corresponding union of souls.[26]

Conclusion

The last 10 days of Poe's life constitute the most conspicuous blank spot in his biography. He arrived in Baltimore on a steamer from Richmond on September 28, 1849; on October 3, Joseph W. Walker found him in a tavern, "in need of immediate assistance" (Thomas and Jackson, 844). From there, Poe was taken to Washington College Hospital, where he died four days later. Little else is known, except through questionable sources, mainly the melodramatic and contradictory accounts of the hospital's attending physician.[27] Appropriately, the death of this writer so closely associated with mystery and detection remains an enigma. As recently as 1996 Poe's death made headlines with an insubstantial but widely debated theory that he had died of rabies.[28] Poe's death triggered controversy among his contemporaries as well. Rufus Griswold, one of Poe's literary rivals and his successor as editor of *Graham's,* wrote a scandalous obituary in which he depicted Poe as friendless, melancholic, and deranged; in the preface to a new edition of Poe's works that he prepared the next year, Griswold emphasized Poe's alcoholism and greatly exaggerated other character flaws. N. P. Willis, Graham, and others defended Poe in print, but as Griswold's edition was reprinted year after year, his image of Poe reached more readers and persisted far longer than the images provided by friends.[29]

While Griswold's defamation certainly tainted Poe's reputation and led many critics to dismiss or misinterpret his work, Poe's infamy also attracted a number of nineteenth-century readers, biographers, and poets. In 1880 J. H. Ingram published a well-documented biography that vociferously defended Poe's character, but Ingram's admiration for Poe made his account nearly as distorted as Griswold's. On the other hand, the influential symbolist poet Charles Baudelaire worshiped Poe largely *because* of his decadent reputation and gained Poe a large French readership by translating and promoting his major works. Poe biography continued to be marked by partisanship well into the twentieth century, and, as any English teacher can attest, questions about Poe's personal habits continue to distract and entice students. As an editor, Poe had courted controversy as a way to sell magazines, and to some extent the same principle has helped publishers sell collections of his work ever since his death.

In considering Poe's posthumous reputation, we encounter yet another dichotomy: between the alcoholic madman and writer of immoral tales on the one hand and the devoted husband and son-in-law, the seeker of supernal beauty on the other. We might take yet another step back and posit a split between the shadowy pop culture icon alluded to in movies, songs, novels, and television shows and the body of work that inspires meticulous scholarly research—and endless debate, as we have seen. There are, of course, many Poes, not only because he was a kind of literary ventriloquist but because readers bring such a variety of expectations to his poems and tales. Still, Poe encourages us to think in terms not of multiplicity but of dichotomy: the self we know versus the self we don't know; everyday experience versus the reality of dreams and art; the mathematician versus the poet; the desire to reach a mass audience versus disdain for that same audience; the impulse for survival versus the impulse for self-destruction; faith in the transmigration of the soul versus fear of the "conqueror worm."

And yet even this tendency is only half of another opposition, another dichotomy, for the same writer who surveyed the divisions in human consciousness also argued for the necessity of unity in the products of human consciousness, namely works of art and theories of the cosmos. At the point in "The Psyche Zenobia" when Mr. Blackwood is explaining how to imitate transcendentalists, he tells Zenobia: "Put in something about the Supernal Oneness. Don't say a syllable about the Infernal Twoness" (*CW,* 2:342). Like the transcendentalists he loved to hate, Poe put in quite a bit about Supernal Oneness, particularly at the beginning and end of his career; and yet it is his insight into the Infernal Twoness that fueled his best writing. Paradoxically, Poe's exploration of self-division, in all its manifestations, unifies his work.

Notes and References

Chapter One

1. On "old" family money backing entrepreneurs in this era, see Edward Pessen, *Riches, Class, and Power before the Civil War* (Lexington, Mass.: Heath, 1973), 130–50. On the materialism of the "typical" Jacksonian, see, for instance, Pessen, *Jacksonian America: Society, Personality, and Politics* (Homewood, Ill.: Dorsey, 1969), 29–32. On the Jacksonians' belief in the importance of being "self-made," see, for instance, Jack Larkin, *The Reshaping of Everyday Life, 1790–1840* (New York: Harper & Row, 1988); Lewis Perry, *Boats against the Current: American Culture between the Revolution and Modernity, 1820–1860* (New York: Oxford University Press, 1993), 13–14; David G. Pugh, *Sons of Liberty: The Masculine Mind in Nineteenth-Century America* (Westport, Conn., and London: Greenwood, 1983), 23–34; and Richard Slotkin, *The Fatal Environment: The Myth of the Frontier in the Age of Industrialization, 1800–1890* (New York: Atheneum, 1985). On John Allan's business, his place in Richmond society, and his early relationship with Poe, see Kenneth Silverman, *Edgar A. Poe: Mournful and Never-ending Remembrance* (New York: HarperCollins, 1991), 9–28.

2. For example, upon the family's arrival in Scotland, Allan wrote his partner, Charles Ellis, "Edgar says Pa say something for me, say I was not afraid coming across the Sea" (Dwight Thomas and David K. Jackson, *The Poe Log: A Documentary Life of Edgar Allan Poe, 1809–1849* [Boston: G. K. Hall, 1987], 26; hereafter cited in text).

3. Ibid., 61. On this change in Poe and Allan's relationship, see Silverman, *Edgar A. Poe*, 23–28.

4. All quotations from Poe's poetry are from *The Collected Works of Edgar Allan Poe*, 3 vols., ed. Thomas Ollive Mabbott (Cambridge, Mass., and London: Harvard University Press, 1969–1978). Subsequent references to poems will be cited by line numbers; other references to Mabbott's edition will be cited in text as *CW*. See Thomas and Jackson, *Poe Log*, 62–63, for the dating of these lines. According to Silverman, Poe was called "Edgar Allan" at schools in England (*Edgar A. Poe*, 25).

5. Silverman, *Edgar A. Poe*, 36.

6. Poe's side of the correspondence can be read in its entirety in *The Letters of Edgar Allan Poe*, ed. John Ward Ostrom (New York: Gordian, 1966); hereafter cited in text as *Letters*. Excerpts from both men's letters can be found in Thomas and Jackson, *Poe Log*, 77–129.

7. Allan married Louisa Patterson on October 5, 1830. In January 1831, Poe sent Allan a long, vitriolic letter in which he promised to "neglect

177

my studies and duties at this institution—if I do not receive your answer in 10 days—I will leave the point [West Point] without" (*Letters,* 1:42).

8. Thomas and Jackson estimate a press run of under 1,000, with 131 copies going to cadet subscribers (*Poe Log,* 116–17).

9. Richard Wilbur, ed., *Poe: Complete Poems* (New York: Dell, 1959), 119.

10. Ibid., 10.

11. David Ketterer, *The Rationale of Deception in Poe* (Baton Rouge: Louisiana State University Press, 1979), 27–30.

12. These are lines 5–8 in Poe's original version, which begins with a stanza he later deleted.

13. See Kent P. Ljungquist, *The Grand and the Fair: Poe's Landscape Aesthetics and Pictorial Techniques* (Potomac, Md.: Scripta Humanistica, 1984), 149–60.

14. William Carlos Williams, *In the American Grain* (New York: New Directions, 1956).

15. See Robert Morrison, "Poe's 'The Lake: To ——,' " *Explicator* 7 (December 1948): item 22.

16. Wilbur, ed., *Poe,* 124.

17. See Daniel Hoffman, *Poe Poe Poe Poe Poe Poe Poe* (1972; reprint, New York: Paragon House, 1990), 38–40, hereafter cited in text; and Ljungquist, *Grand,* 152–54.

18. Wilbur offers a helpful explication in the notes to his regrettably out of print edition of Poe's poetry (*Poe,* 124–27).

19. See Edward H. Davidson, *Poe: A Critical Study* (Cambridge, Mass.: Harvard University Press, 1957), 13, 17–19.

20. See Ketterer, *Rationale,* 161.

21. See Roy Harvey Pearce, *The Continuity of American Poetry* (Princeton, N.J.: Princeton University Press, 1961), 142. See also Neil Harris, *The Artist in American Society: The Formative Years, 1790–1860* (1966; reprint, New York: Simon & Schuster, 1970).

22. Mabbott's note indicates that it is a wooden, painted bird (*CW,* 1:128–29).

23. See Davidson, *Poe,* 31; Silverman, *Edgar A. Poe,* 68–69.

24. See, for instance, Davidson, *Poe,* 31, 39; and Mabbott's introduction, *CW,* 1:155–207.

25. See also Ljungquist, *Grand,* 149–60.

26. Edgar Allan Poe, *Poetry and Tales,* ed. Patrick F. Quinn (New York: Library of America, 1984), 10; hereafter cited in text as *PT.*

27. See Michael Allen, *Poe and the British Magazine Tradition* (New York: Oxford University Press, 1969).

28. In the 1831 version, these lines read, "To the beauty of fair Greece, / And the grandeur of old Rome."

29. See Ljungquist, *Grand,* 168–72.

30.   David Ketterer argues that "[t]he line between hell and heaven, life and death, can be made to disappear. . . . [line 4] is intended to erase such distinctions" (*Rationale,* 176).

31.   Wilbur, ed., *Poe,* 7–39.

32.   See J. Gerald Kennedy, *Poe, Death, and the Life of Writing* (New Haven, Conn., and London: Yale University Press, 1987), esp. 73–74.

33.   The phrase, which Poe placed in quotation marks, is from a letter to Isaac Lea (*Letters,* 1:19).

Chapter Two

1.   There is no evidence that Poe was actually jailed—he might have used the word to mean something like "accosted," or he might have lied to Allan (see Arthur Hobson Quinn, *Edgar Allan Poe: A Critical Biography* [1941; reprint, New York: Cooper Square, 1969], 190).

2.   See Edward Pessen, *Riches, Class and Power.*

3.   See Andie Tucher, *Froth and Scum: Truth, Beauty, and the Ax Murder in America's First Mass Medium* (Chapel Hill: University of North Carolina Press, 1994), 7–20. For more on advances in publishing during this period, see Ronald J. Zboray, *A Fictive People: Antebellum Economic Development and the American Reading Public* (Oxford: Oxford University Press, 1993), 3–16.

4.   Frank Luther Mott, *A History of American Magazines, 1741–1850* (Cambridge, Mass.: Harvard University Press, 1966), 341–42.

5.   See Silverman, *Edgar A. Poe,* 140.

6.   See Alexander Hammond, "Edgar Allan Poe's *Tales of the Folio Club:* The Evolution of a Lost Book," *Library Chronicle* 41 (1976): 13–43.

7.   The *Southern Literary Messenger,* for instance, included "A Tale of a Nose" by Pertinax Placid, a pseudonym for Edward V. Sparhawk (*Southern Literary Messenger* 1 [1835]: 445–48), and, in the same issue, as "Lionizing," "A Prodigious Nose" by Democritus Jr. (468).

8.   See Terence Martin, "The Imagination at Play: Edgar Allan Poe," in *The Naiad Voice: Essays on Poe's Satiric Hoaxing,* ed. Dennis W. Eddings (Port Washington, N.Y.: Associated Faculty, 1983), 29–30; and Davidson, *Poe,* 146.

9.   Allen, *Poe and the British Magazine Tradition*; G. R. Thompson, *Poe's Fiction: Romantic Irony in the Gothic Tales* (Madison: University of Wisconsin Press, 1973).

10.   Poe's use of the name "Joseph Miller," which was synonymous with practical jokes—not to mention the fact that Miller's middle initial progresses through the alphabet with each mention of his name—would have alerted most readers not to take the article at face value.

11.   Davidson, *Poe,* 144.

12.   David Ketterer notes that the balloon is made out of newspaper and that it is shaped like a "fool's cap" (a cheap type of paper). He also points out

that Pfaall arrives at the idea of the voyage only after reading a pamphlet on "speculative astronomy"; that newspapers destroy Pfaall's trade as a bellows mender (there is obvious double meaning in Pfaall's observation that fires are now fanned with newspapers); and that Pfaall compares his water-alarm system to the art of printing ("Poe's Usage of the Hoax and the Unity of 'Hans Pfaall,' " in *The Naiad Voice: Essays on Poe's Satiric Hoaxing,* ed. Dennis W. Eddings [Port Washington, N.Y.: Associated Faculty, 1983], 88–96).

13. *Collected Writings of Edgar Allan Poe,* Vol. 1: *The Imaginary Voyages,* ed. Burton R. Pollin (Boston: Twayne, 1981), 427; hereafter cited in text as *IV.*

14. Neil Harris, *Humbug: The Art of P. T. Barnum* (Chicago and London: University of Chicago Press, 1973). See also Terence Whalen, "Edgar Allan Poe and the Horrid Laws of Political Economy," *American Quarterly* 44 (1992): 381–417.

15. *Southern Literary Messenger* 1 (1835): 580.

16. See Ketterer, "Poe's Usage," 95.

17. Edgar Allan Poe, *Essays and Reviews,* ed. G. R. Thompson (New York: Library of America, 1984), 1256; hereafter cited in text as *ER.*

18. John T. Irwin, *The Mystery to a Solution: Poe, Borges, and the Analytic Detective Story* (Baltimore and London: Johns Hopkins University Press, 1994), 111–14.

19. See Ketterer, *Rationale,* 223; and W. K. Wimsatt Jr., "Poe and the Chess Automaton," *American Literature* 11 (1939): 150.

20. Irwin, *Mystery,* 108.

21. See Robert D. Jacobs, *Poe: Journalist and Critic* (Baton Rouge: Louisiana State University Press, 1969), 94.

22. For a full discussion of the "*Norman Leslie* incident," see Sidney P. Moss, *Poe's Literary Battles* (1963; reprint, Carbondale: Southern Illinois University Press, 1969), 85–131.

23. See Jacobs, *Poe: Journalist and Critic,* 3–19.

24. Ibid., 134–58.

25. Terence Whalen, "Fables of Circulation, Strategies of Power: Poe, Capitalism, and the Selling of Intellectuals," paper presented at the Modern Language Association Convention, San Diego, Calif., December 27, 1994.

26. See Allen, *Poe and the British Magazine Tradition.* Also, Poe describes "Loss of Breath" as a satire "of the extravagancies of Blackwood" in a letter to John Pendleton Kennedy (*Letters,* 1:84). Bruce I. Weiner demonstrates that although *Blackwood's* published some sensational fiction, such stories were not actually representative of the magazine's contents ("Poe and the *Blackwood's* Tale of Sensation," in *Poe and His Times: The Artist and His Milieu,* ed. Benjamin Franklin Fisher IV [Baltimore: Enoch Pratt Free Library and the University of Baltimore, 1990], 45–65).

27. Kennedy, *Poe,* 5–17; Grace Farrell, "Mourning in Poe's *Pym,*" in *Poe's Pym: Critical Explorations,* ed. Richard Kopley (Durham, N.C.: Duke University Press, 1992), 107–16.

28. Kennedy, *Poe,* 10. See also Karen Halttunen, *Confidence Men and Painted Women: A Study of Middle-Class Culture in America, 1830–1870* (New Haven, Conn.: Yale University Press, 1982).

29. Charles May, *Edgar Allan Poe: A Study of the Short Fiction* (Boston: Twayne, 1991), 24.

30. David Ketterer describes this consciousness as "arabesque reality" throughout *Rationale*.

31. Kennedy, *Poe*, 23–24.

32. See Mabbott's introduction, *CW*, 2:192, and Kennedy, *Poe*, 20–21.

33. Thompson, *Poe's Fiction*, 80–87; Clark Griffith, "Poe's 'Ligeia' and the English Romantics," in *The Naiad Voice: Essays on Poe's Satiric Hoaxing*, ed. Dennis W. Eddings (Port Washington, N.Y.: Associated Faculty, 1983), 1–17.

34. Ketterer, *Rationale*, 182.

35. Richard P. Benton argues that "The Assignation" is "a kind of allegorical parody" ("Is Poe's 'The Assignation' a Hoax?" in *The Naiad Voice: Essays on Poe's Satiric Hoaxing*, ed. Dennis W. Eddings [Port Washington, N.Y.: Associated Faculty, 1983], 18–21).

36. Poe told T. W. White that "[t]he Tale originated in a bet that I could produce nothing effective on a subject so singular, provided I treated it seriously." Mabbott adds that "[t]he basis of this challenge pretty surely was a scandal in Baltimore about the 'robbing of graves for the sake of obtaining human teeth' for dentists" (*CW*, 2:207).

37. See May, *Edgar Allan Poe*, 64.

38. J. Gerald Kennedy, "Poe, 'Ligeia,' and the Problem of Dying Women," in *New Essays on Poe's Major Tales*, ed. Kenneth Silverman (Cambridge and New York: Cambridge University Press, 1993), 118–23; see also Griffith, "Poe's 'Ligeia.' "

39. Thompson, *Poe's Fiction*, 87.

40. Joel Porte, *The Romance in America: Studies in Cooper, Poe, Hawthorne, Melville, and James* (Middletown, Conn.: Wesleyan University Press, 1969), 74.

41. Kennedy, "Poe, 'Ligeia,' " 123, 124.

42. Leland S. Person Jr., *Aesthetic Headaches: Women and a Masculine Poetics in Poe, Melville, and Hawthorne* (Athens and London: University of Georgia Press, 1988), 30.

43. Porte, *The Romance in America*, 73.

44. For a complementary reading, see Cynthia S. Jordan, *Second Stories: The Politics of Language, Form, and Gender in Early American Fictions* (Chapel Hill and London: University of North Carolina Press, 1989), 135–39.

45. Gary Lindberg, *The Confidence Man in American Literature* (New York: Oxford University Press, 1982), 49.

Chapter Three

1. Even *Pym*'s status a "major text" is rather slippery: critical attention has come to it relatively recently (it was virtually ignored until the 1950s) and its "classic" status would still likely be challenged even by many Poe specialists.

2. Silverman, *Edgar A. Poe*, 132.

3. For information on the conditions under which Poe wrote *Pym* and substantiated theories regarding distinct phases of composition, see Joseph V. Ridgely, "The Growth of the Text," in *IV,* 29–36.

4. Burton R. Pollin traces similarities of style and other details to 36 sea narratives that Poe could have found compiled in five anthologies in his note on the text in *IV,* 37–47. *Pym* (the last chapters especially) should also be read in light of contemporary interest in ancient Egypt and hieroglyphics: see John T. Irwin, *American Hieroglyphics: The Symbol of the Egyptian Hieroglyphics in the American Renaissance* (New Haven, Conn.: Yale University Press, 1980), 43–235. Joseph J. Moldenhauer argues that Poe's use of picture-writing on Tsalal was influenced by contemporary publications concerning the "Picture Rock" near Dighton, Massachusetts, in *"Pym,* the Dighton Rock, and the Matter of Vinland," in *Poe's* Pym: *Critical Explorations,* ed. Richard Kopley (Durham, N.C.: Duke University Press, 1992), 75–94.

5. See Bruce I. Weiner, "Novels, Tales, and Problems of Form in *The Narrative of Arthur Gordon Pym,"* in *Poe's* Pym: *Critical Explorations,* ed. Richard Kopley (Durham, N.C.: Duke University Press, 1992), 44–56, for more on Poe's (and his contemporaries') awareness of the novel's conventions.

6. See, for instance, Richard Wilbur, introduction to *The Narrative of Arthur Gordon Pym* by Edgar Allan Poe (Boston: Godine, 1973); reprinted in *Responses: Prose Pieces 1953–1976* (New York: Harcourt Brace Jovanovich, 1976), 195.

7. Wilbur, introduction, 195; Burton R. Pollin, "Poe's Life Reflected in the Sources of *Pym,"* in *Poe's* Pym: *Critical Explorations,* ed. Richard Kopley (Durham, N.C.: Duke University Press, 1992), 93–103.

8. Alexander Hammond, "Consumption, Exchange, and the Literary Marketplace: From Folio Club Tales to *Pym,"* in *Poe's* Pym: *Critical Explorations,* ed. Richard Kopley (Durham, N.C.: Duke University Press, 1992), 165. See also Silverman, *Edgar A. Poe,* 136–37; and Wilbur, introduction, 213.

9. J. Gerald Kennedy, The Narrative of Arthur Gordon Pym *and the Abyss of Interpretation* (New York: Twayne, 1995), 78; see also Paul Rosenzweig, " 'Dust within the Rock': The Phantasm of Meaning in *The Narrative of Arthur Gordon Pym,"* *Studies in the Novel* 14 (1982): 137–51.

10. David Ketterer, "Tracing Shadows: *Pym* Criticism 1980–1990, with Bibliography: A Checklist of *Pym* Criticism," in *Poe's* Pym: *Critical Explorations,* ed. Richard Kopley (Durham, N.C.: Duke University Press, 1992), 237.

11. See Ketterer, *Rationale,* 134. See also Kennedy's discussion of inconsistencies in the *Grampus* chapters in *Narrative,* 45–51. Several critics have focused on the importance of the mysterious note as trope for unreadability or the displacement of meaning from writing: see, for instance, Irwin, *American Hieroglyphics,* 43–235; John Carlos Rowe, *Through the Custom House: Nineteenth-Century American Fiction and Modern Theory* (Baltimore and London: Johns Hopkins University Press, 1982), 91–110; J. Gerald Kennedy, *Poe,* 145–76; and Michael J. S. Williams, *A World of Words: Language and Displacement in the Fiction of Edgar Allan Poe* (Durham. N.C.: Duke University Press, 1988), 125–27.

12. Weiner, "Novels," 50. As Weiner points out, those "natural causes" in *Pym* sometimes prove as frightening as any flight of imagination, as is the case with Augustus's death (53).

13. Ibid., 56.

14. Patrick F. Quinn, *The French Face of Edgar Poe* (Carbondale: Southern Illinois University Press, 1957).

15. Ketterer, *Rationale*, 127.

16. See Rosenzweig, " 'Dust within the Rock,' " 141; and Kennedy, *Narrative*, 42.

17. Joseph J. Moldenhauer ("Imagination and Perversity in *The Narrative of Arthur Gordon Pym*," *Texas Studies in Literature and Language* 13 [1971]: 267–80) and J. Gerald Kennedy (*Narrative*) maintain that the *Grampus* symbolizes Pym's mind or consciousness, and that the hold of the ship suggests the irrational or subconscious part of the mind.

18. Kennedy, *Narrative*, 49.

19. Ibid.

20. Ibid., 47–51.

21. Rosenzweig, " 'Dust within the Rock,' " 138.

22. Ibid., 149. See also Kennedy, *Narrative*, 79; and Sidney Kaplan, who concludes that "there was in the Bible no prophecy of black damnation clear enough for [Poe's] needs, and he therefore wrote his own" (introduction to *The Narrative of Arthur Gordon Pym* by Edgar Allan Poe [New York: Hill and Wang, 1960]: xxiii).

23. Poe was almost certainly familiar with John Cleves Symmes's theory that the earth was hollow, with openings at the poles. An 1820 novel entitled *Symzonia: A Voyage of Discovery by Adam Seaborn* (a pseudonym, possibly for Symmes) described a utopia located within the South Pole, inhabited by purely white people (Kaplan, introduction, xiii). Rudy Rucker's 1992 novel *The Hollow Earth* (New York: Avon) utilizes this theory and features Poe as a character.

24. John T. Irwin, "The Quincuncial Network of Poe's *Pym*," in *Poe's Pym: Critical Explorations*, ed. Richard Kopley (Durham, N.C.: Duke University Press, 1992), 187.

25. See Kennedy, *Poe*, 172. See also Jean Ricardou, "The Singular Character of the Water," trans. Frank Towne, *Poe Studies* 9 (1976): 1–6; Rowe, *Through the Custom House;* Irwin, *American Hieroglyphics;* and Dennis Pahl, *Architects of the Abyss: The Indeterminate Fictions of Poe, Hawthorne, and Melville* (Columbia: University of Missouri Press, 1989).

26. Marie Bonaparte, *The Life and Works of Edgar Allan Poe: A Psychoanalytic Interpretation*, trans. John Rodker (London: Imago, 1949), 341.

27. Richard Kopley, "The Secret of *Arthur Gordon Pym*: The Text and the Source," *Studies in American Fiction* 8 (1980): 203–18; "The Hidden Journey of Arthur Gordon Pym," in *Studies in the American Renaissance 1982*, ed. Joel Myerson (Boston: Twayne, 1982), 29–51; "The 'Very Profound Undercurrent'

of *Arthur Gordon Pym,*" in *Studies in the American Renaissance 1987,* ed. Joel Myerson (Charlottesville: University Press of Virginia, 1987), 143–75.

28.   Wilbur, introduction, 213.

29.   John Carlos Rowe ("Poe, Antebellum Slavery, and Modern Criticism," in *Poe's Pym: Critical Explorations,* ed. Richard Kopley [Durham, N.C.: Duke University Press, 1992], 117–38) and Joan Dayan ("Amorous Bondage: Poe, Ladies, and Slaves," *American Literature* 66 [1994]: 239–73) argue that race is a key issue throughout Poe's work and that Poe scholars traditionally have ignored or denied its importance. The Poe Studies Association made "Poe and Race" the topic of one of its panels at the American Literature Association conference in 1996.

30.   Considerable controversy has surrounded the authorship of a review in the *Southern Literary Messenger* in 1836, bearing the title "Slavery" and discussing proslavery books by James Kirke Paulding and William Drayton. Bernard Rosenthal ("Poe, Slavery, and the *Southern Literary Messenger:* A Reexamination," *Poe Studies* 7 [1974]: 29–38) and others contend that Poe probably wrote this unequivocal endorsement of slavery based on the supposed inferiority of blacks. J. V. Ridgely ("The Authorship of the 'Paulding–Drayton Review,' " *PSA Newsletter* 20 [1992]: 1–3, 6) supports, with persuasive evidence, the claim made by William Doyle Hull II ("A Canon of the Critical Works of Edgar Allan Poe with a Study of Poe as Editor and Reviewer," Ph.D. diss., University of Virginia, 1941) that the review was written by Judge Beverly Tucker. But the fact remains, as Rowe points out, that Poe admired proslavery spokesmen such as Tucker and Thomas R. Dew and edited a magazine that promoted their ideas ("Poe, Antebellum Slavery," 119–20). In his forthcoming book *Edgar Allan Poe and the Masses,* Terence Whalen devotes a chapter to Poe's views on race, slavery, and literary nationalism. Whalen agrees that Tucker wrote the Paulding-Drayton review.

31.   Kaplan, introduction, xvii. For more on Poe's use of racist caricature and the proslavery defense in the Tsalal episode, see Sam Worley, "*The Narrative of Arthur Gordon Pym* and the Ideology of Slavery," *ESQ* 40 (1994): 219–50.

32.   Ibid. "Too-wit" is also a likely pun on "to wit" and "two-wit," the latter, as Kennedy points out, suggesting the character's "two-faced" nature (*Narrative,* 289). Pollin questions Kaplan's translation of Klock-Klock, and points out the possibility that "the spelling is intended to make an ironic point about a village outside of time" (*IV,* 322). Tsalemon also puns on "Solomon."

33.   Kaplan, introduction, xix.

34.   Ibid.

35.   Ibid., xix–xxi.

36.   Dana D. Nelson, *The Word in Black and White: Reading "Race" in American Literature, 1638–1867* (New York and Oxford: Oxford University Press, 1992), 90–108.

37.   Ibid., 98–99.

38.   Ibid., 99.

39. Ibid., 99–100.

40. Oliver Sacks, *An Anthropologist on Mars: Seven Paradoxical Tales* (New York: Knopf, 1995), 3–42.

Chapter Four

1. William Charvat, *Literary Publishing in America, 1790–1850* (1959; reprint, Boston: University of Massachusetts Press, 1993), 23.

2. Silverman believes Poe was a novice as a cryptographer, commenting that the ciphers he solved were rather easy (*Edgar A. Poe*, 152–53). Poe's interest in cryptography has gained notable attention recently: see Terence Whalen, "The Code for Gold: Edgar Allan Poe and Cryptography," *Representations* 46 (1994): 35–57; and Shawn Rosenheim, *The Cryptographic Imagination: Secret Writing from Edgar Poe to the Internet* (Baltimore and London: Johns Hopkins University Press, 1997).

3. See John Ward Ostrom, "Edgar A. Poe: His Income as Literary Entrepreneur," *Poe Studies* 15 (1982): 1, 3. Ostrom calculates Poe's total income from February 1841 through March 1842 (the period he was employed by Graham) to have been $1,177 (3). See also Bruce I. Weiner, *The Most Noble of Professions: Poe and the Poverty of Authorship* (Baltimore: Enoch Pratt Free Library, Edgar Allan Poe Society, and the Library of the Unversity of Baltimore, 1987).

4. Silverman, *Edgar A. Poe*, 178.

5. Ibid., 179.

6. A. B. Harris, "Edgar A. Poe," *Hearth and Home* 8 (1875): 24; quoted in Thomas and Jackson, *Poe Log*, 358.

7. David S. Reynolds, *Beneath the American Renaissance: The Subversive Imagination in the Age of Emerson and Melville* (New York: Knopf, 1988), chapter 8, esp. 230; T. J. Matheson, "Poe's 'The Black Cat' " as a Critique of Temperance Literature," *Mosaic* 19 (1986): 69–81; John Cleman, "Irresistible Impulses: Edgar Allan Poe and the Insanity Defense," *American Literature* 63 (1991): 640.

8. Mark Twain, *Tales, Speeches, Essays, and Sketches*, ed. Tom Quirk (New York: Penguin, 1994), 120.

9. Poe added an autobiographical wrinkle to the story by giving the Wilsons his own birthday and using the name of the school he attended as a boy in England, the Manor House School of the Reverend John Bransby at Stoke-Newington (Mabbott, *CW*, 2:449).

10. Valentine C. Hubbs, "The Struggle of the Wills in Poe's 'William Wilson,' " *Studies in American Fiction* 11 (1983): 74.

11. Ibid., 78. Ruth Sullivan argues that since the moral awareness the narrator shows throughout the story must come from the superego, Wilson II must be the narrator: "Loosely, William Wilson's superego tells the story of William Wilson's id" ("William Wilson's Double," *Studies in Romanticism* 15 [1976]: 254).

12. Ralph Waldo Emerson, *Selected Essays,* ed. Larzer Ziff (New York: Penguin, 1982), 104.

13. See Mary Kupiec Cayton, "The Making of an American Prophet: Emerson, His Audience, and the Rise of the Culture Industry in Nineteenth-Century America," in *Ralph Waldo Emerson: A Collection of Critical Essays,* ed. Lawrence Buell (Englewood Cliffs, N.J.: Prentice Hall, 1993), 77–100.

14. See Theron Britt, "The Common Property of the Mob: Democracy and Identity in Poe's 'William Wilson,' " *Mississippi Quarterly* 48 (1995): 197–210, esp. 205–6.

15. Emerson, *Selected Essays,* 96.

16. Ibid., 177.

17. Alexis de Tocqueville, *Democracy in America,* ed. J. P. Mayer and Max Lerner, trans. George Lawrence (New York, Evanston, and London: Harper & Row, 1966), 478.

18. See Julia Stern, "Double Talk: The Rhetoric of the Whisper in Poe's 'William Wilson,' " *ESQ* 40 (1994): 185–218. Stern relates Poe's rhetoric in "William Wilson" to Antebellum American politics, particularly the issue of secession.

19. Ibid., 195–96.

20. Kennedy, *Poe,* 199.

21. See D. H. Lawrence, "Edgar Allan Poe," in *Studies in Classic American Literature* (1923; reprint, New York: Penguin, 1977), esp. 81–85.

22. G. R. Thompson detects an element of burlesque in Poe's use of "The Mad Trist," suggesting that Poe deliberately overdoes his Gothic effects to create ironic distance from his material (*Poe's Fiction,* 93–95).

23. See Richard Wilbur, "The House of Poe," in *The Recognition of Edgar Allan Poe: Selected Criticism since 1829,* ed. Eric W. Carlson (Ann Arbor: University of Michigan Press, 1966), 255–77; Hoffman, 295–316; Thompson, *Poe's Fiction,* 87–98. Thompson's discussion of "Usher" became the subject of an exchange between himself and Patrick F. Quinn regarding (primarily) the narrator's reliability. See Quinn, "A Misreading of Poe's 'The Fall of the House of Usher,' " 303–12; Thompson, "Poe and the Paradox of Terror: Structures of Heightened Consciousness in 'The Fall of the House of Usher,' " 313–40; and Quinn, " 'Usher' Again: Trust the Teller!" 341–53, all in *Ruined Eden of the Present: Hawthorne, Melville, and Poe,* ed. G. R. Thompson and Virgil Lokke (West Lafayette, Ind.: Purdue University Press, 1981).

24. In discussing the narrator's escape from the house, Hoffman likens him to Poe rather than to the reader (*Poe,* 314).

25. In a review of *The Gift for 1842,* in which "Eleonora" appeared, Poe admitted that the tale "is not ended so well as it might be—a good subject spoiled by hurry in the handling" (*CW,* 2:635).

26. See Richard Wilbur, "Eleonora," in *Critical Essays on Edgar Allan Poe,* ed. Eric W. Carlson (Boston: G. K. Hall, 1987), 138–42; and Wilbur's introduction to *Poe: Complete Poems,* 14–16. According to Wilbur, "Ermengarde . . .

is a young woman of the real world subjectively transformed or "Pythagorized" by the hero. He *sees* her as Eleonora" (*Poe*, 16).

27. Wilbur refers to the story as a "hybrid" of poem and tale ("Eleonora," 140).

28. Kennedy discusses the painting, the narrative in the book, and the narrator's "gaze" as successive "translations" (*Poe*, 60 – 63).

29. May, *Edgar Allan Poe*, 52.

30. Person, *Aesthetic*, 41 – 44. See also Elisabeth Bronfen, *Over Her Dead Body: Death, Femininity and the Aesthetic* (New York: Routledge, 1992), 111–17.

31. Ketterer, *Rationale*, 8, 10.

32. Joan Tyler Mead, "Poe's 'The Man That Was Used Up': Another Bugaboo Campaign," *Studies in Short Fiction* 23 (1986): 286 n.

33. Ketterer identifies the old man as the narrator's double (*Rationale*, 103).

34. See May, *Edgar Allan Poe*, 76 – 78; Kennedy, *Poe*, 132–35; Ketterer, *Rationale*, 195. See also E. Arthur Robinson, "Poe's 'The Tell-Tale Heart,' " *Nineteenth-Century Fiction* 19 (1965): 369 – 78.

35. Wilbur, ed., *Poe*, 132 n.

36. Kennedy, *Poe*, 132–33.

37. May, *Edgar Allan Poe*, 78. See also Robinson, "Poe's 'The Tell-Tale Heart,' " 377.

38. Matheson, "Poe's 'The Black Cat,' " 70 – 74.

39. See Susan Amper, "Untold Story: The Lying Narrator in 'The Black Cat,' " *Studies in Short Fiction* 29 (1992): 475 – 85.

40. See also William Crisman, who argues that the black cat is the object of the narrator's jealousy (" 'Mere Household Events' in Poe's 'The Black Cat,' " *Studies in American Fiction* 12 [1984]: 87–90).

41. Amper claims that the bas relief image is actually the wife buried behind the wall ("Untold Story," 481).

42. Ibid., 478 – 79, 483 – 84.

43. Jean-Paul Sartre, *No Exit and Three Other Plays* (1944; New York: Vintage, 1992), 45.

44. Christopher Benfey, "Poe and the Unreadable: 'The Black Cat' and 'The Tell-Tale Heart,' " in *New Essays on Poe's Major Tales*, ed. Kenneth Silverman (Cambridge and New York: Cambridge University Press, 1993), 43. Benfey examines this theme of "The Black Cat" with extended reference to a Robert Frost quotation and Rainer Maria Rilke's *The Notebooks of Malte Laurids Brigge*.

45. Michael Clifton, "Down Hecate's Chain: Infernal Inspiration in Three of Poe's Tales," *Nineteenth-Century Literature* 41 (1986): 224.

46. May, *Edgar Allan Poe*, 96.

47. Clifton, "Down Hecate's Chain," 224; Jeanne M. Malloy, "Apocalyptic Imagery and the Fragmentation of the Psyche: 'The Pit and the Pendulum,' " *Nineteenth-Century Literature* 46 (1991): 82–83; Ketterer, *Rationale*,

203–5. See also David H. Hirsch, "The Pit and the Apocalypse," *Sewanee Review* 76 (1968): 632–52.

48.   Hirsch, "Pit and the Apocalypse," 650.

49.   Ibid., 639–44. See also May, *Edgar Allan Poe*, 96.

50.   Killis Campbell, "Marginalia on Longfellow, Lowell, and Poe," *Modern Language Notes* 42 (1927): 520; Fred Madden, " 'A Descent into the Maelström': Suggestions of a Tall Tale," *Studies in the Humanities* 14 (1987): 134.

51.   See Gerald M. Sweeney, "Beauty and Truth: Poe's 'A Descent into the Maelström,' " *Poe Studies* 6 (1973): 22–25; Ketterer, *Rationale*, 119–21; Kenneth V. Egan Jr., "Descent to an Ascent: Poe's Use of Perspective in 'A Descent into the Maelström,' " *Studies in Short Fiction* 19 (1982): 157–62. Tracy Ware surveys "Maelström" criticism to help establish a strong, original argument that uses elements of both the providential and ironic readings while showing the shortcomings of each (" 'A Descent into the Maelström': The Status of Scientific Rhetoric in a Perverse Romance," *Studies in Short Fiction* 29 [1992]: 77–84).

52.   May, *Edgar Allan Poe*, 102–3; Kermit Vanderbilt, "Art and Nature in 'The Masque of the Red Death,' " *Nineteenth-Century Fiction* 22 (1968): 379–91.

53.   Joseph Patrick Roppolo, "Meaning and 'The Masque of the Red Death,' " *Poe: A Collection of Critical Essays,* ed. Robert Regan (Englewood Cliffs, N.J.: Prentice-Hall, 1967), 140.

54.   Ibid., 137. See also Walter Blair, "Poe's Conception of Incident and Tone in the Tale," *Modern Philology* 41 (1944): 228–40.

55.   Roppolo, "Meaning," 141.

56.   J. Gerald Kennedy argues that "Masque" presents death as "a presence-as-absence whose meaning is forever denied to presence and already accomplished in absence" (*Poe*, 203).

Chapter Five

1.   See N. Bryllion Fagin, *The Histrionic Mr. Poe* (Baltimore: Johns Hopkins University Press, 1949) on the influence of theater on Poe's work, particularly his approach to comedy.

2.   Stuart Levine and Susan F. Levine, "Comic Satires and Grotesques," in *A Companion to Poe Studies,* ed. Eric W. Carlson (Westport, Conn., and London: Greenwood, 1996), 134.

3.   See Jean-Paul Weber, "Edgar Poe or the Theme of the Clock," trans. Claude Richard and Robert Regan, in *Poe: A Collection of Critical Essays,* ed. Robert Regan (Englewood Cliffs, N.J.: Prentice-Hall, 1967), 79–81.

4.   William Whipple, "Poe's Political Satire," *Texas University Studies in English* 35 (1956): 88–91. For a broader sociopolitical reading, see Katrina E. Bachinger, "The Aesthetics of (Not) Keeping in Step: Reading the Consumer Mobocracy of Poe's 'The Devil in the Belfry' against Peacock," *Modern Language Quarterly* 51 (1990): 513–33.

5. Robert Regan, "Hawthorne's 'Plagiary'; Poe's Duplicity," in *The Naiad Voice: Essays on Poe's Satiric Hoaxing,* ed. Dennis W. Eddings (Port Washington, N.Y.: Associated Faculty, 1983), 73–87.

6. See Whipple, "Poe's Political Satire," 91–95; Cornelia Varner, "Notes on Poe's Use of Contemporary Materials in Certain of His Stories," *Journal of English and Germanic Philology* 32 (1933): 77–80; and Jonathan Auerbach, *The Romance of Failure: First-Person Fictions of Poe, Hawthorne, and James* (New York: Oxford University Press, 1989), 53–55.

7. Kennedy, *Poe,* 115; May, *Edgar Allan Poe,* 35. See also John E. Reilly, "Poe in Pillory: An Early Version of a Satire by A. J. H. Duganne," *Poe Studies* 6 (1973): 9–12. Reilly reprints and analyzes Duganne's satiric portrait of Poe, which begins, "With tomahawk upraised for deadly blow, / Behold our literary Mohawk, Poe!"

8. See also William Whipple, "Poe, Clark, and Thingum Bob," *American Literature* 29 (1957): 312–16, and Moss, *Poe's Literary Battles,* chapter 4, for a full discussion of Poe's reference to Clark and his brother, Willis Gaylord Clark.

9. Timothy H. Scherman, "The Authority Effect: Poe and the Politics of Reputation in the Pre-Industry of American Publishing," *Arizona Quarterly* 49.3 (1993): 14.

10. See Halttunen, *Confidence Men,* 1–55; and Lindberg, *Confidence Man,* 48–69.

11. David M. Reese, *Humbugs of New York* (1838; reprint, Freeport, N.Y.: Books for Libraries Press, 1971), vi, 17.

12. Quoted in Lindberg, *Confidence Man,* 6.

13. See Lindberg, *Confidence Man,* 93–96.

14. See A. J. Leo Lemay, "Poe's 'The Business Man': Its Context and Satire of Franklin's Autobiography," *Poe Studies* 15 (1982): 29–37.

15. Charles Goodrum and Helen Dalrymple, *Advertising in America: The First 200 Years* (New York: Abrams, 1990), 18, 21.

16. See Terence Whalen, "Poe's 'Diddling' and the Depression: Notes on the Sources of Swindling," *Studies in American Fiction* 23 (1995): 195–201.

17. See Lindberg, *Confidence Man,* 62–63.

18. See J. Marshall Trieber, "The Scornful Grin: A Study of Poesque Humor," *Poe Studies* 5 (1972): 32–34; and Hoffman, *Poe,* 181–82.

19. See Thomas and Jackson, *Poe Log,* 259; and Silverman, *Edgar A. Poe,* 138.

20. Pollin, introduction to *The Journal of Julius Rodman,* in *IV,* 512.

21. Ketterer, *Rationale,* 141–45; Stuart C. Levine, *Edgar Poe: Seer and Craftsman* (Deland, Fla.: Everett/Edwards, 1972), 252–60, and Ljungquist, *Grand,* 10–14, 44–46.

22. Thomas and Jackson, *Poe Log,* 458–61; and Charles F. Heartman and James R. Canny, *A Bibliography of First Printings of the Writings of Edgar Allan Poe* (Hattiesburg, Miss.: Brook Farm, 1943), 85.

23. Edgar Allan Poe, *Collected Writings of Edgar Allan Poe*, Vol. 2: *The Brevities: Pinakidia, Marginalia. Fifty Suggestions and Other Works*, ed. Burton R. Pollin (New York: Gordian Press, 1985), 175; hereafter cited in text as *Brevities.*

24. May, *Edgar Allan Poe*, 45.

25. G. R. Thompson suggests that "A Tale of the Ragged Mountains" is intentionally ludicrous, partly because it parodies *Edgar Huntly* by Charles Brockden Brown; he also argues that Templeton murdered Bedloe (*Poe's Fiction*, 149–52).

26. Ibid., 150.

27. May, *Edgar Allan Poe*, 48.

28. Ibid., 48–49.

29. See Mabbott, *CW*, 3:971; and Kennedy, *Poe*, 33–40.

30. Kennedy, *Poe*, 54, 55.

31. David Van Leer, "Detecting Truth: The World of the Dupin Tales," in *New Essays on Poe's Major Tales*, ed. Kenneth Silverman (Cambridge and New York: Cambridge University Press, 1993), 65–66; Thomas Joswick, "Moods of Mind: The Tales of Detection, Crime, and Punishment," in *A Companion to Poe Studies*, ed. Eric W. Carlson (Westport, Conn., and London: Greenwood, 1996), 238, See also Howard Haycraft, *Murder for Pleasure: The Life and Times of the Detective Story* (New York: D. Appleton-Century, 1941); and Robert A. W. Lowndes, "The Contribution of Edgar Allan Poe," in *The Mystery Writer's Art*, ed. Francis M. Nevins (Bowling Green, Ohio: Bowling Green University Popular Press, 1970), 1–18.

32. See Bonnie Shannon McMullen's intriguing analysis, "Lifting the Lid on Poe's 'Oblong Box,' " *Studies in American Romanticism* 23 (1995): 203–14. J. Gerald Kennedy focuses on "The Man of the Crowd" and "The Oblong Box" as transitional stories, signaling the beginning and end of Poe's experiments with tales of ratiocination ("The Limits of Reason: Poe's Deluded Detectives," *American Literature* 47 [1975]: 184–96).

33. Kennedy, *Poe*, 118.

34. Patrick P. Quinn, *French Face of Edgar Poe*, 230.

35. See David Leverenz, "Poe and Gentry Virginia," in *The American Face of Edgar Allan Poe*, ed. Shawn Rosenheim and Stephen Rachman (Baltimore and London: Johns Hopkins University Press, 1995): 210–36, esp. 224–28; Linda Patterson Miller, "The Writer in the Crowd: Poe's Urban Vision," *ESQ* 44 (1979): 325–39; and Robert H. Byer, "Mysteries of the City: A Reading of Poe's 'The Man of the Crowd,' " in *Ideology and Classic American Literature*, ed. Sacvan Bercovitch and Myra Jehlen (Cambridge and New York: Cambridge University Press, 1986), 221–46.

36. Amy Gilman, "Edgar Allan Poe Detecting the City," in *The Myth-making Frame of Mind: Social Imagination in American Culture*, ed. James Gilbert et al. (Belmont, Calif.: Wadsworth, 1993), 72.

37. See Halttunen, *Confidence Men*, 33–55; and Reynolds, *Beneath the American Renaissance*, 82–84. On direct sources for "Rue Morgue" and more

commentary on its allusions to newspapers, see Richard Kopley, *Edgar Allan Poe and the Philadelphia Saturday News* (Baltimore: Enoch Pratt Free Library, Edgar Allan Poe Society, and the Library of the University of Baltimore, 1991).

38. Gilman, "Edgar Allan Poe," 77.

39. Stephen Rachman, " 'Es lässt sich nicht schreiben': Plagiarism and 'The Man of the Crowd,' " in *The American Face of Edgar Allan Poe*, ed. Shawn Rosenheim and Stephen Rachman (Baltimore and London: Johns Hopkins University Press, 1995), 55.

40. Van Leer, "Detecting Truth," 78–82. See also Laura Saltz, " '(Horrible to Relate!)': Recovering the Body of Marie Rogêt," in *The American Face of Edgar Allan Poe*, ed. Shawn Rosenheim and Stephen Rachman (Baltimore and London: Johns Hopkins University Press, 1995), 237–67.

41. Irwin, *Mystery*, 1.

42. Ibid., 196.

43. Liahna Klenman Babener, "The Shadow's Shadow: The Motif of the Double in Edgar Allan Poe's 'The Purloined Letter,' " in *The Purloined Poe: Lacan, Derrida, and Psychoanalytic Reading*, ed. John P. Muller and William J. Richardson (Baltimore and London: Johns Hopkins University Press, 1988), 323–34.

44. Ibid., 332–33.

45. Ibid., 333.

46. See Kennedy on rivalry in "The Purloined Letter" (*Poe*, 120–28).

47. Jacques Lacan, "Seminar on 'The Purloined Letter,' " trans. Jeffrey Mehlman, in *The Purloined Poe: Lacan, Derrida, and Psychoanalytic Reading*, ed. John P. Muller and William J. Richardson (Baltimore and London: Johns Hopkins University Press, 1988), 32; Jacques Derrida, "The Purveyor of Truth," in *The Purloined Poe: Lacan, Derrida, and Psychoanalytic Reading*, ed. John P. Muller and William J. Richardson (Baltimore and London: Johns Hopkins University Press, 1988), 179–81; Irwin, *Mystery*, 7.

48. Weiner, "Most Noble," 18–21.

49. Whalen, "Code for Gold," 40, 49.

50. Michael Williams, " 'The *Language* of the Cipher': Interpretation in 'The Gold Bug,' " *American Literature* 53 (1982): 655–57.

51. Ibid., 646–60.

Chapter Six

1. Silverman, *Edgar A. Poe*, 237.

2. Critics tend to read "The Philosophy of Composition" ironically. See, for instance, Hoffman, *Poe*, 88–92; Ketterer, *Rationale*, 233; and Silverman, *Edgar A. Poe*, 296–97. For a full discussion of "Philosophy" as a rewriting of "The Raven," see Leland S. Person Jr., "Poe's Composition of Philosophy: Reading and Writing 'The Raven,' " *Arizona Quarterly* 46 (1990): 1–15.

3. See Auerbach, *The Romance of Failure*, 61.

    4. Ostrom, "Edgar A. Poe," 5.
    5. Silverman, *Edgar A. Poe,* 276.
    6. Ibid., 290.
    7. Ibid., 290–91.
    8. See Thomas and Jackson, *Poe Log,* 623; and Silverman, *Edgar A. Poe,* 290–91.
    9. Silverman, *Edgar A. Poe,* 313, 328.
   10. Ibid., 301, 329.
   11. Ibid., 340–44.
   12. See also Silverman, *Edgar A. Poe,* 379–82.
   13. Ibid., 374.
   14. Ibid., 363–65.
   15. Ibid., 386–88.
   16. Ibid., 408.
   17. Ibid., 415.
   18. Ibid., 416–19.
   19. Ibid., 426–27.
   20. Ibid., 427.
   21. Ibid., 433, 430.
   22. *Collected Writings of Edgar Allan Poe,* Vol. 3: *Writings in* The Broadway Journal, *Nonfictional Prose,* ed. Burton R. Pollin (New York: Gordian, 1986), 68; hereafter cited in text as *BJ.*
   23. Silverman, *Edgar A. Poe,* 255.
   24. Burton R. Pollin, "Poe as Author of the 'Outis' Letter and 'The Bird of the Dream,' " *Poe Studies* 20 (June 1987): 10–15; Silverman, *Edgar A. Poe,* 251. The most persuasive case against Poe's authorship of the Outis letter is Kent Ljungquist and Buford Jones, "The Identity of 'Outis': A Further Chapter in the Poe–Longfellow War," *American Literature* 60 (1988): 402–15. Ljungquist and Jones identify Lawrence Labree, editor of the New York *Rover,* as Outis.
   25. Quoted in Moss, *Poe's Literary Battles,* 153.
   26. *Weekly Mirror,* 1 (February 15, 1845), 306. See Weiner, "Most Noble," 8.
   27. See, for instance, Francis B. Dedmond, " 'The Cask of Amontillado' and the War of the Literati," *Modern Language Quarterly* 15 (1954): 137–46; Kennedy, *Poe,* 138, 143; and Silverman, *Edgar A. Poe,* 316. As Kennedy also suggests, the story's equation of wine with death also has autobiographical significance (*Poe,* 141.)
   28. Kennedy, *Poe,* 143.
   29. Ibid., 140.
   30. See, for instance, Walter Stepp, "The Ironic Double in Poe's 'Cask of Amontillado,' " *Studies in Short Fiction* 13 (1976): 447–53; Kennedy, *Poe,* 141–43; and May, *Edgar Allan Poe,* 79–81.
   31. Kennedy, *Poe,* 142.

32. Ibid., 142–43.

33. Patrick White, " 'The Cask of Amontillado': A Case for the Defense," *Studies in Short Fiction* 26 (1989): 552. White theorizes that the snake represents the Montresors. Charles E. May, on the other hand, speculates that if "the foot signifies Montresor, then the snake Fortunato who has bitten him still has his fangs embedded" (*Edgar Allan Poe,* 81).

34. Ketterer, *Rationale,* 111. Ketterer retains Poe's original spelling of "Luchresi," which he later changed to "Luchesi."

35. Ibid., 112–14; see also May, *Edgar Allan Poe,* 38–39.

36. Joan Dayan, "Romance and Race," in *The Columbia History of the American Novel,* ed. Emory Elliott (New York: Oxford University Press, 1991), 104.

37. Elise Lemire placed "Rue Morgue" in the context of whites' fear of miscegenation in " 'The Murders in the Rue Morgue': Detective Fiction and Amalgamation Discourse in Jacksonian Philadelphia," a paper given at the Modern Language Association Convention, San Diego, Calif., December 29, 1994.

38. See Jerome Denuncio, "Fact, Fiction, Fatality: Poe's 'Thousand-and-Second Tale of Scheherazade,' " *Studies in Short Fiction* 27 (1990): 365–70.

39. See Andrew Levy, *The Culture and Commerce of the American Short Story* (Cambridge and New York: Cambridge University Press, 1993), 10–26.

40. David Long, "Poe's Political Identity: A Mummy Unswathed," *Poe Studies* 23 (1990): 8.

41. See, for instance, Poe's 1844 letter to James Russell Lowell, in which he states, "I cannot agree to lose sight of man the individual, in man the mass" (*Letters,* 1:256–57).

Chapter Seven

1. See also G. P. Putnam's account of Poe's solicitation of the *Eureka* manuscript in Thomas and Jackson, *Poe Log,* 731.

2. See Ketterer, *Rationale,* 255 n, for a list of critics (writing before 1979) who regard *Eureka* as the key to the Poe canon. Joan Dayan devotes a 60-page chapter of her book *Fables of Mind: An Inquiry into Poe's Fiction* (New York: Oxford University Press, 1987) to *Eureka;* John Limon, whom Ketterer cites for an earlier study, discusses *Eureka* at length in *The Place of Fiction in the Time of Science* (Cambridge and New York: Cambridge University Press, 1990), 70–120.

3. See Ketterer on Poe's use of irony, *Rationale,* 255–77, esp. 258. Beverly Hume argues that we should read against the "narrator" of *Eureka* as we would other unreliable narrators in Poe ("Poe's Mad Narrator in *Eureka,*" *Essays in Arts and Sciences* 22 [October 1993]: 51–65). See also Hoffman, who reads *Eureka* as one of Poe's tales, a "tale which is a poem" (*Poe,* 274).

4. *Letters,* 2:361–62; Davidson, *Poe,* 224–26; Williams, *A World of Words,* 146–47; Silverman, *Edgar A. Poe,* 339–40; Jacobs, *Poe: Journalist and*

Critic, 415. See also Silverman's analysis of *Eureka (Edgar A. Poe,* 531–34); and Barbara Cantalupo's survey of attempts to summarize or outline the text in "*Eureka:* Poe's Novel Universe," in *A Companion to Poe Studies,* ed. Eric W. Carlson (Westport, Conn., and London: Greenwood, 1996), 324–26.

    5. See Hoffman, Poe, 280.

    6. Ketterer, *Rationale,* 256.

    7. Dayan, *Fables,* 27.

    8. See Cantalupo, "*Eureka,*" 334–35. See also Susan Welsh, "The Value of Analogical Evidence: Poe's *Eureka* in the Context of a Scientific Debate," *Modern Language Studies* 21 (1991): 3–15.

    9. See Barbara Cantalupo, " 'Of or Pertaining to a Higher Power': Involution in *Eureka,*" *ATQ* 4 (1990): 81–90.

    10. Hume, "Poe's Mad Narrator," 51–65.

    11. See Silverman, *Edgar A. Poe,* 531–34; and Hoffman, who claims Poe projects onto the cosmos the conflict between Eros and Thanatos, "between the life-wish and the will to self-destruction" (*Poe,* 289).

    12. Emerson, *Selected Essays,* 39.

    13. Ketterer, *Rationale,* 272.

    14. Robert Frost, "The Figure a Poem Makes," in *Complete Poems of Robert Frost* (New York: Holt, Rinehart and Winston, 1956), vi.

    15. See Jules Zanger, "Poe's American Garden: 'The Domain of Arnheim,' " *American Transcendental Quarterly,* no. 50 (1981): 94.

    16. Jeffrey A. Hess, "Sources and Aesthetics of Poe's Landscape Fiction," *American Quarterly* 22 (1970): 177–89.

    17. Andrew Horn, " 'A Refined Thebaid': Wealth and Social Disengagement in Poe's 'The Domain of Arnheim,' " *ESQ* 27 (1981): 194. See also Dayan, *Fables,* 96–107.

    18. James Russell Lowell, *The Complete Poetical Works of James Russell Lowell* (Boston and New York: Houghton, Mifflin, 1896), 140.

    19. Silverman, *Edgar A. Poe,* 535.

    20. Ibid.

    21. See [Theodore Watts-Duncan], "Poetry," *Encyclopedia Britannica,* 11th ed. (1910–1911), vol. 21, 880, cited in Mabbott's introduction, *CW,* 1:409.

    22. As Mabbott notes, it is a reworking of "To —— " ("Should my early life seem") of 1829 (*CW,* 1:450).

    23. See Silverman, *Edgar A. Poe,* 240–41.

    24. See Kennedy, *Poe,* 71–73; and Silverman, *Edgar A. Poe,* 336–37.

    25. See Wilbur, ed., *Poe,* 150 n.

    26. Richard Wilbur reads the entire Poe canon in similar terms. See his introduction to *Poe* and his essays "Edgar Allan Poe" and "The House Of Poe."

    27. On the attending physician's unreliability, see W. T. Bandy, "Dr. Moran and the Poe-Reynolds Myth," in *Myths and Reality: The Mysterious Mr. Poe,* ed. Benjamin Franklin Fisher IV (Baltimore: Edgar Allan Poe Society,

1987), 26–36. See also Scott Peeples, "Life Writing/Death Writing: Biographical Versions of Poe's Final Hours," *Biography: An Interdisciplinary Quarterly* 18 (1995): 328–38.

    28. See Blake Eskin, "Mad Dogs and English Professors," *Lingua Franca*, December/January 1997, 10–11.

    29. See Ian Walker, "The Poe Legend," in *A Companion to Poe Studies,* ed. Eric W. Carlson (Westport, Conn., and London: Greenwood, 1996), 19–42.

Selected Bibliography

PRIMARY SOURCES

The Collected Works of Edgar Allan Poe. 3 vols. Edited by Thomas Ollive Mabbott. Cambridge, Mass.: Harvard University Press, 1969–1978. Definitive scholarly edition of the poetry and short fiction, with excellent introductions and notes.

The Collected Writings of Edgar Allan Poe. 4 vols. to date. Edited by Burton R. Pollin. Boston: Twayne; New York: Gordion, 1981– . Picks up where Mabbott left off. So far Pollin has edited *Pym,* "Hans Pfaall," "Rodman" (in one volume), the Marginalia and other "brevities," and the *Broadway Journal* prose.

The Complete Works of Edgar Allan Poe. 17 vols. Edited by James A. Harrison. New York: Thomas Y. Crowell, 1902. The "standard" edition prior to Mabbott and Pollin, still used by scholars, especially for essays and reviews not yet edited by Pollin.

Essays and Reviews. Edited by G. R. Thompson. New York: Library of America, 1984. Best edition in print of most of Poe's essays and reviews.

Eureka: A Prose Poem by Edgar Allan Poe. Edited by Richard P. Benton. Hartford, Conn.: Transcendental Books, 1974. Scholarly edition with line numbers and an essay by Benton.

The Letters of Edgar Allan Poe. 2 vols. Edited by John Ward Ostrom. New York: Gordian, 1966.

Poetry and Tales. Edited by Patrick F. Quinn. New York: Library of America, 1984. Reliable text with sparse but helpful notes; includes *Pym* and *Eureka.*

Poetry, Tales, and Selected Essays. Edited by Patrick F. Quinn and G. R. Thompson. New York: Library of America, 1996. Paperback "college edition" of *Poetry and Tales* along with four major essays.

SECONDARY SOURCES

Reference Works

American Literary Scholarship: An Annual. Durham, N.C., and London: Duke University Press, 1963– . Includes an annual review of Poe scholarship, currently written by Benjamin Franklin Fisher IV.

Carlson, Eric W., ed. *A Companion to Poe Studies.* Westport, Conn., and London: Greenwood, 1996.

Dameron, J. Lasley, and Irby B. Cauthen Jr. *Edgar Allan Poe: A Bibliography of Criticism, 1827–1967.* Charlottesville: University Press of Virginia, 1974.

Frank, Frederick S., and Anthony Magistrale. *The Poe Encyclopedia.* Westport, Conn., and London: Greenwood, 1997.

Hyneman, Esther F. *Edgar Allan Poe: An Annotated Bibliography of Books and Articles in English, 1827–1973.* Boston: G. K. Hall, 1974.

"International Poe Bibliography." (Formerly "Current Poe Bibliography.") *Poe Studies* (Journal), 1971– . Annotated listing of Poe scholarship, last updated through 1993.

Pollin, Burton R. *Word Index to Poe's Fiction.* New York: Gordian Press, 1982.

————. *Images of Poe's Works: A Comprehensive Descriptive Catalogue of Illustrations.* Westport, Conn.: Greenwood, 1989.

Smith, Ronald L. *Poe in the Media: Screen, Songs, and Spoken Word Recordings.* New York: Garland, 1990.

Wiley, Elizabeth. *Concordance to the Poetry of Edgar Allan Poe.* Selinsgrove, Penn.: Susquehanna University Press, 1989.

Books and Parts of Books

Allen, Michael. *Poe and the British Magazine Tradition.* New York: Oxford University Press, 1969. Analyzes the influence of *Blackwood's* and other British magazines on Poe, arguing that Poe's magazine writing was shaped by his efforts to reach both elite readers and the masses.

Bonaparte, Marie. *The Life and Works of Edgar Allan Poe: A Psychoanalytic Interpretation.* Translated by John Rodker. London: Imago, 1949. Fearless (and for many readers preposterous) Freudian analysis of Poe, treating his works as dreams.

Carlson, Eric W., ed. *The Recognition of Edgar Allan Poe: Selected Criticism since 1829.* Ann Arbor: University of Michigan Press, 1966. Excellent collection of Poe criticism through the mid-1960s. Includes influential essays by Allen Tate, W. H. Auden, and Richard Wilbur, among others.

Charvat, William. *Literary Publishing in America, 1790–1850.* 1959. Reprint, Boston: University of Massachusetts Press, 1993. Groundbreaking study that helps establish a context for Poe's writing and career.

Davidson, Edward H. *Poe: A Critical Study.* Cambridge, Mass.: Harvard University Press, 1957. One of the first major book-length critical studies of Poe; impressive close readings focusing on Poe's philosophy and aesthetics.

Dayan, Joan. *Fables of Mind: An Inquiry into Poe's Fiction.* New York: Oxford University Press, 1987. Philosophical study that sheds light particularly on lesser-known works.

————. "Romance and Race." In *The Columbia History of the American Novel,* edited by Emory Elliott. New York: Columbia University Press, 1991. Influential essay on racism and slavery in Poe.

Eddings, Dennis W., ed. *The Naiad Voice: Essays on Poe's Satiric Hoaxing*. Port
    Washington, N.Y.: Associated Faculty, 1983. Includes 15 essays by such
    reputable Poe scholars as Richard P. Benton, Eddings, Benjamin Franklin
    Fisher IV, Clark Griffith, J. Gerald Kennedy, David Ketterer, Kent P.
    Ljungquist, Robert Regan, Claude Richard, and Bruce I. Weiner.
Fisher, Benjamin Franklin, IV, ed. *Poe and His Times: The Artist and His Milieu*.
    Baltimore: Enoch Pratt Free Library and the University of Baltimore,
    1990. Collection of essays on specific contexts of Poe's work and possible
    influences.
Gilman, Amy. "Edgar Allan Poe Detecting the City." In *The Mythmaking Frame
    of Mind: Social Imagination in American Culture*, edited by James Gilbert et
    al. Belmont, Calif.: Wadsworth, 1993. Analyzes Poe's urban vision and
    casts Dupin as "the ultimate modern man."
Hoffman, Daniel. *Poe Poe Poe Poe Poe Poe Poe*. 1972. New York: Paragon House,
    1990. Insightful and refreshingly irreverent study of Poe with psychoan-
    alytic emphasis.
Irwin, John T. *American Hieroglyphics: The Symbol of the Egyptian Hieroglyphics in
    the American Renaissance*. New Haven, Conn.: Yale University Press,
    1980. Influential study of *Pym* in particular; combines historical research
    with a poststructural emphasis on writing and indeterminacy.
————. *The Mystery to a Solution: Poe, Borges, and the Analytic Detective Story*. Bal-
    timore and London: Johns Hopkins University Press, 1994. A tour de
    force of literary detective work and close reading.
Jacobs, Robert D. *Poe: Journalist and Critic*. Baton Rouge: Louisiana State Uni-
    versity Press, 1969. Thorough chronological survey of Poe's nonfiction.
Jordan, Cynthia S. *Second Stories: The Politics of Language, Form, and Gender in
    Early American Fictions*. Chapel Hill and London: University of North
    Carolina Press, 1989. Chapter on Poe traces his treatment of women's
    voices through "Ligeia," "The Fall of the House of Usher," and the Dupin
    tales.
Kaplan, Sidney. Introduction to *The Narrative of Arthur Gordon Pym*, by Edgar
    Allan Poe. New York: Hill and Wang, 1960. Early exploration of race
    and slavery issues implicit in *Pym*.
Kennedy, J. Gerald. *Poe, Death, and the Life of Writing*. New Haven, Conn.: Yale
    University Press, 1987. Deftly combines research on nineteenth-century
    mourning rituals and modern death anxiety with a poststructuralist
    approach to writing.
————. The Narrative of Arthur Gordon Pym *and the Abyss of Interpretation*.
    New York: Twayne, 1995. Clear, concise overview of the novel's historical
    context and the range of critical responses it has provoked, followed by
    an analysis that stresses the problems of reading and interpretation raised
    by *Pym*.
Ketterer, David. *The Rationale of Deception in Poe*. Baton Rouge: Louisiana State
    University Press, 1979. Argues that Poe sought to reveal the deceptive-

ness of our senses while his work points toward a transcendent "arabesque" reality.

Kopley, Richard, ed. *Poe's Pym: Critical Explorations*. Durham, N.C.: Duke University Press, 1992. Essays originally presented at a conference on *Pym* represent an impressive range of critical perspectives. Contributors include John Barth, Grace Farrell, John T. Irwin, J. Gerald Kennedy, Burton R. Pollin, John Carlos Rowe, and G. R. Thompson.

Lawrence, D. H. *Studies in Classic American Literature*. 1923. Reprint, New York: Penguin, 1977. Includes a provocative psychoanalytic reading of "Ligeia" and "Usher."

Levine, Stuart C. *Edgar Poe: Seer and Craftsman*. Deland, Fla.: Everett/Edwards, 1972. Wide-ranging analysis of the Poe canon with helpful references to cultural context.

Levy, Andrew. *The Culture and Commerce of the American Short Story*. Cambridge and New York: Cambridge University Press, 1993. Chapter 1 concerns Poe's role in establishing the short-story form in light of his unrealized *Penn/Stylus* magazine project.

Limon, John. *The Place of Fiction in the Time of Science*. Cambridge and New York: Cambridge University Press, 1990. Includes an extended analysis of *Eureka*.

Lindberg, Gary. *The Confidence Man in American Literature*. New York: Oxford University Press, 1982. In chapter 2, "Poe's Credentials," Lindberg analyzes Poe's use of trickery and deception as themes and as techniques.

Ljungquist, Kent P. *The Grand and the Fair: Poe's Landscape Aesthetics and Pictorial Techniques*. Potomac, Md.: Scripta Humanistica, 1984. Careful treatment of an often overlooked facet of Poe's art.

May, Charles. *Edgar Allan Poe: A Study of the Short Fiction*. Boston: Twayne, 1991. Concise, insightful readings of Poe's tales; also includes excerpts from Poe on elements of fiction and essays by three other critics.

Moss, Sidney P. *Poe's Literary Battles*. 1963. Reprint, Carbondale: Southern Illinois University Press, 1969. Accessible and informative account of Poe's feuds with Lewis Gaylord Clark, Thomas Dunn English, Henry Wadsworth Longfellow, and others.

Muller, John P., and William J. Richardson, eds. *The Purloined Poe: Lacan, Derrida, and Psychoanalytic Reading*. Baltimore and London: Johns Hopkins University Press, 1988. Collection of essays related to "The Purloined Letter" with emphasis on Lacan's seminar and the responses it generated. Also includes Liahna Klenman Babener's influential essay " 'The Shadow's Shadow': The Motif of the Double in . . . 'The Purloined Letter.' "

Nelson, Dana D. *The Word in Black and White: Reading "Race" in American Literature, 1638–1867*. New York and Oxford: Oxford University Press, 1992. In chapter 5, Nelson explores the racial implications of blackness and whiteness in *Pym*.

Person, Leland S., Jr. *Aesthetic Headaches: Women and a Masculine Poetics in Poe, Melville, and Hawthorne.* Athens and London: University of Georgia Press, 1988. Includes a persuasive feminist reading of the dying-woman tales.

Porte, Joel. *The Romance in America: Studies in Cooper, Poe, Hawthorne, Melville, and James.* Middletown, Conn.: Wesleyan University Press, 1969. An insightful chapter emphasizes gender issues in Poe's fiction.

Quinn, Arthur Hobson. *Edgar Allan Poe: A Critical Biography.* New York: D. Appleton-Century, 1941. Reprint, New York: Cooper Square, 1969. Thorough and reliable, the standard Poe biography prior to Silverman; still valuable.

Quinn, Patrick F. *The French Face of Edgar Poe.* Carbondale: Southern Illinois University Press, 1957. Makes a lasting case for Poe's significance while analyzing the response of French critics (pre-Lacan) to Poe.

Reynolds, David S. *Beneath the American Renaissance: The Subversive Imagination in the Age of Emerson and Melville.* New York: Knopf, 1988. Examines Poe's relationship to sensational literature of his time.

Rosenheim, Shawn. *The Cryptographic Imagination: Secret Writing from Edgar Poe to the Internet.* Baltimore and London: Johns Hopkins University Press, 1997. Explores the implications of Poe's fascination with cryptography.

Rosenheim, Shawn, and Stephen Rachman, eds. *The American Face of Edgar Allan Poe.* Baltimore and London: Johns Hopkins University Press, 1995. Uneven but provocative and challenging collection of essays; contributors include Barbara Johnson, John T. Irwin, Joan Dayan, David Leverenz, and Gillian Brown.

Rowe, John Carlos. *Through the Custom-House: Nineteenth-Century American Fiction and Modern Theory.* Baltimore and London: Johns Hopkins University Press, 1982. Includes an influential poststructuralist reading of *Pym.*

Silverman, Kenneth. *Edgar A. Poe: Mournful and Never-ending Remembrance.* New York: HarperCollins, 1991. The most readable and responsible narrative biography of Poe.

Silverman, Kenneth, ed. *New Essays on Poe's Major Tales.* Cambridge and New York: Cambridge University Press, 1993. Each essay in this collection is notable: Christopher Benfey on "The Black Cat" and "The Tell-Tale Heart," Louise J. Kaplan on "Usher," David Van Leer on the Dupin tales, David S. Reynolds on "The Cask of Amontillado," and J. Gerald Kennedy on "Ligeia."

Thomas, Dwight, and David K. Jackson. *The Poe Log: A Documentary Life of Edgar Allan Poe 1809–1849.* Boston: G. K. Hall, 1987. Fascinating collection of the evidence on which Poe biography is based; extremely useful.

Thompson, G. R. *Poe's Fiction: Romantic Irony in the Gothic Tales.* Madison: University of Wisconsin Press, 1973. Influential study that uncovers the pervasive irony in Poe's fiction.

Weiner, Bruce I. *The Most Noble of Professions: Poe and the Poverty of Authorship.* Baltimore: Enoch Pratt Free Library, Edgar Allan Poe Society, and the

Library of the University of Baltimore, 1987. Examines Poe's attitude toward his profession.

Wilbur, Richard. Introduction and Notes to *Poe: Complete Poems*. New York: Dell, 1959. Unfortunately out of print, one of the best introductions to Poe's poetry.

——. *Responses: Prose Pieces 1953–1976*. New York: Harcourt Brace Jovanovich, 1976. Reprints two essays on Poe, one of which is his introduction to an edition of *Pym*.

Williams, Michael J. S. *A World of Words: Language and Displacement in the Fiction of Edgar Allan Poe*. Durham, N.C.: Duke University Press, 1988. Insightful deconstructionist reading of Poe's fiction.

Williams, William Carlos. *In the American Grain*. New York: New Directions, 1956. Williams was ahead of his time in seeing Poe "in the American Grain," and his chapter on Poe reveals a surprising kinship between the two writers.

Articles

Amper, Susan. "Untold Story: The Lying Narrator in 'The Black Cat.' " *Studies in Short Fiction* 29 (1992): 475–85. An attempt to discover the true story beneath the narration.

Hammond, Alexander. "Edgar Allan Poe's *Tales of the Folio Club*: The Evolution of a Lost Book." *Library Chronicle* 41 (1976): 13–43. Careful examination of Poe's never-realized book project.

Hirsch, David H. "The Pit and the Apocalypse." *Sewanee Review* 76 (1968): 632–52. Explicates the apocalyptic imagery of "The Pit and the Pendulum" and relates the story to existential philosophy.

Hubbs, Valentine C. "The Struggle of Wills in Poe's 'William Wilson.' " *Studies in American Fiction* 11 (1983): 73–79. Lucid analysis of repression in "William Wilson."

Hume, Beverly. "Poe's Mad Narrator in *Eureka*." *Essays in Arts and Sciences* 22 (October 1993): 51–65. Argues that Poe ironically undermines the narrator in his cosmology as he does in much of his fiction.

Kennedy, J. Gerald. "The Limits of Reason: Poe's Deluded Detectives." *American Literature* 47 (1975): 184–96. Argues that Poe went through a ratiocination phase in the early 1840s but that even his detective tales reveal his skepticism toward the power of reason.

Kopley, Richard. "The Secret of *Arthur Gordon Pym*: The Text and the Source." *Studies in American Fiction* 8 (1980): 203–18.

——. "The Hidden Journey of Arthur Gordon Pym." In *Studies in the American Renaissance 1982*. Edited by Joel Myerson. Boston: Twayne, 1982.

——. "The 'Very Profound Undercurrent' of *Arthur Gordon Pym*." In *Studies in the American Renaissance 1987*. Edited by Joel Myerson. Charlottesville: University Press of Virginia, 1987. Taken together, these essays make a strong case for a unity of design and a spiritual "undercurrent" in *Pym*.

Long, David. "Poe's Political Identity: A Mummy Unswathed." *Poe Studies* 23 (1990): 1–22. Argues that Poe was philosophically attuned to American Whiggery.

Manning, Susan. " 'The Plots of God Are Perfect': Poe's *Eureka* and American Creative Nihilism." *Journal of American Studies* 23 (1989): 235–51. Argues for the entropic power of writing in *Eureka*.

Ostrom, John Ward. "Edgar A. Poe: His Income as Literary Entrepreneur." *Poe Studies* 15 (1982): 1–7. Calculates Poe's meager earnings, year by year.

Pollin, Burton R. "Maria Clemm, Poe's Aunt: His Boon or Bane?" *Mississippi Quarterly* 48 (1995): 211–24. Important biographical reassessment.

Ridgely, J. V. "Tragical-Mythical-Satirical-Hoaxical: Problems of Genre in 'Pym.' " *American Transcendental Quarterly*, no. 24 (1974): 4–9. Straightforward analysis of one of the basic difficulties *Pym* presents.

———. "The Authorship of the 'Paulding-Drayton Review.' " *PSA Newsletter* 20 (1992): 1–3, 6. Concludes that Poe did not write the infamous proslavery review.

Robinson, Douglas. "Reading Poe's Novel: A Speculative Review of 'Pym' Criticism, 1950–1980." *Poe Studies* 15 (1982): 47–54. Influential survey that pointed to new directions *Pym* scholarship would take in the 1980s and 1990s. See also David Ketterer's overview of *Pym* criticism in the 1980s in *Poe's* Pym: *Critical Explorations*, ed. Richard Kopley (Durham, N.C.: Duke University Press, 1992).

Roppolo, Joseph Patrick. "Meaning and 'The Masque of the Red Death.' " *Tulane Studies in English* 13 (1963): 59–69. Reprinted in *Poe: A Collection of Critical Essays*, edited by Robert Regan (Englewood Cliffs, N.J.: Prentice-Hall, 1967), 134–44. Coherent interpretation of symbolism in "Masque."

Rosenthal, Bernard. "Poe, Slavery, and the *Southern Literary Messenger:* A Reexamination." *Poe Studies* 7 (1974): 29–38. Makes a case for Poe's authorship of the proslavery Paulding-Drayton review.

Rosenzweig, Paul. " 'Dust within the Rock': The Phantasm of Meaning in *The Narrative of Arthur Gordon Pym*" *Studies in the Novel* 14 (1982): 137–51. Stresses the lack of a true ending and the more general problem of meaning in *Pym*.

Scherman, Timothy H. "The Authority Effect: Poe and the Politics of Reputation in the Pre-Industry of American Publishing." *Arizona Quarterly* 49.3 (1993): 1–19. Discusses Poe's efforts to publish "Tales of the Folio Club" in light of the politics of the mid-nineteenth-century literary marketplace.

Stern, Julia. "Double Talk: The Rhetoric of the Whisper in Poe's 'William Wilson.' " *ESQ* 40 (1994): 185–218. Argues that "William Wilson" had contemporary political implications, specifically for the secession debate.

Thompson, G. R. "Romantic Arabesque, Contemporary Theory, and Postmodernism: The Example of Poe's 'Narrative.' " *ESQ* 35 (1989): 163–271. Wide-ranging discussion that stresses Poe's genre-bending techniques in *Pym.*

Ware, Tracy. " 'A Descent into the Maelström': The Status of Scientific Rhetoric in a Perverse Romance." *Studies in Short Fiction* 29 (1992): 77–84. A strong, original argument that uses elements of both the providential and ironic readings of the story.

Whalen, Terence. "Edgar Allan Poe and the Horrid Laws of Political Economy." *American Quarterly* 44 (1992): 381–417. Reads Poe's detective fiction in light of the emergence of urban capitalism and the commodification of information.

———. "The Code for Gold: Edgar Allan Poe and Cryptography." *Representations* 46 (1994): 35–57. Deciphers a previously unsolved cryptogram to establish a new Poe text and examines "The Gold Bug" in the context of antebellum financial crises.

Whipple, William. "Poe's Political Satire." *Texas University Studies in English* 35 (1956): 81–95. Historical explications of "Four Beasts in One," "King Pest," "The Devil in the Belfry," and "The Man That Was Used Up."

Zanger, Jules. "Poe's American Garden: 'The Domain of Arnheim.' " *American Transcendental Quarterly,* no. 50 (1981): 93–103. Focuses on levels of allusion in Poe's garden imagery and on the character of Ellison.

Index

The Author

Scott Peeples is assistant professor of English at the College of Charleston. He received his Ph.D. in American Literature from Louisiana State University in 1994, and has published essays in *The Southern Quarterly* and *Biography: An Interdisciplinary Quarterly*.

The Editor

Nancy A. Walker is director of women's studies and professor of English at Vanderbilt University. A native of Louisiana, she received her B.A. from Louisiana State University and her M.A. from Tulane University. After receiving her Ph.D. from Kent State University in 1971, she taught American literature, American studies, and women's studies at Stephens College, where she also served as assistant to the president and chair of the Department of Languages and Literature.

A specialist in American women writers, Walker is the author of *A Very Serious Thing: Women's Humor and American Culture* (1988) and *Feminist Alternatives: Irony and Fantasy in the Contemporary Novel by Women* (1990), which won the first annual Eudora Welty Prize. She has published numerous articles in such journals as *American Quarterly, Tulsa Studies in Women's Literature, American Literature,* and *American Literary Realism,* and several essays on women's autobiography. With Zita Dresner, she edited *Redressing the Balance: American Women's Literary Humor from the Colonial Period to the 1980s* (1988).